# THE DAWN OF LANGUAGE

*Sverker Johansson*

# THE DAWN OF LANGUAGE

## How we came to talk

*Translated from the Swedish by*
*Frank Perry*

MACLEHOSE PRESS
QUERCUS · LONDON

First published as *På spaning efter språkets ursprung* by Natur & Kultur, Stockholm, in 2019
First published in Great Britain in 2021 by

MacLehose Press
An imprint of Quercus Publishing Ltd
Carmelite House
50 Victoria Embankment
London EC4Y 0DZ

An Hachette UK company

This publication is sponsored by

A CIP catalogue record for this book is available from the British Library.

ISBN (HB)   978 1 52941 139 3
ISBN (TPB)  978 1 52941 140 9
ISBN (Ebook)  978 1 52941 142 3

10 9 8 7 6 5 4 3 2 1

Designed and typeset in Scala by Libanus Press Ltd, Marlborough
Printed and bound in Great Britain by Elcograf S.p.A.

# Contents

# Foreword

"Dad, why is that thing hanging by its tail?"

"It's hanging by its tail because that's more convenient when you're climbing trees and picking fruit."

"Dad, why is it picking fruit?"

"Because fruit is what that monkey eats."

"Dad, why do you call it a monkey?"

"Because it is a monkey. We call that kind of animal monkeys."

"Dad, why do we call them monkeys?"

"Because that's what we were taught when we were little: that they're called monkeys."

"Dad, is its name Monkey?" She turns to the monkey. "Monkey, hello Monkey." No response from the monkey.

"Dad, why isn't the monkey answering?"

"Because it doesn't understand what you are saying."

"Dad, why doesn't it understand what I'm saying?"

"Because monkeys can't talk."

"Dad, why can't monkeys talk?"

"Because animals can't talk."

"Only, Dad, yesterday you said people are a kind of animal. So how come people can talk?"

That's when Dad gives up. You'd need an entire book to answer that question. That's the book you've got in your hands right now.

Most children go through a period at some point about the age of four when they ask "why" about everything. They are not satisfied even when they get an answer and each answer just leads on to a new "why". Eventually Dad gets tired of answering, and eventually the children get tired of asking because they never get a proper answer. In any case they usually stop asking fairly soon after they start school.

I never got tired. I continued to ask "why" and am still doing it today, just over fifty years later. A lot of that would have to do with the fact that my father never grew tired of answering and explaining. And I continued to ask him questions from time to time but nowadays I do most of my thinking about things no-one knows the answer to, and not even Dad would have. So I try and find out the answers myself.

The things I speculate about, the questions I ask, have frequently been about origins, about how the world works in the final analysis. I was fairly young when I started reading books about fossils and outer space, and I still have some of my favourite books from when I was five or six. I continued reading about evolution and cosmology and I must have been a fairly unbearable pupil at primary school – most of my teachers soon wearied of my questions, and I got bored of asking them. So I read up on the subjects instead.

Eventually this led to a brief first scientific career as a particle physicist. But soon after I finished my doctorate in 1990 on the production of lepton pairs in proton collisions in a particle accelerator in Switzerland, I discovered something that was more exciting than physics: language. Although I had not thought very much about language until that point, I decided to take an evening course in general linguistics, mostly for fun. It was on that course that I discovered how exciting the study of language could be and how many unanswered questions remained about how language worked. It was the origin of language, above all, that was still shrouded in darkness. This would eventually lead me to completely alter the course of my research work and resulted in this book.

Today we know a great deal more about the origin of language than we did then, even if many pieces of the puzzle are still missing. I hope in this book to be able to show the reader both how fascinating language is and how much detective work goes into finding all the pieces of that puzzle. While the pieces that frame the puzzle emerge, we will also get some idea of how many other pieces we have yet to put in place.

# Introduction

What is it that makes us human beings? We like to think of ourselves as special, unique, unlike all the other animals. Even referring to us as "animals" can still cause offence to some people, but I am going to be doing that in this book if only because anything else would be absurd in biological terms. We are nevertheless extremely unusual animals, not least because of our extraordinary success and the impact we have had on our planet.

What, then, is the key to our success? What is it that makes us special? Over the years, scientists and philosophers have proposed long lists of the supposedly unique qualities of the human being, both in terms of the body and the soul. Possessing a soul is the kind of quality that is assumed to be uniquely human – if we do possess a soul, that is, and if other animals do not: two questions to which there are no clear answers.

Although we are a bit on the odd side when it comes to our bodies, we are not really radically different from the other apes. That did not stop thinkers in previous ages from attempting to discover bodily parts that are unique to us, although no idea of this kind has ever survived a more rigorous examination. So no, what may be unique to us is not located in the body.

Morality, courage, consciousness, intelligence, feelings, personality, empathy, love and piety are some of the mental qualities that have been considered uniquely human. None of them have ever really measured up. In order to maintain that something is uniquely human, we have first to be able to show that the quality is unambiguously present in humans and, second, that it is just as unambiguously absent in other animals. But these qualities are difficult to define and hard to measure in people, let alone in animals. There is still no definitive consensus among scientists about a concept as relatively robust as intelligence. Not to mention how we would be able to define and measure – and thus be able to exclude – courage in a blue whale or morality in a shrew.

All the same, it is hard for us not to feel that there is something in our heads that is different to the other animals, that our brains are in some way better equipped. But that is a feeling we should be suspicious of. We are very quick to use ourselves as measuring sticks and to consider ourselves the norm, and this can lead us to see anything different as inferior.

It is not just other animals we look down on. As soon as one group of humans meets another, they regard each other as lesser beings. *Us* against *The Others* is a particularly gratifying trope our minds are always far too ready to remind us of, as they have been doing from time immemorial. Two thousand years ago the Romans considered the Germanic barbarians to be beneath them, while the Germanic tribes no doubt considered the feeble Romans to be second-rate . . . and this is by no means the earliest example. Neandertals and early *Homo sapiens* probably considered each other to be inferior barbarians when the opportunity first arose around 100,000 years ago. And so it has gone on – right up to the present. Most of us – but far from everyone – have, however, begun to realise that the intuitive sense that *The Other* is inferior is just an illusion, a toxic chimera that undermines human relationships across borders.

Barbarians were called barbarians by the Romans – and before them by the Greeks – because the barbarians' language did not sound to them like a real language in the Greco-Roman sense, but like an incomprehensible bar-bar-bar-bar instead. It was language that distinguished the civilised *Us* from the barbarian *Others*. The Romans and the Greeks saw their own languages as the norm, and so anyone who spoke differently was a barbarian. As far as they were concerned, language was the key to civilisation.

Language plays an important role in the Bible stories as well. It is used there, too, to distinguish *Us* from *The Others*. There is an account in Judges, chapter twelve, of the correct pronunciation of the word "shibboleth" being a matter of life and death – anyone mispronouncing it was executed.

The Bible also has a story about language being created specifically to separate human beings from one another. The starting point for the story of the Tower of Babel is that human beings had only one single language in the beginning and this common tongue was such a powerful tool it opened up vast opportunities for the human race: "If as one people all sharing a common language they have begun to do this, then nothing they plan to do will be beyond them . . ." (NET Bible, Genesis 11:6). But their God did not approve so he made sure of their subjugation by scattering them and giving them a wealth of different languages so they could not understand one another. A very efficient way of sowing discord in the world. This is the Biblical explanation of why there are so many languages.

Though the Bible has no explanation for why language exists in the first place. "In the beginning was the Word, and the Word was with God, and the Word was fully God." (John 1:1). And one of Adam's first tasks in the Garden of Eden was to name all the animals (Genesis 2:19), a linguistic task that assumes Adam already had a language. At this point in the story Adam could have been two days old at most, so presumably he was born with a ready-made language in his head (apart from the names of the animals, that is).

So language plays a key role in the Bible and is the first human quality to be highlighted, as in the case of Adam. It is the human being who names the animals, and not the animals that name the humans. And even today language is one of the very few attributes that clearly distinguish people from other animals. Language may be the key to what makes us human.

But to find an answer to the question why people have language, we will have to look elsewhere than the Bible. To understand the origins of language we have to understand what language is, its structure and nature, but we also need to achieve insight into the nature and evolutionary origins of the human being. We will have to gain an understanding of the way we think and how our brains work. In order to answer the question it is necessary to consider the scientific evidence from a wide range of different fields, not just linguistics but evolutionary biology as well as paleoanthropology, archaeology, primatology, genetics, anatomy, ethology, neuroscience, cognitive science, psychology and social anthropology, just to name the most important ones. This makes it rather hard to gain an overall understanding of the issue, not least for the person who is a specialist in just one of these scientific fields and unfamiliar with the others. This book cannot delve deeply into all of them, but we will have occasion to dip into a number of different subject areas at least, though inevitably these will only be dips. I have been obliged to simplify matters both to keep the scale of the book within reasonable bounds and so that the core of the argument does not get lost amidst a wealth of detail. In most instances I have been fully aware of the complexities and shades of meaning involved. I have chosen nonetheless to try to provide an overall view of the state of research that captures enough of the heart of the matter without making it more complex than is absolutely essential.

\* \* \*

The nature of language has been a central issue in philosophy for as far back as we can trace the history of the subject. In the fourth century BCE the great Greek philosopher Aristotle foregrounded language as a key dividing line between humans and animals. A generation later Epicurus would set out the oldest known theory on the origin of language. Language began, in his view, because people had innate reactions to things they experienced; a particular experience would make them utter a particular sound, generating different sounds for different experiences. This range of innate sounds for various experiences became the nucleus from which language then developed. He fails to mention where those innate reactions came from, however.

Two thousand years later, several of the philosophers of the Enlightenment would express renewed interest in how language arose. In 1710, Gottfried Wilhelm Leibniz, better known for his mathematical discoveries, published his ideas on language in which he attempted to locate its origin in the onomatopoeic words – such as "miaow" and "cuckoo" – a number of which still form part of our vocabulary.

In 1746, the French philosopher Étienne Bonnot de Condillac discussed the origins of language in his *Essai sur l'origine des connaissances humaines*, in which he speculated on the possibility that its roots lay in gestures and mime that had then been refined into a form of sign language. By 1765 the Scots philosopher Thomas Reid was expressing similar ideas; it remains unclear whether he came up with them himself or had been influenced by the somewhat older Condillac. Reid would speculate on the links between language and art as well.

The Swiss political philosopher Jean-Jacques Rousseau, famous for the idea of the noble savage, also entered the debate, in a polemic with his almost exact contemporary Condillac. Rousseau imagined an original stage in which the noble savage used both gestures and cries to communicate. The gestures were supposed to express needs while the cries expressed feelings. Rituals and song would then have played a vital role in developing these gestures and cries into a real language.

Yet another contemporary thinker was the Scot James Burnett, Lord Monboddo, who unlike the gentlemen referred to above (ladies being, sadly, conspicuous by their absence) was not simply a general philosopher who happened to speculate about language on the side. Monboddo was one of the first philosophers who can really be called a linguist and he helped lay the foundations of modern comparative and historical linguistics.

While Monboddo was giving thought to the history of the various human languages, it seemed obvious to think about the very first beginnings of language as well. He placed the emphasis on the social functions of language and considered imitation to be a crucial skill. Interestingly, Monboddo got the inspiration for many of his ideas from observing the way orang-utans communicate in captivity. This was decades before Darwin was born, and so the notion of seeking an evolutionary origin for language, or that that evolutionary origin would have anything to do with apes, would have been far from obvious. Monboddo, however, engaged with several evolutionary ideas, although none would be fully developed in his work.

The next eighteenth-century thinker to tackle the origin of language was Johann Gottfried Herder, who would have to be called a German even though Germany did not exist at the time and his birthplace, Morąg, currently forms part of Poland. He was a friend of Goethe's and contributed to the development of German nationalism and a pride in all things Germanic with what are to us familiar consequences. Herder himself was, however, politically radical and a supporter of the French Revolution.

Although Herder was most influential as a literary scholar, in 1772 he would also publish an entire book devoted to the origin of language: *Abhandlung über den Ursprung der Sprache*. In this work he discusses what he calls "natural languages", all the various sounds that animals and humans use to express their feelings – cries of pain, pleasure and so on. His aim was not, however, to look for the roots of human language in this natural language, but to try to discover instead what it is that distinguishes Man from the animals and could explain why we have real languages while animals only have the natural language of their emotions.

Herder's solution to the problem is an interesting one which has parallels with modern theories of human evolution. He considers other animals to be specialised to a considerable degree; they have instincts for finding their food in a particular and restricted way and possess the sounds they need for their specific way of subsisting. The human being, on the other hand, is a generalist and is not subject to the same limitations, nor a slave to his or her instincts, but capable of using reason to discuss new situations and come up with new solutions. It is here, according to Herder, that we find the key to language: in our need to communicate beyond the boundaries of what is instinctively given. Reason also means that we can take a step backwards and reflect on a situation; we are not immediately forced to do what instinct commands but can think about what confronts us and create words for new experiences. Herder does appear, however, to assume that people possess one instinct at least, an instinct to give things names, an innate drive to find words for everything.

Although the philosophers of the Enlightenment gave a lot of thought to the origin of language, their ideas are for the most part pure speculation, imaginative scenarios about how language could have arisen that lack a firm grounding in any more profound knowledge about the way language works or how humans came into being. This is hardly surprising when you consider that almost nothing was known about these issues in the eighteenth century. As a result, if your aim was to write about the origin of language, all you could really do was speculate.

In the nineteenth century, *linguistics* – the study of language – developed into a scientific field of its own in tandem with very different requirements as to evidence and rigour. Unsupported speculation was no longer welcome. The origin of language therefore fell into disrepute as an area of research and was even banned by the Linguistic Society of Paris in 1866. To all intents and purposes the subject would remain taboo for more than a century, during which time no ideas of any serious merit about how language arose would be put forward. And yet, during that same period, enormous progress was also being made in terms of our knowledge about human beings, language and evolution, which should have provided a more solid foundation for tackling the origin of language. But it would be a long time before research into the origin of language was considered acceptable and could resume.

Even though the occasional attempt to broach the issue would be made from the 1960s onwards by researchers such as Eric Lenneberg and Derek Bickerton,[1] it was only in the 1990s that research into this field really took off.

Two key figures in this relaunch of the origin of language as the subject of scientific enquiry were Steven Pinker and Jim Hurford, although both would play entirely different roles. Pinker is a professor of psychology at Harvard, and in 1990, together with Paul Bloom, he published an article on the evolution of language that attracted a great deal of attention from researchers.[2] The same article was turned into a popular science book, *The Language Instinct* (1994), which became a best-seller. It was this book that also got me thinking about the origin of language – even though I did not agree with Pinker's conclusions.

Pinker is a polymath who ranges over a broad academic terrain; he has also published books on heredity and the environment, on cognition, and on war and peace. Because he does not linger in one field, he remained an important source of inspiration for research into the origin of language rather than an active leader.

The role of leader was assumed instead by Jim Hurford, Professor of Linguistics at Edinburgh University, who, beginning in 1990, established a dedicated research group and research institute in Edinburgh and set up a series of international scientific

1 Unlike Lenneberg, Bickerton would remain a key figure in the science of the evolution of language until his recent death. He continued to undertake research until the end and published his last book in 2016, when he was 90. We will meet him again at several points in this book.

2 Pinker, S. & Bloom, P. "Natural language and natural selection". *Behavioral & Brain Sciences* 13: 707–84 (1990).

conferences on the origin of language. These Evolang-conferences, as they are called (Evolution of Language International Conferences), became the arena in which researchers from all over the world with an interest in the origin of language would meet to exchange ideas and continue to build on one another's work, which is crucial to establishing a new field of scientific research. The conferences are still arranged every other year, and I last attended in 2018, in Toruń in Poland.

The new wave of research initiated by Jim Hurford and others in 1990 brought together a miscellaneous team of scientists from various fields who shared a common interest in the evolution of language. During the almost thirty years that have passed since, we have exchanged ideas, carried out experiments, compiled research findings, run computer simulations and in these and other ways attempted to acquire the knowledge that is essential if we are to be able to make statements about the origin of language that are more than pure speculation, and so get around the ban imposed in 1866.

This book is based on the findings of this research journey, and my goal has been to provide an overall picture of where we are today, how we conceived of our work and what we know and do not know about the origin of language. There are many strands of thought from many academic fields that need to be woven together in the course of this journey. On occasion we may have to untangle some of those different threads and it may take a while before it becomes obvious what they have to do with language. This will not be a straightforward linear journey, but something more like a tapestry in which a pattern will gradually emerge. I have not included midwives, robots, squid or the left-handed for fun, but because they actually do have something to tell us about the origin of language. In the end it will all come together.

# PART ONE

# ON LANGUAGE

# Human Language

My youngest daughter Aina is sitting on my lap as I write this. She is six months old, happy, and curious about everything; it's hard to keep her hands away from the keyboard. She keeps making noises. She laughs, she cries, she gurgles and she babbles. She can communicate clearly: she had no difficulty letting me know she wanted to be lifted off her blanket on the floor a little while ago. But she did this without language. She cannot talk yet; those sounds she makes do not constitute a language. She will no doubt be able to say "Daddy" to me in a few months, but not yet.

At what point can we say that a child has begun to use language? Every parent knows that learning to speak is a long process for a child; it takes several years from that first babbling *da da da* until children can express themselves fluently in complete sentences in their mother tongue. The child gradually develops from a language-less baby to a language-equipped three-year-old who never stops talking. Children usually start by babbling, practising speech sounds, when they are more or less the same age as Aina. The first recognisable words tend to appear around their first birthday, and by the second they start putting together words into simple phrases. Grammar – in the more adult sense of complete sentences – gets going at about three years old. The exact ages can vary enormously from one child to another, but most children go through more or less the same stages in roughly the same order although at different rates.

Whether the child is learning one or more languages seems to have little impact on the process, nor does it make much difference whether the language is signed or spoken. Children are good at learning languages, irrespective of the particular form and circumstances as long as they grow up surrounded by language. They are remarkably good at learning languages compared with how much effort and conscious practice is required for many other skills, such as mathematics or music, which are actually no more complicated than language.

Nevertheless, it still takes a couple of years for children to acquire language. At what point during this process can we call what children are doing *language*? The first time the child utters sounds? Hardly; the cries of the newborn in the maternity ward are not language in any meaningful sense. The first time the child achieves a complete and grammatically correct sentence? Hardly that either; children can speak at full throttle long before their grammar is up and working. It would have to be somewhere along the journey between those points. But establishing a definitive moment that we can point to is difficult. I will not be able to write in my diary in a few months: "Today Aina started using language." I may be able to write: "Today Aina said *Daddy* for the first time." But if we are going to call the first word she uses language, we would have to be agreed that it is the production of words that defines language, and that is by no means obvious.

We face the same problem when talking about the origin of language in ancient times. We descend from ape-like ancestors, and over the course of several million years our branch of the family tree has gradually evolved into the human beings we are today. Those apes in our lineage were no more capable of language than chimps or baboons are today; we, on the other hand, can talk. Somewhere along that evolutionary journey language must have arisen.

We cannot draw an absolutely clear dividing line between the apes and humans among our ancestors. An increasing number of human characteristics and behaviours gradually emerge with the passage of millions of years. Perhaps the same is true of language.

Perhaps there never was a single ape-man who could be called the first speaker, in just the same way that no one day will be the first day my daughter speaks. Or it may be purely a matter of definition as to who was the first person ever to speak.

It is possible, in principle, that language suddenly appeared fully formed during human evolution without any gradual or intermediate forms. That notion, a linguistic Big Bang, has been championed by linguists such as Noam Chomsky. But it is extremely improbable, biologically speaking, that such a complex characteristic as our capacity for speech just popped up out of nowhere. It is more likely that language evolved in several stages in the same way, for instance, as our large brains did or our tool-making ability. This may have been a process similar to the one children go through, or the process may have been entirely different and involved intermediate forms. But some form of evolution must have occurred on the journey from non-speaking ape to speaking humans. At some point there must have been linguistic precursors, simpler forms of language. There must also have been a protolanguage, the first one that could be called a language.

In that case, what was it that evolved? Language, of course, but what more concretely? There are several aspects of language that are important to distinguish here. The sounds transmitted through the air when someone speaks are the only aspect of language that is directly observable. But that is not its most interesting dimension. There are at least two more important aspects. One is the language faculty to be found in our brains which means that we can use and understand language. The other is language as a social system: the system that allows people to reach agreement on what means what so that we are able understand one another.

Noam Chomsky regards the language faculty in our brains as the most important aspect and the one that has to be explained by linguistics. This turns the origin of language into a purely biological issue: How did our brains evolve to contain a language module? Many other scientists doing research into the origin of language consider the social system of language to be more interesting. From that perspective the key question instead is how the social interactions of human beings evolved in such a way that our shared system of communication became a language.

People differ from other apes both biologically and socially. A young chimp lacks a biological language faculty and can never really learn to use language even when it is brought up in a human social environment. But a human child that is forced to grow up without human social contact and communication does not learn to use language either. Meeting both the biological and social requirements is essential to language. And so both the biological and social changes that underpin language need to be taken into account in the search for its origin.

The human voice and capacity to utter sounds are an obvious biological adaptation to spoken language. Chimps can, of course, make sounds, and very loud ones at that, but they are incapable of articulating the wide range of speech sounds in rapid sequence that characterises human language. This was long thought to be a consequence of a number of differences between humans and other apes in relation to the gullet, the mouth and the tongue that provide us with a capacity to produce greater variation in the production of sounds. But it is actually more to do with differences in our brains and in the connections between the brain and the organs of speech.

The nature of the other factors that make up the biological dimension of our language faculty is a controversial issue among linguists. Do we possess an innate "language instinct" and, if so, what does it consist of? This is a key question in relation to the origin of language.

## THE CONCEPTS OF LANGUAGE

We need to have terms for the various constituent parts of language if we are going to look at its origin. Linguists have developed a conceptual framework to do just that, and this section explains the concepts that will be used in this book. Readers who are already familiar with the terminology can skip to the next section.

The structure of language can be analysed on a number of different levels. I choose to begin with the word, since this is a concept most people are familiar with and its meaning in linguistics is very like the everyday meaning of the term. If "word" is to be defined: it refers to the smallest linguistic unit that can stand, and be pronounced, on its own. Words, however, can seem very different in different languages, and it is far from simple to arrive at a strict definition that will serve in every context. But "word" in its everyday sense will do for now.

There are various kinds of words, various **parts of speech**. The most important of these are:

**Nouns**. Words for things, both concrete and abstract. Examples: *word, book, language, person, universe, idea.*

**Pronouns**. Short simple words that replace nouns, that take the place of a noun in a sentence, either because it remains undecided which noun it should be (*someone*) or just to save time and effort (*she*).

**Verbs**. Words for actions, events, states and processes. Examples: *run, read, happen, smell, wipe, exist, disappear.*

**Prepositions**. Words that typically tell us where something happens, sometimes literally and sometimes figuratively. Examples: *to, on, in, over, from, for.* "Lisa drove *to* town *on* Wednesday and bought cakes *for* Peter."

**Conjunctions**. Words that join together two parts of a statement. There are coordinating conjunctions and subordinating conjunctions (nowadays sometimes referred to as

**subjunctions**). The coordinating conjunctions join together two parts of the sentence that are of the same kind on equal terms, so that they are arranged side by side or juxtaposed. Examples: *and, but, or.* The subordinating kind do what their name suggests: they turn part of a sentence into an appendix to another part. Examples; *that, if, since, although.*

**Adjectives.** Words that designate the characteristics or qualities of something. Examples: *red, fine, happy, abstract.*

**Adverbs.** Words that designate the characteristics of things other than nouns. This is a rather sprawling classification that contains words that do not share a great deal in common. Examples: *quickly, recently, rather, badly, not.*

The parts of speech can take different forms in different languages, and it is common for one or more parts of speech to be missing. That does not mean that languages that lack adjectives, say, cannot express characteristics, but they do so in a slightly different way and not by using a separate part of speech.

Going down another level, there is a meaningful unit that is smaller than a word: that is the morpheme. Sometimes a word consists of several components that help to make up the meaning of the word. A morpheme is the smallest meaningful unit, the smallest unit that can be usefully said to convey any meaning. A word like "speech" consists of a single morpheme; there is no part of the word that conveys anything by itself. In contrast a compound word such as "speechlessness" consists of several morphemes: speech-less-ness in which each separate unit conveys its share of the meaning of the word as a whole. The core of the word is "speech" again, to which the morpheme "-less" is added to indicate an absence and finally the morpheme "-ness" tells us the word is an abstract noun.

By definition a morpheme cannot be subdivided further in terms of meaning. On the other hand it can be divided into syllables, and then into sounds. In sign language the morpheme can be divided in the same way but using gestures instead of sounds; for the sake of simplicity, however, let us stick to spoken language here. In principle a syllable always contains a vowel or a vowel-like sound at its centre. Around the vowel there are a varying number of consonants. Vowels are those speech-sounds that are pronounced with an unobstructed flow of air through the mouth – a, e, i – whereas consonants are formed by cutting off or compressing the flow of air in various ways – p, f, g, s.

Every language uses a particular set of speech sounds, with different sets being used by different languages. Almost all sounds are vowels or consonants, but some languages also use clicks and other noises. A good many languages also distinguish different tones; what we might think is the same vowel can sound like very different sounds to the speakers of those languages, depending on whether it is pronounced with a high or low tone, or in some other tonal variant.

The number of sounds in a particular language can vary from a dozen to over one hundred. English has around forty-four sounds whereas Swedish has thirty-five or so, depending in both cases on dialect, and even the lower figure is rather more than the average. English does not use tones to distinguish meaning, whereas Swedish uses tones to distinguish words but not individual sounds.

The sounds of speech can be described on two different levels, both as phonemes and as the sounds that are actually uttered. A phoneme is the smallest unit of sound that can distinguish one meaning from another, or one word from another. It is a common feature of language that what we experience as the same sounds are actually pronounced in various different ways depending on context. These variants are the same phoneme even though they sound slightly different. Even though the sounds represented by the p in "pin" and the p in "spin" are pronounced slightly differently, we interpret both variants as though they were the same p sound, they belong to the same phoneme.

Speech sounds can be broken down further in purely acoustic terms on the basis of which tones they contain and in terms of how and where they are produced in the human vocal tract. But we can get by without any of that for the moment.

If we go up a level from the word instead, words can be put together in phrases, clauses and sentences. Anyone who has learned to write knows what a sentence is: a row of words that when written starts with a capital letter and ends with a full stop (or, on occasion with some other punctuation mark). In linguistic terms a sentence is the smallest unit that is grammatically complete and that does not leave any loose grammatical threads hanging. An utterance will frequently consist of several sentences that are connected in terms of meaning although the sentences are grammatically separate.

This leads us on to the nature of grammar. Grammar is the set of rules that determine how words can be assembled into larger units, as well as the rules for how words can be composed from morphemes, and how words may be inflected depending on the grammatical context.

Grammar is sometimes subdivided into syntax and morphology. Here, syntax has to do with how words are combined into sentences, while morphology deals with the form and structure of individual words and includes endings and so on. This division works well in English and Swedish but is not valid for all languages.

Going back to phrases, clauses and sentences, a sentence may consist of a number of clauses. Each clause basically describes something that is happening, with a verb that indicates what is occurring and one or more nouns around it that tell us who or what is involved in the event. "Lisa is driving the car" is a clause that can also be a complete sentence, consisting of just the one clause. But you could also expand it with another clause. "Lisa is driving the car that Peter bought yesterday." The second clause: "that Peter bought yesterday" is subordinate to the first and cannot stand as a sentence on its own. In principle an infinite number of clauses can be added on in the same sentence.

Phrases, finally, are units that the rules of grammar treat as though they were a single word. If we write "Lisa is driving the little green car with patches of rust on the bonnet", "the little green car with patches of rust on the bonnet" is a phrase which functions grammatically as though it were a single noun – a noun phrase. In the sentence "Lisa would have preferred to fly", "would have preferred to fly" is a phrase that functions grammatically just like a single verb – a verb phrase.

This is as far as we can go with an analysis of the formal structure of language without taking into account what is actually being said and what it means, or being concerned with the way language is actually used between people. It is possible to invent formally and grammatically correct sentences that are entirely meaningless and that would never occur to anyone to use. Noam Chomsky employed an example that has become so famous it has a Wikipedia article of its own: *Colorless green ideas sleep furiously*. This sentence is both perfectly correct in terms of English grammar and complete nonsense, which is Chomsky's point – in his theory of language, grammar is entirely autonomous and completely independent of the meaning of what is said.

But it isn't quite that simple. Meaning occasionally has a bearing on grammar. In Swedish, as in numerous other languages, nouns have grammatical gender, marked by using *en* or *ett* as an article before a noun, with *den* or *det* as the corresponding pronouns. In Swedish, just as in English, however, the choice of pronoun is different when the pronoun refers to a human being: whether you use "he" or "she" as the pronoun for a secretary depends on the actual gender of the secretary in question, not on the grammatical gender of the word "secretary".

Marginal effects on grammar of this kind aside, the point of language is, after all, that what we say actually means something and that it contains a message that the listener can both comprehend and interpret. The branch of linguistics that deals with the meaning of language is called semantics.

Two further branches of linguistics are worth mentioning here:

- Prosody, which deals with pronunciation at a level above the individual speech sounds, and thus with intonation: how we use variations in pitch across an entire utterance to communicate a message on a level that goes over and above the formal content of language. You can say "You're coming tomorrow" either as a statement, as a command or as a question, and what distinguishes the pronunciation of the question from the statement is prosody.

- Pragmatics, which deals with what is appropriate to say and when. What greeting should I use when I ring someone up? Should I use the same phrase to my boss as to my mother? Should a remake of the movie version of *The Adventures of Tom Sawyer* use the words for African Americans and Native Americans that Twain employs in his original novel? These are issues of pragmatics.

## THE DIVERSITY OF LANGUAGES

There is an extraordinary diversity of human languages, with thousands existing around the world. The question "How many languages are there?" has no exact answer, and very definitely no answer that everyone is agreed on. There is no clear dividing line between what is a language in its own right and what is just a dialect of another language. What are regarded as separate languages is more a question of politics than a linguistic matter. In purely linguistic terms there are far greater differences between different dialects of Chinese than between the Scandinavian languages, and linguists normally treat a number of Chinese "dialects" as separate languages. How linguistic boundaries should be drawn is a controversial matter within Sweden as well. It is by no means self-evident whether Elfdalian (*älvdalska*) should be seen as a dialect of Swedish or as a language of its own; as a Swede from the south of the country who moved north to Dalecarlia, I find Elfdalian harder to understand than Danish, even though I live in the province where it is spoken. On the western bank (the Swedish side) of the Torne, what they speak in the river valley is regarded as a language in its own right – *Meänkieli* – while on the eastern bank it is seen as a dialect of Finnish.

Not all linguistic variation is geographically determined. In the place where I grew up I find it easy to hear differences in the speech of different social classes, and I can even hear whether the person speaking grew up in the town or the country. In Stockholm, the linguistic distance between the upper-class suburb of Lidingö and the immigrant neighbourhood of Rinkeby is considerably greater than the few minutes it takes to travel by underground between the two.

An old joke often gets trotted out when linguists are asked to define what a language is: "a language is a dialect with an army". That joke is no longer quite so funny; the issue has become a matter of life and death rather too often, as in Yugoslavia, for instance, when the country disintegrated in the 1990s. For as long as the country was unified, the Yugoslavs spoke different dialects of Serbo-Croat. But one by one these dialects acquired armies of their own, a devastating civil war ensued, and Serbo-Croat has now split into at least four separate languages. And all of this took place without any change at all in the way people actually spoke – the formation of the languages was a purely political process.

If one is forced to try and come up with a linguistic definition of the difference between a dialect and a language, then it would have to do with mutual understanding. If two people can understand one another without further ado when talking, they are speaking the same language, and otherwise they are not. However, that definition fails to provide any clear-cut boundaries between languages and will by no means always correspond with what are officially defined as languages. Frequently there will be a continuum of dialects across national borders, with people in one village invariably understanding the dialect spoken in a neighbouring one irrespective of any borders that may separate them, whereas people in villages that are further apart will find it more difficult to understand each other's dialects. An interconnected chain of mutually comprehensible neighbouring dialects of this kind can be drawn all the way from Portugal through Spain via Catalonia and across France to Italy. In this sense Portuguese, Spanish, Catalan, French and Italian could be considered to form a single language even though the Italians and the Portuguese cannot understand one another. And although a Sicilian and a Parisian cannot communicate, people in Nice and Ventimiglia manage to do so pretty well. So how are we to count the number of languages in this region?

However they are counted, there is a vast array of languages in existence. Using a restrictive definition that lumps dialects together might produce only 4,000 languages, whereas a more generous one would result in twice as many. Ethnologue,[3] a catalogue of languages that is frequently cited, lists 7,000 languages, and that figure is as good as any.

All these languages differ widely in terms of vocabulary and grammar. It is mainly the grammar that can differ more radically than many people would suppose. All the European languages we tend to learn at school – French, German, Spanish and so on – are rather closely related and have the same underlying structure, their grammars go about things in much the same way although the details may differ quite a bit. They have verbs and nouns that function in more or less similar fashion: the verbs are inflected

3  http://www.ethnologue.com/

with endings to show their tense and the nouns have endings to show that they are plural. Word order (and to some degree case endings and other forms of inflection) is used to show who is doing what with whom in a sentence.

These may seem like obvious points to someone who is only familiar with European languages, but languages from other families can operate in completely different ways. Some languages have no endings at all, no tenses of the verb and no plural form for nouns but make use of other tools to show when something is happening and how many things it is happening to. While yet others can form entire sentences and not just alter the tense but also who is doing what to whom and in what way by adding different suffixes to verbs – a single long word may correspond to an entire sentence in French or German, say. Other languages again have words that basically consist of just a few consonants. To achieve what Swedish or English do with various endings, different vowels are inserted at various points between these consonants. There is an almost infinite amount of variation among the world's thousands of different languages.

Why are there so many languages? The nature of the human faculty for language must be such that it has the capacity to handle many different kinds of language. And what does all this diversity tell us about its origin? The evolution of language must have been such that it led naturally to a versatile and flexible linguistic faculty, which then led naturally to the development of languages – in the plural.

## THE FEATURES OF LANGUAGE

A hotly debated topic among linguists is what characteristics all these 7,000 languages have in common and what the constraints are that define those characteristics. Can a language take on any guise at all or are there fundamental features that characterise every language?

In the 1960s, the linguist Charles Hockett published a list of the "design features" he regarded as characteristic of human languages, and that could be used to define what a language is. Hockett's list was published in several different versions that contained up to sixteen different features and was very influential in its time. Below is the most frequently used version of the list, with thirteen features (in my wording):

1  Vocal-auditory. Communication occurs by means of voice and hearing.
2  Undirected. Transmission is undirected (anyone in the vicinity can hear) although reception is directed (the listener can identify the person speaking.)
3  Transitory. The sound immediately disappears, unlike scent trails, for instance.
4  Bidirectional. Anything that can be heard can be said – unlike a peahen, for instance, which cannot "say" the message she receives from a peacock when displaying his fan.
5  Monitorable. Speakers can perceive their own signals (hear their own voices) unlike deer, for example, which emit warning signals by showing their white rumps to other members of the herd. They cannot see their own hind-quarters.
6  Intentional. Communication is deliberate, unlike laughter and tears, or the backside of the deer I just mentioned for that matter.
7  Semantic. Each signal is linked specifically to a particular meaning.
8  Arbitrary. There is no particular pattern to which signals are linked to which meanings.
9  Composite. Language is built up of components that are perceived as discrete elements. There are two levels of composition in language from speech sounds to words and from words to sentences.

10  Displaced. Communication can be about things that are not present at this time.

11  Learnable. Language can be learned and passed on as a tradition within the group. Children learn languages from adults. Adults can also learn new languages from other adults.

12  Unreliable. You can lie using language.

13  Reflexive. Language can be used to communicate about language.

Hockett maintained that even if many individual features in the list could be found in the communication systems of different animals, only human language shared all of them.

The list has its weaknesses, however. Even the very first point is incorrect: sign languages are human languages that are not transmitted by the voice and hearing. And not every use of language is transitory: written language can last for millennia. All the first five features treat spoken language as the given and ignore the other forms of language that humans use. These features cannot therefore be considered as universal characteristics of language – it is entirely possible to think of languages that fail to demonstrate all five.

More generally, Hockett has been criticised because his list focuses on the superficial features of language and not on the more profound aspects of its content and structure, nor on the way language is processed in our brains. Several of the features in Hockett's list can be explained as superficial consequences of more fundamental properties of language.

The almost boundless expressiveness of language, its capacity to express an infinite multitude of different messages, is one such fundamental aspect – language is free to expand by including new words and putting those words into new sentences without ever encountering any limitation other than the purely practical. Several of Hockett's features are quite simply the inevitable consequences of this expressiveness. A language that was not semantic (Hockett 7) – with specific meanings tied to linguistic signals – would not be capable of expressing many messages at all. A language that was not arbitrary (Hockett 8) – in which there was a direct and self-evident connection between each signal and what it signifies – would have difficulty expressing any significant proportion of what human languages can and do convey. It would be restricted to signals that directly resemble what they signify and limited in consequence to messages that could be expressed by signals that resemble the message in question. There are "languages" which possess elements of this kind of non-arbitrary signal. Many road signs for instance have a meaningful link to what they signify – a sign that warns road users about elks will show a picture of an elk, a sign that tells you to turn right will show an arrow pointing right and so on. But not even a "language" as limited as that of road signs can manage without arbitrary conventions. In Europe triangular signs warn of danger while circular signs indicate what road users may or may not do, but that is not the case in the United States. The connection between form and meaning here is entirely arbitrary. Ordinary human language possesses a tiny minority of words that are *iconic*: that are like what they signify. These are most often words for various sounds: "miaow", "bang" and so on. Sign languages may possess quite a large proportion of words like this because there are many more concepts that can be imitated with a gesture rather than a word. But sign languages, too, consist for the most part of arbitrary conventions.

A language that was not composite and made up of discrete units (Hockett 9) could never be as expressive as real human languages. Without the combinatory arrangements of sounds into words, each word in a spoken language would have to be a sound of its own and the human throat is not capable of producing the tens of thousands of different and distinct sounds that would be necessary. Without the capacity to combine words into sentences we would have needed as many words as there are messages to be expressed, and we have neither the time to learn the millions of different words that would be required nor the memory capacity to remember them.

A language that could not be learned (Hockett 11) would have to be passed on between the generations in some other way than by children learning it. Although it is common for fairly complex behaviours to be innate in animals, these are passed on genetically between generations and not by learning. There are limits to how much complexity can be stored by biological evolution in the genes, however, and human language with all its words and grammatical ingenuities is many orders of magnitude beyond those limits. The same limitation can be observed in birds: in species that produce simple sounds, these sounds are often innate, whereas the song of songbirds that produce more complex sounds is not innate but has to be passed on, with a new generation learning it from the previous one. Instead of an innate song, the nightingale possesses an inborn ability – and drive – to learn the complex songs of its species.

A language that possesses the infinite expressive possibilities of human language, can, of course, use that same flexibility to discuss itself. Hockett 13 does not therefore qualify to be on the list as a distinctive feature either.

* * *

Two bonobos – dwarf chimpanzees – are mating behind a bush in the jungle on the south bank of the Congo river. The coupling animals are a male and female, not something that can be taken for granted among bonobos – what humans refer to as bisexuality is the norm among this species. The female utters loud screams during the act; it sounds as though she is enjoying what the alpha male is up to. The noise has attracted the attention of other members of the troop, which is the point – the female is keen for

them to know who she is mating with. But they fail to notice that
the alpha female in the troop is having a bit of fun with a young
female behind another bush at the same time, because she is
keeping quiet. Sex with a low status partner is not something to
yell about.[4]

These mating cries do not resemble language in themselves –
what they call to mind instead is the sounds humans make in
the corresponding situation – but they share Hockett 12 with
language in that they are being employed both flexibly and tactically. Bonobos can use their cries – or their silence – to "lie", and
not many animals can do that. Or, to be more precise, there are
very few animals that show signs of *deliberately* lying, who can
choose to lie, that is. In fact, lies in the form of false messages
are far from rare in the animal kingdom. The striped abdomen
of the wasp signals a genuine warning – you need to keep clear –
but the abdomen of a hoverfly, which is similarly striped, is
broadcasting a false note of caution because hoverflies are quite
harmless. In a sense the hoverfly is using its colours to "lie",
but it cannot choose to do so. The hoverfly shows the deceptive
colours evolution has provided it with, whether it wants them
or not, and is presumably blissfully ignorant of the fact that it is
sailing under a false flag.

   We need to devote some space to lying at this point because
the ability to lie is actually a crucial feature of language and one
we need to pay special attention to in relation to the evolution of
the human faculty for language.

   What was the first practical use Man made of [speech]?
   Remember he was, by that time, past-master in all arts of
   camouflage known to the beasts. [. . .] In short he could act
   any kind of lie then extant. I submit, therefore, that the

---

4   This little tale is based on observations of wild bonobos in the Congo carried out
by the British primatologist Zanna Clay.

first use Man made of his new power of expression was to tell a lie – a frigid and calculated lie.[5]

Animals can communicate in many different ways, but in most cases their communications are honest – not because other animals are that much more honest than we are but because animal signals have most frequently evolved in such a way that they are impossible to lie with. Elk bulls transmit a message via their antlers; one with twelve points "is saying" with its headgear: *Look how big and strong I am since I can wear a crown this large, if you are a female I will be a great dad for your calves, if you are a male there's no point you trying to fight me because you're bound to lose.* Elks cannot lie with their antlers for the simple reason that an elk that is not actually big and strong will be incapable of developing and wearing tines that are that large. The lie would give itself away. The same applies to the calls of the blackcock or the song of the nightingale – singing and calling for hours is *hard work* and a male has to be in peak form to be able to do it.

So wouldn't all animals be able to save a lot of energy if they evolved signals that were less costly instead? Well, yes, they would – but no-one would take the "cheap" signals seriously. Let's say that elks evolve a cheap signal to demonstrate their strength: instead of a heavy and impractical set of antlers with a great many tines, they show a number of patches on their breast with as many spots as they would have had antler points. The patches would cost almost nothing to possess. And they'd be so much more practical! And so it would prove for a short while . . . until evolution started helping a weak little elk bull by giving him a lot more patches than he actually merits. Younger elk bulls give way to the little fellow and the females let him have his way . . . and the genes for possessing an entirely undeserved number of patches spread rapidly through the elk population. Soon, within a few generations, all elk bulls

5 Kipling, R., *A Book of Words: Selections from Speeches and Addresses Delivered Between 1906 and 1927* (1928).

have got a huge number of patches, and the same spots have become entirely meaningless as a sign of strength. They all stop bothering about the patches and pit their strength against one another the hard way instead. Costly signals that cannot be used to mislead provide the only stable evolutionary route for elks.

But human language does not work that way. Talk is cheap and we lie at will – and yet human communication does not fall apart as it would in the case of the spotted elks. We listen to one another and trust each other, more or less, even though lying is so easy. Human language is an evolutionary paradox in this regard and one that demands an extraordinary explanation. However language evolved, it did not do so the way elk antlers or birdsong or the communication systems of most animals have done.

Hockett 12, which relates to the unreliability of language, therefore stands the test as a key feature of language. This is closely connected to the fact that language is cheap to use. *Human language with all its potential for lying could not have evolved until we trusted one another sufficiently.*

Hockett 6, which tells us that language is used intentionally, and Hockett 10 that language can handle matters other than the here and now are two further features that pass muster and require explanation. There is no need for a more profound explanation directly connected with language when it comes to Hockett 6, as a lot of primate communication also appears to be intentional. The difficulty here lies rather in explaining where intentions come from, but that would require a book of its own.

The fact that language is not limited to the here and now is an important point. This can be stated in more general terms as language being characterised by what is known as triadic (three-sided) communication. The communications of animals are mostly dyadic (two-sided), they involve only the "speaker" and the "listener" and do not refer to any third party or to anything outside those immediately involved. Human triadic communication on the other hand almost always involves something more than the speaker and the listener: most sentences in language refer to a third party, someone or something else separate from the individuals who are directly engaged in the conversation. We are conspicuously fond of talking about people who are absent, which is something animals do extremely rarely.

There are isolated examples of triadic communication among animals. Warning cries may be the clearest example – a "speaker" utters a cry when danger approaches. And a "listener" comprehends that the cry refers to the approaching danger. Here, the danger serves as the third party that makes the communication triadic. But this is the exception, and the absolute freedom to refer to anything at all that human language enjoys is entirely absent among other animals.

The speaker and the listener are always here and now, and for that reason dyadic communication is restricted to the present time and current place. The capacity to communicate triadically is therefore a prerequisite for being able to talk about that which is not here and now.

## UNIVERSALS

The features Hockett included in his list were all rather abstract and general. The extent to which any more specific features exist that all languages share – linguistic universals – is a hotly debated topic among language specialists. Many universals have been proposed by various researchers, but when a broader and more diverse range of languages has been examined exceptions have been found to almost all of them. Here are a couple of examples:

- All languages were thought to possess both consonants and vowels. *Exception*: Sign language. Although when it comes to spoken languages it does appear to be true that all of them distinguish between consonants and vowels.

- All languages were thought to be able to begin a syllable with a consonant. *Exception*: in addition to sign language, the syllables of the Australian Aboriginal language *Arrernte* never begin with a consonant.

- All languages were believed to possess a structure of main clauses to which subordinate clauses can be added along with sub-subordinate clauses and so on in many layers. "This book is written by a writer who lives in Falun, which is a town in Dalecarlia, which is a province in Sweden, which is a country in Europe, which . . ." *Exception*: the Brazilian language *Pirahã*, perhaps, which lacks subordinate clauses and similar constructions according to the linguist Daniel Everett.

There are, however, a few all-encompassing universals that do appear to be strictly valid:

- All languages have words in some form, although the form may vary enormously and it is sometimes difficult to draw firm boundaries around individual words.

- All languages distinguish between nouns and verbs. This is not, however, undisputed and depends on exactly how nouns and verbs are defined, but when using the generally accepted definitions all languages appear in some way to differentiate between words for things – nouns – and words for doing something – verbs.

- All languages have interjections – exclamations such as: Wow! Damn! Bam! – which exist somewhat apart from the actual grammar of the language.

- All languages possess a hierarchy of linguistic building blocks. Individual sounds (or gestures and hand shapes in sign language) can be combined into words, words can be combined into phrases and phrases combined into sentences. The hierarchy in almost all languages has several levels but the above three at least can be found in all of them. This universal is essentially the same as Hockett 9.

All languages have some kind of structure that determines how the building blocks can be put together; language is not just a long sequence of disconnected sounds and words that can be rearranged at will; there are always rules for how the building blocks on one level can be combined on the next one.

- All languages are open systems, such that a speaker can coin new words and other components and try to get them accepted in the language.

- All languages are flexible systems, such that a speaker has considerable room for manoeuvre in how to put a thought into words: "The woman is driving the car", "The car is being driven by the woman", "That is the woman who is driving the car", "That is the car being driven by the woman", "Driving is what the woman does with the car", and so on. All these variants are essentially describing the same event using the same words but employing the flexibility of English to provide different perspectives and emphases on various aspects of the event. Flexibility can take extremely varied forms in different languages but is always present in one way or other.

- Grammatical rules are valid for phrases and not for individual words. One example is the rule in English for making a question out of a statement. A question can be made of "Lisa is in the car" by altering the sentence to "Is Lisa in the car?" However, although the grammar rule behind this does not say the first two words have to switch places but that (simplified) the subject phrase and the verb have to change places. "The little girl with brown eyes is in the car," becomes "Is the little girl with brown eyes in the car?" The phrase "the little girl with brown eyes" is the subject so the whole phrase has to switch places with the

verb "is". Simply changing around the first two words –
"Little the girl with brown eyes is in the car" – would just
be silly. This is what is meant by saying that the rules of
grammar apply to phrases. This applies to all the grammatical rules for the sequence of words in all languages
(even though the form a phrase may take can be extremely
varied in different languages).

- All languages can express an infinite number of different
  thoughts; almost every human thought can be put into
  words in every human language.

Even if there are not that many universals which are valid in the
strict sense, the ones that *do* exist still need to be explained in some
way, particularly for anyone trying to discover the origin of human
language. And in addition to the universals that seem to be valid
for *all* languages, there are many more that are valid for the vast
majority of them, as well as a great many patterns and connections
between the various grammatical rules in a language. An example
of a grammatical pattern that exists in most languages is the existence of a link between how words are arranged in various kinds of
pairings. An adjective normally belongs with a noun – "red house"
– just as a preposition does with a noun – "to the house" – and a
verb frequently has an object, the object of the action that the verb
describes. In a sentence like "the woman is driving the car", "the
car" is the object of the verb "is driving". Different languages may
put these pairings in various orders. In English we say, "the woman
is driving the car", but roughly half the world's languages do the
opposite and say the equivalent of "The woman the car is driving".[6]

6 It is by no means self-evident either that "the woman" should stand first in the
sentence. Every conceivable permutation of subject+verb+object appears in at least
one language across the globe. Filipino languages, for example, most often have the
sequence: "Is driving the woman the car" and Fijian has "Is driving the car the woman".
Having the object first is considerably less common and only occurs in isolated
languages. Even so it is popular in science fiction to have aliens talk just like that – object
first word order the character Yoda in the *Star Wars* films uses, and in *Star Trek* the
object+verb+subject word order has the Klingon language.

Similarly, many languages do the opposite with adjectives and prepositions (which are then known as postpositions): "house red" and "house to". The point here is that there are connections between these different word pairings, so that a language that has the verb-object word order usually also has the preposition-noun order and the noun-adjective order. Languages with the order object-verb usually have the order noun-postposition instead along with the order adjective-noun. Like Swedish, English does not conform entirely to the first pattern but most languages follow one or other of these two patterns. These patterns, too, need to be explained in some way – they are far too consistent to be pure matters of chance.

## PUZZLING, SPEAKING AND WRITING

A crucial question in relation to language is how linguistic communication actually works. Two major lines of inquiry can be distinguished here: on the one hand, language as a code; on the other, what is referred to as ostensive-inferential communication.

If language is a code then the linguistic expression itself conveys all the information communicated. The speaker converts his or her message into the linguistic code; the listener then decodes what has been said and thus understands the speaker's message. Ostensive-inferential communication works in an entirely different way to a code. Much of the actual message in this form of communication is not conveyed by the purely linguistic expression but by all the circumstances that surround the utterance, and the listener has to piece together a puzzle in order to reconstruct the speaker's intended message.

The ostensive aspect involves the speaker. The mere fact that the speaker is speaking demonstrates an intention to communicate, and everything the speaker does in relation to the communication helps to make clear the intentions of the speaker in addition to what is contained in the purely linguistic message. All communication takes place in a context as well, and the speaker uses both the context and the situation to get his or her message across.

The inferential aspect relates to the listener, who does not simply passively decode what has been said but also takes in everything the speaker does and the communicative context as a whole. The listener then draws conclusions (inferences) from the whole process, not just from the linguistic content, about what the speaker intended. The speaker in their turn can exploit this to tailor the message so that the listener draws the correct conclusions. In practice, this "tailoring" is frequently used to simplify communication, with the speaker leaving out parts of the message that the listener can be expected to have worked out.

These two sorts of communication could be likened to two ways of transmitting an image to a recipient. In terms of language as a code, the equivalent would be sending a complete picture so that the recipient can immediately see what it represents. Whereas in ostensive-inferential communication, the image is treated more as a puzzle. The sender does not transmit a puzzle that has been laid and completed but exactly as many pieces of the puzzle as are necessary for the recipient to have enough clues to figure out what the image in the puzzle is supposed to represent. The pieces of the puzzle are clues, obviously, but so is everything else the sender does, including which clues to select. The recipient then pieces together the various clues into a message. That is why ostensive-inferential communication could also be called "puzzle communication", which is I what I intend to call it throughout this book. We will frequently have cause to return to piecing the bits of the puzzle together.

\* \* \*

It is important to keep the distinction between spoken and written language in mind when seeking to explain language in general and grammar in particular. Spoken language, the kind we use in natural everyday conversation, differs a good deal from formal written language. The spoken (or signed) word is normally used face to face, and the speaker and the listener both have a relationship of some kind and a shared context for their conversation. These are the ideal circumstances for puzzle communication: the listener has many of the pieces to put together in addition to the words themselves, and the speaker has a good grasp of which pieces the listener already has at their disposal. This is why it is often possible in spoken language to leave out large sections of the message and still be confident that the listener can piece the whole thing together. So spoken language frequently contains what would in the written language be regarded as incomplete and ungrammatical fragments. These fragments function perfectly well nonetheless because the listener already has all the other bits of the puzzle required, and they should not be considered ungrammatical when used in spoken language.

The written word is more or less permanent and is often used with a considerable distance existing between the writer and the reader. The writer may not even know who will read the text, and the reader is not familiar with the writer's context. This book can serve as an example – it is intended to be read by many different people with whom I have no relationship outside these pages. You do not know me, I do not know you, and I do not know what pieces of the puzzle you possess apart from the ones in this text. This makes it much harder to communicate in terms of a puzzle. In writing – but also on television, in public lectures and other forms of impersonal communication – language must therefore be used in a more code-like way; the entire message needs to be contained in the words that are actually said, and what is said needs to follow stricter rules.

A grammar that describes coded communication and a grammar that describes puzzle communication will take very different forms because the information structures will be so different. A puzzle grammar in particular will need much more liberal rules about what can be left out or abbreviated. As a result it is frequently difficult to adapt spoken language to the rules of the grammar of written language if one is to remain true to the spoken language.

So what kind of language are we going to uncover when we find its origin? The answer to that question lies in what sort of language the original language was. And there are simply no two ways about it – both written language and television are very recent occurrences. For 99 per cent of the time that has passed since language first emerged, only spoken language existed, used face to face. It is only during the most recent 1 per cent of that existence that written language has even been around, and it is only in the last hundred years that writing has been more than a very marginal event for a tiny elite. Written language is an artificial and relatively novel form that we can leave aside in our search for the origins of language as such.

Written language also differs from spoken in that virtually all human beings learn to talk quickly and almost automatically, while far from all of us will learn to write. The art of writing, unlike the ability to speak, has to be learned by children the hard way. There are also far greater differences between people in their ability to write than in their ability to speak – or rather, greater differences in the ability to communicate impersonally rather than personally. Anyone and everyone can manage personal puzzle communication, face to face, but using the formal structures necessary to be good at *im*personal communication requires both talent and comprehensive training.

*Almost all language use throughout history has been oral conversation face to face, between human beings who know each other well and who share an all-encompassing social context. That is also the sort of language that children are exceptionally good at learning. And that is the kind of language whose origin we are trying to find.*

## THE NATURE OF GRAMMAR

So how does grammar relate to the way language is actually used? Are there rules of grammar in our minds, and if so what kind of rules are they? How does grammar actually work? We will need to devote a few pages to these issues because the answers have a considerable bearing on what kinds of explanation we will then be seeking for the origin of grammar.

When we use language on an everyday basis we rarely think about grammar. If we were not taught a bit of basic grammar at school most of us would not think about grammatical rules at all. Our use of grammar when we speak is normally therefore completely unconscious even if it usually proves to be correct. But not always – every now and then we get sloppy when we're talking, which makes it easy to lose the grammatical thread, particularly when we hesitate or pause in a sentence and then we may end up not getting everything in the right place. On the whole grammar works without the person speaking having to be aware that there is any such thing.

We often become aware of someone else breaking grammatical rules, however. We notice when someone uses the wrong word order or conjugates a verb the wrong way. We may not always be able to put our finger on just what was wrong, and we usually have no problem understanding what was meant, yet we know there was something jarring in what we just heard. How do we know this unless we are consciously aware of grammar?

At one level there is nothing odd about that at all. We know how to do lots of things without having a conscious understanding of the theoretical basis of what we are doing. You can ride a bike without consciously knowing anything about torque or angular momentum, you can throw a ball and hit the target without consciously knowing anything about ballistics, and so on. Most motor skills work that way – we learn how to do them rather than understand them. It isn't even clear that understanding is helpful – I know ballistics and can calculate a trajectory with no problem, but my ball skills are rubbish in practice.

So grammar appears to function in our minds much the same way our motor skills do, as something we learn to employ entirely automatically, without needing to think about it. What grammar also has in common with riding a bike is that when we try to provide a conscious theoretical analysis of what we're doing, the task turns out to be strikingly difficult. No human language can be simply captured with some handy theoretical description.

Linguists all over the world disagree about how grammar is actually structured in our brains. There are several fundamentally different grammatical theories in circulation.

The term "paradigm" as used here is a concept derived from the philosopher of science Thomas Kuhn's 1962 book *The Structure of Scientific Revolutions*. He employs the term to describe a not unusual situation in science when there are profound differences of opinion between scientists. Not only do they disagree about the answers to research problems, they also cannot agree on precisely which questions should be answered. Different paradigms subscribe to such totally different worldviews that communication and comparisons between them are barely meaningful.

This is more or less the place we find ourselves in when it comes to grammar. There is no consensus about the nature of the questions a theory of grammar should answer and even less of one about the answers.

One of the few things there is agreement about, however, is that the grammar in our brains bears little resemblance to the rules of grammar many of us were taught at school, but then views differ radically as to what form it actually takes – the different paradigms speak entirely different languages.

There is also agreement that, in addition to grammar, we also have a lexicon in our heads. After all, every language user knows thousands of words and there must be something in the brain to keep track of all those words, how they sound and what they mean.

We call this something a mental lexicon without actually knowing very much at all about the way it works – and without being able to agree about the relation between the lexicon and grammar.

There are therefore a number of grammatical paradigms on offer; that is, fundamentally different ideas about the way grammar works and which questions a theory of grammar ought to answer.

## Generative Grammar

Generative grammar is the name given to one of the most prominent grammatical paradigms, a family of grammatical theories that have their roots in Noam Chomsky's groundbreaking work from the 1950s onwards. In these theories grammar consists of a set of rules for how grammatical sentences can be generated. Generating sentences involves using the rules of language roughly like a computer, scanning through the regulatory system on a systematic basis in order to form sentences that comply with the rules. This could be compared with a computer program designed to play chess that can use its knowledge of the rules of the game to work out all the positions a player is permitted to move to based on the current state of play on the board. This generation of every possible sentence and every possible position is more theoretical than practical. In relation to both language and chess – both the number of possible sentences and moves are far greater than the capacity of any one brain, or for that matter of any computer. Chess is, however, finite, whereas language is considered to be infinite in the generative paradigm.

Both in chess and in language there are limits to what can be generated. A chess position in which both kings are on adjacent squares is impossible to arrive at according to the rules of the game, and a sentence with the word order "Woman on a driven has road the car" is just as impossible to arrive at if following the rules of English grammar. The pattern of which word orders can and cannot be generated, and how the various word orders are interpreted, are vital clues to the underlying rules.

This is extremely simplified, and modern versions of generative theories are considerably more subtle. But the basic idea remains that grammar is a set of rules, or mathematical operations, that can generate all the grammatical sentences of a language, and that language is defined as the sentences grammar generates. In this view, grammar is considered to be managed by an entirely autonomous module in the brain that is not closely related to the rest of our cognitive capacity, nor directly woven into our lexicon or the process that ultimately converts what we mean to say into actual speech.

Generative grammar is closely associated with the idea that grammar is innate. In that case we are born with that grammar module built in and ready to go. It is, of course, not the grammar of a specific language that is innate, but the general software for managing that grammar which incorporates universal grammatical principles. All children have to do when they learn the grammar of their mother tongue is adjust various settings and parameters in the module, much in the same way that you change the settings of your computer at home.

The basic principle of generative grammar is that language is a code; what is said linguistically should be self-sufficient. Grammatical structure is the core of language and grammar defines language. The paradigm has no place for puzzle communication with all its linguistic shortcuts. The focus is on the written word. Traditionally, grammar has been explored by means of the researcher's own introspective judgements of what feels grammatical or ungrammatical, although other methods have also begun to be employed.

In generative grammar, imperfections and slips of the tongue are dealt with by referral to other mental systems outside grammar itself, which is seen as perfect.

## Connectionist Grammar

A paradigm of an entirely different sort is provided by connectionist grammar. In this paradigm there are in fact no grammatical rules at all. Instead, connectionism starts from the premise that human cognitive abilities, including the linguistic faculty, are based on neural networks. These are networks of nerve cells in the brain, in which each neuron is connected to a large number of others. Every connection between neurons has a certain weight, and the greater that weight, the more the neuron at one end of the connection affects the neuron at the other end. The network is open at both ends so that information can be fed in at one end and a result is produced at the other. The pattern of weights between neurons determines what a neural network does and what results it produces.

According to connectionism, all grammar exists in a network of this kind, in which the brain inputs what you want to say at one end of the network and a fully formulated sentence comes out at the other end – and then vice versa in the brain of the listener. Which language one is speaking is determined by the pattern of connections and connective weights in the network. It is not possible to point to any one spot in the network and say "there is the grammatical rule for the plural"; instead, every rule is distributed throughout the pattern of the network.

Artificial neural networks, in which neurons are simulated in computers, are extensively used in the field of artificial intelligence, particularly when computers are supposed to learn how to recognise patterns or images. Most of us have encountered apps, for example, that can identify where there is a face in an image – the core of such an app is very likely to be an artificial neural network.

A prominent feature of neural networks is that they have no problem dealing with imperfection and variation; on the contrary, it is rather difficult to get a network to deliver anything that is as respectful of the rules as human grammar. The grammar rules that deal with the connections between words that are far removed from each other in a sentence are particularly difficult for connectionist models to deal with, as are sentences with several layers of embedded subordinate clauses.

Studies of the human brain at the microscopic level have, of course, made clear that it is made up of vast numbers of neurons with each neuron connected in turn to large numbers of other nerve cells. To that extent connectionism appears well founded as it stays closer to the actual structure of the brain than other paradigms. The question is not whether there are neural networks in our heads, because there are. Instead, the issue is whether this is a positive and fruitful level at which to describe human language, and that is where many linguists have their doubts.

## Functionalist Grammar

A third paradigm is the functionalist one and, as the name suggests, the focus of this approach is on the communicative function of language. Although this paradigm has been around for almost a century, it was thoroughly crushed by generative grammar in the 1960s. Not totally eradicated, however, it continued to survive in a number of countries. In recent years it has enjoyed a renaissance with the growth of cognitive linguistics, systemic functional grammar and construction grammar.

By and large what cognitive linguistics postulates is the exact opposite of generative grammar. It considers grammar not as existing in some separate module, but as being intimately connected with our general cognitive abilities and conceptual apparatus. Grammar has no real autonomous existence, but is rather a product of our conceptual apparatus and the way concepts relate to each other. Language is a dynamic process that is formed in interaction with our thoughts.

Cognitive linguistics is attractive in many ways and has obvious points of contact with our flexible and highly metaphorical use of language. It is nevertheless difficult to derive a theory of grammar from cognitive linguistics that is sufficiently robust and specific to produce grammatical analyses, or to explore arguments about the origin of grammar.

Construction grammar is one of those more robust theories of grammar that currently belongs within the functionalist paradigm and is fairly close in philosophical terms to cognitive linguistics, even though the original roots of construction grammar belong within the generative paradigm.

The starting point for construction grammar is our mental lexicon. Everyone agrees that in addition to words our lexicon also contains a good number of idiomatic expressions. To "kick the bucket" does not mean knocking over a pail unless you are a domestic cleaner, although neither the word bucket nor the other words in the expression have anything to do with death. The meaning of "to die" is connected to the expression "to kick the bucket" as a whole, and therefore the whole expression must be contained in our mental lexicon in the same way that the *OED* or Merriam-Webster also refers to the expression in its entirety.

What construction grammar does is to generalise from this notion of idiomatic phrases. No distinction is made between grammar and lexicon in construction grammar: everything becomes expressions, which are known as constructions, in this theory. The simplest expressions are individual words as in a standard dictionary. Then there are set phrases which always have the same form such as "by all means" or "you're welcome". The next stage is expressions with variable parts. "To kick the bucket" is a good example because the phrase can vary slightly. That concluding "the bucket" remains the same but you can say, "He kicked the bucket", or "She'll kick the bucket soon", or other variants with different subjects and tenses of the verb and in which you can insert an adverb (e.g "soon") of your choice. The construction is therefore not "To kick the bucket" but "*Subject* kick + *tense* the bucket (*adverb*)", in which the elements in italics indicate that a word of your choice (or a construction of your choice) of the right kind is to be inserted in the construction. The brackets designate an optional element. These constructions can be made more and more abstract and include several optional components. What are considered grammatical rules in other theories become abstract constructions in construction grammar. There is no one rule in this theory that says that the word order in a sentence is normally subject-verb-object. Instead, there is a construction that says "*Subject verb object*" and then other constructions that specify how the subject and the other components may be put together. Although in practice these abstract constructions resemble rules to a considerable extent, the underlying way of thinking about grammar is entirely different.

Puzzle communication feels naturally at home within the functionalist paradigm. The latter is not just about encoding and decoding linguistic utterances, but actively using the whole range of our cognitive abilities. Cognitive linguistics stresses this aspect in particular. Seen from a functionalist perspective, many apparently ungrammatical elements in the informal use of language become a natural consequence of the relative freedom afforded by puzzle communication to omit the sort of thing that recipients can work out by themselves.

Linguistic variation and development are also fairly straightforward to deal with in functionalist terms. There is even a variety of construction grammar called Fluid Construction Grammar that is designed to be able to deal with the evolution of language in both formal and practical terms and that is much used in certain areas of the research devoted to the subject.

## Theories of Grammar and the Origin of Language

There are more grammatical paradigms than the three I have outlined here, but I consider these three to be the most relevant to the aims of this book. In addition, several variants exist within each paradigm. While all these grammatical paradigms have their proponents, none of them has managed to convince an over-whelming majority among the linguists of the world. They are all being actively researched, and the theories are continually being developed and refined.

As for the question of the origin of language, and more part-icularly the origin of grammar, it is vitally important to determine the nature of the grammar whose origin is to be studied. Seeking the origin of a generative grammar would require answers to completely different questions than seeking the origin of a con-nectionist grammar or a construction one.

Within the generative paradigm it is the origin of the grammar module in the main that has to be accounted for. Basically, the grammar module is used solely for linguistic purposes and is con-sidered to be an indivisible unit that cannot be put together piece by piece. This makes the question of if and how the module evolved a particularly hard nut to crack.

The counterpart to the grammar module in the connectionist paradigm poses little difficulty – our brains are, after all, full of neural networks. Here the problem of the origin of grammar becomes more a question of why we devoted so much of our brain capacity to networks that deal purely with grammar, and how these networks evolved to handle apparently rule-governed hierarchies and, furthermore, why we evolved sufficient capacity for this purpose. Why did we end up with such large brains?

Cognitive linguistics considers language to be the natural consequence of our applying general cognitive abilities to social interactions and our mutual desire to communicate with fellow human beings. What needs to be accounted for in this context is our general cognitive and social evolution as a whole; the origin of grammar does not require a more sophisticated explanation of its own.

Construction grammar involves more grammatical machinery that requires explaining, and resembles generative grammar in that sense. But, unlike the latter, the machinery is not isolated in a separate module and may be broken down fairly easily into smaller components that could have evolved one at a time. Instead of one vast question as to the origin that is difficult to solve, this poses many small questions that would be easier for Darwin to crack.

# Language in Other Creatures?

A bee is returning to its hive. It has been out scouting for flowers and has found a rich array in a bed some way away. There is much more nectar to collect than this bee can manage on its own before the flowers wither. Once inside the hive the bee climbs up onto one of the combs and starts to dance back and forth. The dance moves diagonally up the comb, back and forth in a figure of eight as the bee waggles its abdomen. Other bees gather around and watch. When the first bee has finished dancing the bees set off out of the hive. The bees who were watching the dance fly straight to the flower bed and start harvesting nectar and pollen.

* * *

How did the other bees know where to find the flowers? Because the location could be worked out from the dance of the first bee, known as the "waggle dance". There are patterns in the dance that function like a code. If the dance moves straight up the comb, the flowers are exactly in the direction of the sun outside. If the dance moves diagonally upwards to the right, the flowers are just as much to the right of the sun outside. The further the bee dances up the comb, the further the flowers are from the hive. And so on. The dance serves as a detailed route map towards their food source for the other bees.

Is the waggle dance a language? The dance has some of the features of language – it transmits a complex message; it is made up of several components; it deals with things that are not

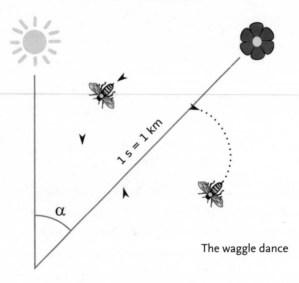

The waggle dance

immediately present. And yet it also lacks other key features – the dance is limited to a set and very small repertoire of messages; it is entirely innate, and there is no flexibility as to the signals used or the meaning. This dance language is well suited to its limited goals but is also an evolutionary cul-de-sac; it would be extremely difficult for the dance to evolve into a more extensive form of language.

In that case why are we considering a cul-de-sac at this point and one, besides, which involves creatures we are only very distantly related to? Because one way of shedding light on the origin of language is to make comparisons with the way other animals communicate. Ways of communicating that share some of the key features of language without actually being languages are especially interesting. They may have something to tell us about the origin of some of those features. We will be considering a few more of these other ways of communicating in this chapter.

\* \* \*

A male nightingale sits on a branch in spring and sings as loud as it can. The song contains a wealth of different sounds that are combined in a constantly varying pattern. An average male nightingale employs about 250 different sounds in its song, which is more than are used in any human language, and he may have a repertoire of 180 different phrases that can then be combined into long snatches of song.

\* \* \*

I think the song of the nightingale is lovely and in that I am not alone; few other birds have had so much poetry dedicated to them. The English poet John Keats (1795–1821) magnificently evokes its song in his poem "Ode to the Nightingale":

> *That thou, light-winged Dryad of the trees*
> *In some melodious plot*
> *Of beechen green, and shadows numberless,*
> *Singest of summer in full-throated ease.*

Not that being the object of human poetry is anywhere near the point for the nightingale when it is singing. Male nightingales sing because female nightingales like singing males. And male nightingales compose complex songs with a great deal of variation because that is what the females prefer. The more intricate a song the male manages to compile, the greater his chances of being chosen as a partner. Sexual selection favours the evolution of the ability to sing. The male that fails to sing well will not father any young, and all young nightingales have a talented vocalist as a sire – and a mother who likes gifted singers. An evolutionary arms race is the outcome and it leads towards ever more sophisticated singing by nightingales.

Is birdsong a language? Like the dance of the bees, birdsong shares several features with speech. Combining sounds into phrases and phrases into songs resembles the way language puts together sounds into words and words into sentences. Each species also has rules of its own that govern how the sounds can be combined; rules that could be likened to a grammar for its song. And yet there is a fundamental difference between birdsong and language – birdsong only contains a single message, and the message is the same no matter how the bird composes its song. The only thing a nightingale is saying with its song is: *Look at me, listen to how beautifully I am singing; I will be a wonderful father for your children.* The song may have infinite variations, but the message does not vary at all – in contrast with the unlimited variation of the messages conveyed by the combinatory systems of human languages.

Unlike the dance of the bees the song of the nightingale may, theoretically, possess the capacity to be as expressive as human languages but what the nightingale lacks is the flexible connection between form and message that characterises our language. And although some bird species at least have the intellectual capacity to learn to connect a certain sound with a certain meaning – which might have laid the foundations for a language evolving – no bird has ever taken that step. Evolution may have restricted the nightingale's options inasmuch as its entire song is a single message and a male nightingale that began to analyse its song and use different parts for different purposes would lose his sex appeal and be unable to mate.

* * *

Two squid, a male and a female, are circling each other above a sandy sea floor near a coral reef in the warm seas off Jamaica. Both the male and the female change colour to make different garish patterns several times during their dance. Another male appears and swims towards the dancing couple. The first male puts himself between the newcomer and the female, turning his flank towards the intruder. On that side he changes colour to a fierce pattern of zebra stripes while on the side turned towards the female he continues to display his courting colours. The newcomer adopts the same zebra-striped pattern, signalling his readiness to fight.

\* \* \*

Squid of the species *Sepioteuthis sepioidea* communicate with patterns of colour. They change colour like chameleons – rather better in fact than chameleons themselves do – in order to send various messages to each other. They can produce a wide range of different patterns and many whose meaning we do not understand. Zebra stripes are an aggressive signal; certain other patterns are amorous but when it comes to most of their signals only the squids know what they mean.

Do these patterns constitute a language? We do not know. The fact that that possible language is made up of visual signals rather than of sounds is not a barrier. You are reading a book right now and thus absorbing language through visual patterns; a process that seems to work rather well in our case. Sign languages are another instance of visual languages, in which "the speaker" shows visual patterns to "the listener", that also function perfectly well; sign languages are complete languages with all the features and refinements possessed by spoken languages (and a few more). The system used by squid has the potential to communicate with the same complexity as a language, but we know too little about how the system is structured and how it is employed. The cephalopods, squid and octopuses that is, are also exceedingly intelligent creatures, particularly when compared with their closest relatives, mussels and snails, and they are capable of solving complex problems both in the wild and in the laboratory. They can use tools and they are difficult to keep in captivity because they are able to work out how to escape from a standard aquarium. There is a video on YouTube showing a tiny octopus locked inside an ordinary jam jar with a screw-top lid – it escapes by unscrewing the lid from the inside with its suckers. However, we have found nothing to indicate that the social interactions of squid are more complex or more differentiated than those of other animals without language. Perhaps they do not need a fully developed language even though they meet all the technical requirements?

\* \* \*

A little vervet monkey is sitting on the ground beneath an acacia tree in Tanzania, eating fallen seeds. One of the other monkeys in the troop suddenly utters a series of short croaks. The first vervet drops the seeds and climbs as fast as she can high up the tree and out on to the thinnest branches. All the other vervet monkeys that were on the ground do the same thing. They then sit there in safety waiting for the leopard to get tired and slink away. There was, in fact, a leopard nearby; that was what those croaking sounds meant.

A while later and the little vervet is still up in the tree. The leopard has long since disappeared, but there happens to be plenty of food up there so she stays where she is. Then she hears a series of muffled grunts from one of the other monkeys in the tree. This time she needs to get down to the ground as quickly as possible and hide in the bushes, because there is an eagle hovering above: that is what those grunts meant.

\* \* \*

Like many other animals, these vervet monkeys possess a range of sounds that they use to warn other members of the troop that danger is lurking. But the warning cries of the vervet are not just general warnings because each kind of cry warns of a specific danger. They allow these monkeys to make the right choice – climbing out onto the thinnest branches is a safe way to escape from a leopard but would be an idiotic thing to do if an eagle were in the air.

Are warning cries a language? Once again they have features

that resemble language. And unlike bird song, the warning cries actually mean something. But warning cries are a bit like the bees' dance – both their number and the complexity of the messages they contain are very restricted. Unlike the bees' dance the warning cries are also limited to what is occurring in the here and now. A vervet monkey cannot use the leopard warning to discuss the leopard that almost got them yesterday, or to ask its friend if it thinks there could be a leopard in the thicket over there. Although the warning cries in themselves are innate, a young vervet has to learn to use the right cry in the right situation, and sometimes they make mistakes.

What sets limits to the linguistic development of these monkeys is first and foremost that they have no simple way to expand their "vocabulary". They have no means of adding new cries with new meanings to it, except through the very slow changes wrought by evolution. Nor do they show any appetite for using the existing cries flexibly in new situations. The latter may reflect the fact that they are warning cries. Using them for purposes other than warning would be like crying wolf for fun – soon no-one would bother to listen to you. This locks the vervet monkeys into a closed system.

* * *

A school of dolphins is swimming in the sea off the island of Bohol in the Philippines. They spread out beside a small coral reef and start hunting for fish. They stay in contact using a broad range of whistling and chattering sounds. Some of the sounds are used by all of them – but each dolphin also possesses its own "signature tune" that it whistles every now and then in order to say "Here I am". The various dolphins recognise each other's signature tunes and that is how they check on the whereabouts of the other members of their school even when they are outside visual range in the labyrinth of coral.

A dolphin that has been away from the school for a while is on the way back. He whistles his signature tune as he approaches. His friends hear him and respond both by repeating his signature and by sounding their own. That is how the friends confirm that they remember and recognise him while also signalling where they are. The signature tune serves as a dolphin's name in many respects. Dolphins recognise each other's tunes even when a computer-generated copy is played back to them so the voice of the dolphin in question does not provide any clues. And they use the tunes both to signal their own identity and to communicate with another dolphin whose "name" is a particular tune.

A shark is in the water behind a coral cliff nearby. One of the dolphins discovers the shark using its sonar and then turns towards the school and broadcasts a pattern of sounds to the others which is a representation of the echo it got back from the shark. The others realise there is a shark in the vicinity and make sure to gather all their young together to keep them safe.

*  *  *

Most animals possess ways of communicating with other members of their species. Sometimes this is done using very basic means that need be no more complicated than the very whiteness of a white swan, which communicates the message: *I am an adult swan*, or a female butterfly that releases an aromatic substance into the air to inform interested males that she exists. This kind of communication probably occurs unconsciously and neither the swan nor the butterfly has any choice in the matter; they simply transmit their message to anyone in the neighbourhood. They cannot alter the message either, apart from the way in which the swan altered the message by becoming adult with the result that his plumage changed from grey to white.

But as the examples referred to earlier in this chapter demonstrate, animal communication can also be quite sophisticated. A number of features that resemble those found in human language appear in the communication systems of some species of animal. Both bees and birds assemble their messages from several components and, with regard to the bees at least, the nature of the message is determined by which elements are combined. Monkeys, dolphins and squid can use flexible forms of communication as a social tool that operates within the group. Monkeys, dolphins and bees can send messages that have a goal of some kind and that "point to" something outside themselves: food or predators or friends. All these are properties that are shared with human language.

Our closest relatives among the apes can communicate with a small number of sounds and a slightly larger number of gestures. Unlike the warning cries of the vervet, which function like a code, the way chimps communicate is more like piecing together the parts of a puzzle. As far as we know, their gestures do not have any fixed coded meaning but are used flexibly to produce different messages in different situations with the result that the recipient has to interpret what the communicative intent is behind the gestures.

Something that corresponds to most of the individual features of human language can be found in at least one kind of animal. Hockett's entire list of design features, which we discussed earlier, can be found distributed throughout the animal kingdom, although no single animal species displays more than a handful of them in the way they communicate. And nothing has been found in any other animal that is known to correspond to an essential feature of human language: the infinite possibilities it offers to express every conceivable message.

Or maybe not? Let us return to the dolphins for a moment. While the dolphins are swimming around they continually emit tiny pulses of sound and listen to the returning echoes of those pulses. This works exactly like the sonar on a boat, and radar, too, works on the same principle (though using radio waves instead).

Dolphins are incredibly skilled echolocators and can detect very small objects in the water or swim at high speed without colliding with anything even when the sea is full of obstacles and the water is too cloudy to see anything with their eyes. Dolphins do indeed have eyes, but in their natural environment they benefit more from echolocation and are able to "see" their surroundings primarily using their own form of sonar.

Scientists have recently discovered that dolphins can use their echolocating skills to emit patterns of echoes that resemble what they have "seen" using those same skills. We still do not know if they are actually using this technique to communicate, as in the episode I described with the shark in the dolphin story above, but that should be entirely possible. A dolphin that wants to tell another dolphin about something he has discovered should be able to use his own echolocating equipment to transmit a copy of the echo he received when he made the discovery. This fake echo might then allow the other dolphin to "see" what the first dolphin saw using its own sonar. It is more or less as though people were communicating by making little drawings for each other. This is after all something we can actually do if we want to – games such as Pictionary are based on that ability – although with only moderate accuracy when it comes to more abstract concepts.

Do dolphins have a language? They have a comprehensive system of different sounds that are used in different contexts, and they are very teachable and able to learn new sounds easily. They may be able to communicate non-abstract concepts using sonar images and also identify one another by their signature tunes. These elements might serve as the foundation for fairly advanced communication. But we know too little about how dolphins communicate in their natural environment to determine how much they can actually do with their system of communication, or to what extent it is like a language.

Perhaps we are being a bit too anthropomorphic when we ask whether dolphins have a language? Their system of sonar images has the potential to be just as powerful as a language but in an entirely different way. The manner in which dolphins communicate should be studied on its own terms and not be judged solely by whether or not it is like a language.

## CAN ANIMALS LEARN LANGUAGES?

Parrots are famous for being able to learn to talk – but they are also known to simply imitate sounds without understanding them, so well known indeed that the verb "parrot" means exactly that: to imitate without understanding. Parrots are good at imitating every conceivable sound, not just human speech – they can reproduce any sound imaginable and frequently with astonishing accuracy. They did not, of course, evolve their talent for imitation so that humans could teach them how to talk – parrots use those imitated sounds instead more or less like other species of bird employ song. Being able to sing as beautifully as possible and with as much variation as possible is considered sexy among nightingales – whereas what parrots find sexy is being able to imitate as many sounds as possible and as accurately as possible. Attempting to imitate – and to outdo any rivals in producing that imitation – forms part of the social interaction between parrots. For this reason they will often imitate all the sounds in their environment, particularly sounds they hear in a social context. It is that instinct which is exploited by humans who want to train parrots – let a parrot hear a human phrase a sufficient number of times while interacting with its trainer and it will probably start to imitate the phrase.

Has the parrot acquired language as a result – in any meaningful sense? Hardly. What a parrot normally learns is simply a number of set phrases that it keeps repeating, clearly without any understanding of what they mean and without the capacity to develop or make use of the words it has learned in new situations.

The fact that the parrot can imitate human speech is amazing though. It is an ability that is rare in the animal kingdom. There are quite a few birds that can imitate new sounds that they hear – apart from parrots this would include hummingbirds and some species of songbird – but most avians cannot do so, and there are few other species as good at it as parrots. There are also a handful of mammalian species that can imitate sounds, seals being one of them. But most animals are incapable of imitation; they are unable to control their vocal organs to produce a copy of a sound they have heard. The ability of primates to "ape" the sounds others make is very modest indeed, limited by and large to minor adjustments to the normal sounds primates make in order to adapt to the "dialect" of the troop they find themselves in.

People are, however, very good at imitating each other, much better than any other mammal. We are pretty good at imitating new sounds, any kind at all, and we improve with practice. But our imitative talents really come into their own with words – we have no difficulty at all in repeating a new word we have heard, and children who are learning language are imitating words all the time.

*The ability to imitate sounds is absolutely essential for spoken language. If we could not imitate the words we hear, we would never be able to learn new ones and this would mean a child could never develop language. And yet this capacity is lacking among our closest relatives, which means it must have arisen at some point in the course of our evolution as human beings.*

So why did we evolve that ability to imitate? For the sake of language, might seem to be the obvious answer. But here we are faced with which came first: the chicken or the egg? Evolution does not predict the future; characteristics do not evolve because they might be of some future benefit. If the ability to imitate is absolutely essential for spoken language then it must have existed before we began to speak – in which case we need another explanation than spoken language for why we started imitating sounds.

The birds that can imitate sounds clearly do so solely for

purposes of display. Imitation on the part of parrots and other avian species has no obvious practical function. Being skilled imitators is exclusively about making friends and gaining influence and, above all, opportunities to mate. It may be the case that the human ability to imitate has a similar origin, and that the early humans acquired high status by being able to imitate the other animals on the savannah, but we have no real evidence for any such thing. Researchers have also compared the ways modern humans use their ability to imitate in situations other than purely linguistic ones. It is not uncommon for hunter-gatherers to imitate animal sounds both in the context of hunting and when subsequently describing the hunt. Without language the ability to imitate animals might also have been important as a means of planning a hunt together. This is one of the possible origins of our imitative talents.

\* \* \*

"Fetch the striped ball!" The white border collie runs off to the other end of the garden, where there are a number of toys and returns with a striped ball. "Good dog. Fetch the duck." The dog goes searching and after a while comes back with a yellow plastic duck. "Well done! Biscuit?" "Woof" The dog gets its biscuit and lies down beside its owner to chew contentedly.

\* \* \*

Can animals learn language beyond simple imitation? And in that case, what can they learn? A lot of experiments have been carried out in the attempt to teach different animals to use language with varying degrees of success.

One thing that will be immediately obvious to people with any experience of dogs, horses and other pets is that it is entirely possible to teach animals to understand spoken commands. A dog can easily understand the word "Sit!" and with training learn to distinguish it from other similar words, which it is able to prove by not sitting down when we say "Fetch". With sufficient training many mammals manage to learn to obey commands, although some animals are much easier to train than others. Getting a cat to sit on command is considerably more difficult than getting a dog to do so, although based on my experience of cats I suspect that it is the desire that is lacking rather than the ability – taking orders is not really what cats do.

Does the fact that a dog can interpret commands in this way mean that dogs understand language? A very limited form of understanding in that case, it would have to be said. Dogs understand commands to the extent that they know what to do when they hear "Sit" and a few more words besides; many dogs also understand when we talk about giving them their food. There are also isolated examples of dogs understanding hundreds of words: when they are told to go and fetch a specified object, they will return with the right thing.

But this is still only a limited form of linguistic understanding. The dog learns a number of words while also learning to connect each word with something it is supposed to do. There is nothing to suggest that dogs understand any kind of grammar; they cannot understand sentences apart from possibly being able to pick up key words inside them, even if some dog owners choose to believe they understand much more than that. Nor is there anything to suggest that dogs can do anything with words other than connect them directly to actions that take place immediately, either their own such as sitting on command or ours when filling the dog bowl after we have said the word: "food". A key aspect of the human capacity for language is after all to be able to use words for things that may not be happening here and now; that is, however, beyond Fido.

* * *

Two creatures are sitting in front of a little table. There are various small items on the table, mostly toy bricks and balls in different colours.

Creature 1 says, "Give me a red brick", creature 2 picks up a red brick and gives it to the other creature. Creature 1 again: "How many green balls?" 2: "Three. I want a nut." 2 gets a nut. 1 goes on: "How many blue items?" "Two." "On the table there are a blue ball and a blue brick. What are there three of?" "Green balls." "You're so good at this. Here's another nut for you."

* * *

Another reason of course that dogs cannot learn to use a human language is that their vocal apparatus is not the least bit suited to our speech sounds; furthermore, they lack the ability to control their vocal organs so as to produce anything other than the usual sounds dogs make – barks, growls, snarls and howls; that is more or less it.

The above dialogue comes instead from a parrot that is replying to a human's questions. As already mentioned, these birds are perfectly capable of imitating human speech. But this particular parrot is doing something more than simple imitation: to all appearances it is using language "for real"; it seems to both understand the questions and to give sensible replies. The parrot's name is Alex and it was trained for many years by Irene Pepperberg.[7] Alex not only learned a large number of words, he also learned to

---

7 In addition to a number of scientific papers, Irene Pepperberg has also authored books about Alex. *Alex and Me* is a popular science account of Alex's life, while *The Alex Studies* presents a more formal account of what Alex was capable of. Alex died in 2007 at the age of forty, and is probably the only bird to have its obituary published in newspapers such as the *New York Times* and *The Economist*.

The dialogue above is not authentic but was put together by me based on the words spoken in real dialogues to give a more concise overview of the breadth of Alex's talents. Real dialogues with Alex took much more time and the leaps from one kind of question to another did not occur as quickly.

use the words as though he understood what they meant. He could answer several different kinds of question: about shapes, colours and numbers. It was possible to ask him, "How many green balls?" and get the answer "Three" when there were three green balls on the table, even when there were both red balls and green bricks on it as well. It was also possible to ask him, "What are there three of?" and get the answer "Green balls."

It is very hard to explain what Alex could do without coming to the conclusion first that Alex understood a large number of concepts about shapes, colours and numbers and second that he had sufficient linguistic ability to put these concepts into words.

And yet Alex never learned enough language to be able to hold an ordinary conversation about topics other than the ones he had been specifically trained in. While what Alex achieved is rather impressive nonetheless, particularly when you think that we are talking about a creature whose brain is the size of a walnut, he only learned a tiny fraction of human language, and it is far from clear how much grammar he really understood.

There have been many attempts to teach animals to speak – with varying and frequently very modest success. Parrots evidently have a talent for language and are in fact the animals that come closest to being able to learn to speak like people. All the attempts to get apes to speak have ended in complete fiasco: they lack the flexible control of their vocal organs that is required in order to produce speech sounds and combine them into words.

Not even raising a chimp in a human family, as a foster child among the biological children of human parents, made any significant difference. In the classic experiment carried out in the US at the beginning of the 1930s, the chimp managed to keep pace with her human foster brother in every respect save one – language. Gua, as the young chimp was called, learned to understand quite a lot of what her foster parents said but she could never produce any comprehensible sounds of her own. She responded to them instead with chimp sounds and while she learned to use those chimp sounds flexibly in new situations, she could never manage anything that even remotely resembled human speech.

But language is not necessarily synonymous with speech. Language can be expressed by many different means and still be language. And because speech production in particular proved to be such an insurmountable barrier for apes, researchers switched instead to trying to teach them to use language in other ways. Starting in the 1960s a number of experiments were carried out using either sign language or various types of artificial language with special symbols that an ape could produce by pressing a key or by pointing to the correct symbol on a board.

Teaching apes language via a medium that they could actually use worked considerably better than fruitless attempts to teach them to speak. The apes learned to produce a number of signs or symbols without any great difficulty and to do so in the right context.

The chimp Washoe (1965–2007) was a pioneer in the sign language experiments. The basic idea was the same as with Gua: to bring up a young chimp in a human setting that was steeped in language with the difference that this time it was signing that was employed. Washoe learned to use several hundred different signs adapted from ASL, the sign language used by the deaf in the United States. She used these signs for communication purposes in the appropriate context, and she could also combine a couple of signs into more or less meaningful combinations.

Another sign language experiment would prove to be a watershed in the debate on apes and language. The main character in this experiment was the chimp Nim Chimpsky.[8] Nim was taught sign language in much the same way as Washoe but under more laboratory-like conditions and using more formalised tests of his linguistic ability. The experiment was not particularly successful; Nim learned only a fairly small number of signs and did not

8  Distantly related to a certain celebrated linguist.

do very much with them. Herbert Terrace, the scientist running the experiment, concluded that chimps lack the ability to learn language, especially grammar, and that previous experiments had not been performed with sufficient care and the results had been interpreted too optimistically. Not enough attention had been paid to the Clever Hans effect in particular.

\* \* \*

Clever Hans, *der Kluge Hans*, was a horse that lived in Germany just over a hundred years ago. The horse became famous for its mathematical ability, and its owner made a lot of money exhibiting his talented horse. You could ask the horse any mathematical question you liked, and the horse would tap the ground with its hoof as many times as the answer to the question required. If you asked the horse what the square root of twenty-five was, for example, it would correctly tap five times.

One psychologist became suspicious of the horse genius, however, and carried out a number of detailed experiments on the animal. He concluded that while Clever Hans could not count at all, the horse was very good at detecting tiny clues in the behaviour of the questioner. If you asked a question and the horse started tapping its hoof, you would unconsciously stiffen as the horse approached the right answer and then relax when it had tapped the correct number of times. What Clever Hans was doing was simply detecting that relaxation and immediately stopping to tap.

This was discovered by not allowing the horse to see anyone who knew the answer to the question. The horse was then unable to answer the simplest question but just tapped at random. The horse could only answer correctly if it could watch someone who knew the answer.

\* \* \*

This is what is known as the Clever Hans effect: animals that are trained to learn something may not in fact be learning what the trainer thinks but learning instead to detect subtle unconscious clues on the part of the trainer that indicate what they are supposed to do. This could also be a factor when one of the apes is being trained to use sign language, because the trainer is closely involved in social interaction with the ape during the training and may well give off many clues about what the ape is supposed to do to get its reward. To guard against the Clever Hans effect in animal experiments it is vital that the animal be tested "blind" – the animal must have no access to anyone who can provide unconscious clues, and the animal's achievements must be assessed by someone who does not know the correct response.

There was no thought of any such safeguard in the previous experiments and as a result one could not exclude the possibility that Washoe was behaving in the same way as Clever Hans. The scientists were more careful with Nim Chimpsky but even so that did not work out well either. This led many researchers, but not all of them, to conclude that it was pointless to try and teach apes to speak.

A few new experiments were conducted in the 1970s, even though getting funding for these projects was rather difficult after the debacle with Nim Chimpsky. A gorilla by the name of Koko was taught sign language and proved even better at it than Washoe. According to reports provided by her trainer, Koko had over a thousand signs at her disposal by the time of her death in 2018 and could use them both communicatively and creatively for everyday purposes. The Koko experiment would also be criticised, however, for insufficient safeguarding against the Clever Hans effect.

Attempts have also been made to teach language to dolphins in various ways. They proved to be rather good at understanding the language they had learned, whether this was a sign language or a specially designed whistle language. Their understanding reached at least the same level as Alex or the apes. But in purely practical terms it was difficult to find a working means for them to produce a form of language that humans could understand despite the fact that dolphins have some ability to mimic sounds.

Two chimps called Sherman and Austin took part in another experiment, with a different structure and focus, that deserves more attention than it has received. Instead of allowing the young chimps to grow up in a human setting, a language-like communication system adapted to their own chimpanzee environment was introduced into a social setting that they shared with other chimps. Sherman and Austin were in their own rooms when they were given keyboards with a number of symbols on. They could see each other but not go into the other chimp's room, and they each had a screen on which they could see the symbols the other had pressed. This meant the chimps could use those symbols to communicate with each other, which was a lot more fun than always having to answer the stupid questions of human scientists. The chimps swiftly learned to use the symbols between themselves and could even agree on new meanings for them. One day they received a new piece of fruit in their food for which they had no symbol. They held this fruit up so they could both see it and one of them then chose an unused symbol on the keyboard and pressed it. They then quickly reached agreement that the symbol in question would stand for the new fruit.

This is significant because that is more or less the way new words arise in human languages. A new concept appears which means a new word is required in order to talk about the concept. Someone suggests a new word, either explicitly or by simply starting to use it. And other people latch on to the newcomer and a word is born. This is the basis for the richness and flexibility of human language, and something that Sherman and Austin were able to accomplish within the framework of their language of symbols. It is interesting that great apes possess such a language-related aptitude without apparently employing it in their natural environment.

A more celebrated turning point in ape experiments came in the form of the bonobo Kanzi, who was born in 1980. When he was small his adoptive mother took part in an experiment in which she was supposed to learn to use a number of different symbols for the purposes of communication. Each symbol was placed inside a small square on a computer screen (or on a physical board) and she was meant to communicate by pointing to the correct symbol. This did not turn out well and the mother learned next to nothing. But one day the researchers, headed by Sue Savage-Rumbaugh, noticed that the bonobo's little child Kanzi, who had been allowed to accompany his mother to the lessons, had picked up a lot more than she had. The focus of the experiment shifted to young Kanzi who quickly learned the entire board of symbols. He is no longer so little today – correct answers get a sweet as reward and over the years there have been many kilos of sweets – and he can fluently use several hundred symbols besides understanding spoken English at least as well as a human two-year-old.

Kanzi received a great deal of attention both in the media and from other scientists. He is now the core of a small group of apes and primate researchers. They are conducting a great many different experiments together while also running their day-to-day lives using the symbol boards for ordinary everyday communication. The various experiments involving Kanzi are meticulously documented and the researchers have taken precautions against the Clever Hans effect as best they can. These precautions have included tests in which Kanzi was given instructions by telephone in ordinary spoken English, which he then carried out at the end of the call. There was an observer in the room (wearing ear protectors so they could not overhear the conversation) who kept a record of what Kanzi was doing without knowing what Kanzi had been told to do, and who was therefore unable to give him the kind of clues that Clever Hans detected. The fact that Kanzi managed to follow the instructions even under these conditions with reasonable accuracy proves very clearly that he understands English.

Kanzi with his teacher Sue Savage-Rumbaugh. She is holding a symbol board and pointing to one of the symbols, thus "saying" the word to which the symbol corresponds

Naturally the matters discussed were not very profound ones, but neither were the instructions simply trivial. He has proved able to manage tasks such as: "Fetch the carrots on the table in the kitchen and put them in the bowl in the living room."

The fact that he could also handle a phone conversation and obviously understand that there was a person at the other end is no less impressive.

Many accounts of Kanzi's achievements in day-to-day life have been documented with some thoroughness. According to reports he is able to light a fire (using matches), to feed it with wood and then to prepare an omelette over the flames. He can also fashion simple stone tools with a sharp edge and then use the edge to cut a rope. He is also said to be able to play Pac-Man, the computer game.

Whatever the truth about Pac-Man, in more general terms Kanzi can basically learn anything that we imagine *Australopithecus* could do, and a good deal of what *Homo erectus* was able to achieve. And yet no-one has ever seen a chimp in the wild frying an omelette or making a stone knife (or playing Pac-Man). Once again it would seem as though apes have latent abilities that they do not use in their natural state. Kanzi's linguistic ability also goes far beyond any kind of communication we have observed among chimps in the wild.

Human beings, however, also possess quite a few abilities that we do not use "in our natural state" – which in our case would be a hunter-gatherer existence. From solving differential equations to building bombs to writing books like this one – these are all abilities that people clearly have but did not get to use until the modern era.

Alfred Russel Wallace, who discovered evolution and natural selection at the same time as Darwin, devoted a lot of thought to this issue of the "higher mental capacities" of human beings. He concluded that natural selection could not explain how such abilities had evolved and that an explanation that went beyond the natural sciences was required, some form of spiritual explanation, that is. This is a view that only survives today among religious deniers of evolution (Creationists) and even in Wallace's time – he published these ideas in the 1860s – they were not well received by other scientists.

From a scientific perspective these apparently unnecessary abilities can be explained instead as the expressions of a more general ability that would have been used for other purposes by our ancestors. Natural selection has not specifically produced either mathematicians or bomb makers – but it has produced a species that possesses enormous cognitive flexibility, a highly developed general capacity to solve any conceivable problem life can throw at it. Among hunter-gatherers, natural selection favoured that capacity because it made it possible for people to survive and flourish not just in the environment to which they were originally adapted, but in every imaginable setting on the planet: from the Arctic tundra to tropical atolls. The same ability can still be used to solve the problems life confronts us with. Nowadays, however, we face very different problems to the ones our ancestors had to tackle. The reason human beings can solve differential equations may be explained in this way – not because our ancestors had to deal with higher mathematics, but because the intellect that evolved among them in order to solve all the problems they faced can also be used for differential equations if so required.

The cognitive abilities of apes, including their ability to acquire at least some aspects of language, can basically be explained the same way, even if at a more modest level. Nonetheless it is interesting – and of relevance to the evolution of language – that a good many language-related abilities remain latent among our closest relatives and were therefore probably present among our common ancestors five to ten million years ago. This lowers the threshold for the evolution of language while also raising the question of why all these abilities remained latent in chimps but were realised in our human ancestors.

There must have been something about the latter's situation that was different to that of the ancestors of chimps and which meant that we evolved language while they did not. The fact that there must have been a relevant difference between the two evolutionary lineages is useful as a plausibility test for theories on the evolution of language – a good theory not only has to explain why language evolved among humans; it must also explain why it did *not* do so among chimps, nor in any other animal. This plausibility test is often referred to as "the chimp test"!

## ANIMALS, ROBOTS AND SENTIENT CREATURES

One of the features that Hockett assigned to language was that it is used intentionally. But what about the communication systems of animals? Do animals know what they are doing when they communicate? If a marmot utters a warning cry when a hawk appears, is that marmot intentionally warning the others? Or is it purely instinctive and beyond its conscious control? These are questions that do not have easy answers, either in philosophical terms or experimentally. On the philosophical level they raise further questions about whether animals have intentions at all, whether they are sentient, whether they have anything like the free will we humans like to imagine we possess.

Or are animals like robots, merely mechanisms whose behaviour is genetically programmed? Given how much robots have been able to achieve in recent years, simply dismissing the notion of animals as robots has become more difficult. Robots – and here I include both physical robots that run around in the real world and purely software robots that only exist on the internet – can play chess better than we can; they can compose classical music, author texts, vacuum your house and even serve as pets.

Some robots have been constructed to mimic the behaviour of animals, which can certainly work in the case of insects. It is possible to program a robot to do anything a beetle can do. Do we then have any reason to think that the beetle is more sentient than the robot?

Beetles may be; I am not that concerned whether they are just like robots or zombies, scuttling around without knowing what they are doing. But the issue becomes trickier when we consider animals that are more like us. We like to believe that our pets have some kind of awareness – if you look your dog in the eye, it really does feel as though there is someone in there looking back at you, doesn't it?

This is a thorny problem from an evolutionary perspective. We experience ourselves subjectively as sentient beings – we humans are the obvious example of Descartes' "I think therefore I am." And the "I" in Descartes' familiar phrase can hardly be anything but a sentient being. And yet we descend from ancestors with a more limited intellect, and if we go back a billion years or so in history what we find are unicellular ancestors who probably had no intellect at all and can hardly have been sentient beings, no more sentient than an amoeba is today. Sentience, like language, must have arisen somewhere along the way.

But when did sentience arise, and how can we know? Sentience is exceptionally difficult to tackle in objective experiments, and Descartes is no help at all to an external observer. Can we actually know whether our fellow humans are sentient beings? We take for granted that other people are like us, more or less. Strictly speaking, however, the only thing we know is that seen objectively they display all the external signs of having roughly the same kind of inner life we subjectively experience ourselves. Sentience in other animals is an even trickier question in philosophical terms, and one that was discussed by the philosopher Thomas Nagel in his 1974 paper "What Is It Like to Be a bat?"[9] The question in the title of this article is considered by Nagel to be one of the keys to the issue of consciousness – the question "What is it like?" can only be meaningful in relation to sentient creatures. Being a creature without sentience would not be like anything at all. The question "What is it like being a flatworm?" is about as meaningful as asking "What is it like being a lawn mower?" The answer, though, is by no means as self-evident when it comes to bats.

Leaving philosophy aside, experiments on animal sentience tend to be conducted along one of two main tracks. One track targets self-awareness and whether the animal has any notion of its own existence; the other looks instead at whether the animal treats other animals as though they were sentient creatures.

One test commonly used to assess the self-awareness of animals is to check whether they understand what their reflection is. If I grasp that the creature I see in the mirror is *me* then I must have a concept of an "I", some kind of awareness of myself as an individual. The first part of a mirror experiment involves the animal being given access to a mirror for a while, in order to

9  http://www.philosopher.eu/others-writings/nagel-what-is-it-like-to-be-a-bat/

understand how mirrors work in general. Then the animal is anaesthetised and has a coloured mark painted on its forehead, or on some other appropriate part of the body, that the animal can only see with the aid of a mirror. When the animal comes to, it will look at its reflection sooner or later and notice that the creature in the mirror has got a mark on its forehead. If the animal then starts rubbing at its own forehead, we can conclude that the animal understands that it is seeing itself in the mirror and that it has some kind of concept of self.

The mirror experiment has been conducted on various animals. Human children usually pass the test at about the age of two. Many primates also pass the test, but not all. The result can vary even within the same species: some gorillas pass but not others. It is unlikely that only some gorillas are aware of their own existence, and the results are not that easy to interpret. In addition to primates, dolphins, orcas, elephants and magpies have passed the test. While elephants found the test easy, the researchers were hard pressed to produce a big enough mirror and one that was sufficiently elephant-proof. They got through quite a few mirrors before finding a solution.

We humans regularly assume that other humans are thinking beings as well, and we take other people's ideas into account in our plans and arguments. We frequently spend time on something that most closely resembles social chess, and that involves us thinking and planning several steps ahead. If I do something this way, she will think that I think that she knows the secret, and then she will do that, which will lead me to think that she is thinking . . . and so on. Note that each move in this game is based on the understanding that the other person is also a thinking being, with their own ideas and their own sense of what is real – including their own sense of what I am thinking.

Our awareness of other people's sentience comes into play in the way we use language: when we speak, we are constantly taking into account how the listener will understand what we are saying – in the spirit of puzzle communication – and this pre-supposes that we understand that the other person is a thinking being. Language could hardly have evolved in a creature who did not think his peers were sentient, for what would be the point of communicating with a zombie?

*This capacity to perceive other people as sentient, which is known as Theory of Mind, is therefore a prerequisite for the evolution of language.*

Do animals think the same way? Small children do not. Humans need to be about four or five before they can properly understand arguments that involve other people's awareness. Among the last things to gel is frequently the realisation that other people may have a different perception of reality than one-self. It can be extremely difficult for small children to grasp that someone else does not know something the child itself does. One experiment that has been conducted many times and in many different ways goes something like this: The child sees on film a room with a table on which there are some cans in different colours as well as two people – let's call them Ann and Ben – who can see the cans. A third person enters the room and puts a biscuit in the red can. Ben is sent out of the room while Ann remains. The biscuit-hider enters the room again, but this time craftily moves the biscuit from the red to the green can. Ann and the child can see this but not Ben. Then Ben is allowed back in and wants a biscuit. The question is: which can will Ben look in first?

For those of us with conventional perception of the way other people see the world the answer is more or less obvious: Ben saw the biscuit being put in the red can but he didn't see it being moved. So Ben still thinks that the biscuit is in the red can and that is the one he looks in first.

The child knows that the biscuit is in the green can. Before it has reached four years of age, it cannot successfully separate that knowledge from its ability to reason where Ben should search and will say that Ben will look in the green can. Slightly older children can make the distinction.

This particular experiment is difficult to conduct with animals (or very small children) because it is based on the experimental subject being able to say what it thinks Ben should do. But other kinds of experiment have been conducted and after various failures and blind alleys, researchers have been able to prove that chimps at least consider each other to be sentient beings and understand that another chimp can have a sense of reality different from its own.

Can you consider someone else to be a thinking being without being a thinking and aware creature yourself? And, of greater relevance to the origin of language: would the chimp's "theory of mind" provide an adequate foundation for a protolanguage? It probably would – when small children learn to talk their "theory of mind" is still at the same level as a chimp's.

## CAN ROBOTS LEARN LANGUAGES?

Let us go back to those non-sentient robots and zombies we touched on in the previous section and examine how much language they can actually learn. The question of whether robots can learn languages pops up in a number of different contexts. It has elements in common with the question of whether animals are able to learn languages and can be used to shed light on what we actually mean by knowing a language.

If robots can learn to understand and use language, that would tell us something about which characteristics living creatures need to have – and which they do not – in order to learn language. This can in turn shed light on which characteristics our ancestors would have needed at the time in order to speak that first protolanguage.

Here in Sweden, if you phone the train company to book a ticket, the chances are it will be a robot that answers your call. The robot asks where you want to travel to and tries to understand your answer so you can get your ticket issued. In my experience this does not work that well but the robot isn't completely hopeless; it does seem to understand some of what you say. Does this mean we are dealing with a robot who understands my language?

Other robots provide responses in various forums on the Internet. A great many sites have robots that take part in conversations in different ways. This could be the chat function of customer services that will be "manned" by robots in the first instance, or it could be robots that are trying to keep order in chat rooms and make sure that propriety is maintained.

So while robots can deal with more basic linguistic tasks, they cannot handle a language proper. However, it would appear that it is not language as such that is the prime factor constraining them but rather their understanding of situations and contexts; they have a very limited capacity "to read between the lines". They are not at all good at puzzle communication and that also makes their language unnatural. On the one hand this tells us that puzzle communication plays a key role in natural human language and, on the other, that the ability to solve puzzles was essential if our ancestors were to begin speaking the protolanguage.

It is worth noting that successful language robots, such as Google Translate, work in a way that most closely resembles the connectionist paradigm (see p. 49) and learn languages using statistical patterns. Equipping robots with an inbuilt pre-programmed grammar, an "innate" language module, has been tried, but with very limited success.

## CAN ROBOTS DEVELOP A LANGUAGE?

Robots have often been used in research into the origin of language. Here we are not dealing with robots learning to understand normal human languages, but rather whether robots can develop basic precursors to language by themselves. The origin of language is difficult to study directly, after all, because we do not have access either to our ancestors' language or to the rest of their abilities. Instead of vainly attempting to research the question of which traits our ancestors actually possessed that made them ready to evolve a language, many scientists have chosen to use robots to shed light on the same issue but looking at it the other way round. Researchers create robots with different characteristics and abilities; they get the robots to attempt to communicate with each other and then consider how well that works. Based on the results of these experiments, conclusions may be drawn as to what capacities the robots need in order to develop anything resembling a language and, indirectly, what capacities our ancestors must have had when language was first evolving.

Since the 1990s robots have played a prominent role in the research being conducted into the origin of language, both software robots that live entirely inside computers and physical robots that move around in real space. Jim Hurford in Edinburgh, whom we have already encountered, is one of the pioneers in the field, and Luc Steels, an AI-scientist from Belgium, is another.

In a typical experiment, a set of robots with specific characteristics are constructed; these robots are then let loose in a space they can move around in and they try to communicate as best they can with one another about what they find within it. This could be robots with a built-in set of signals they can transmit to one another, in which case their job is to try to agree on which signals mean what. They could also be robots equipped to produce lights or sounds but that have not been pre-programmed as to what counts as a signal. This means they are faced with the daunting task of trying to agree on what constitutes a signal in the first place, even before they can agree on what the signals mean.

A thorny problem in these experiments is how to ensure that the robots have been equipped with just enough linguistic ability from the outset. Without any form of linguistic ability they will get nowhere, but too much linguistic capacity constitutes "cheating" in the sense that the robots have been given too much for free.

It is fruitless to study them as they go about developing a language they already have a built-in capacity to deal with. A continual balancing act has to be achieved while doing these experiments, and there is some dispute every now and then about how to interpret the results.

One very clear result from these experiments, however, is that they will fail completely if the robots do not cooperate; if they do not all share the goal of achieving communication and of trying to help one another in that attempt, while also relying on the honesty of each other's intentions. Without these shared foundations no development takes place at all.

As long as the will to cooperate is present, the robots can be designed in many different ways. But if there is to be any substantial language development in these experiments the robots need something to talk about. They need an environment that is sufficiently complex and varied so they can benefit from one another's experience. If their world is too simple, a robot can explore it completely on its own and then no communication is necessary. And even if the robots want to talk about it, a world that is too simple also fails to generate any really advanced language.

*This would appear to be a fundamental prerequisite for language: it cannot develop without collaboration and mutual good will between the robots. The results of the robot experiments support the conclusion we drew from the earlier argument about lies and lying, that trust is a fundamental prerequisite for human language. And that there need to be things to talk about.*

# PART TWO

# ON ORIGINS

# The Other Apes and Us

The sun is rising over the East African savannah. A young female baboon is yawning as she stretches. She takes a first cautious look around but once she sees that several other members of the troop are active down there among the bushes she hops quickly off the rock ledge on which she spent the night. She grunts a morning greeting and is answered by several other females close by. When she comes across a higher-ranking female she steps off the path and signals submission by baring her teeth. The high-ranking baboon grunts amicably; fortunately she is in a good mood today and the young female sighs with relief. Even though the other baboon is barely adult herself and would not have come out on top, her mother and aunts belong to the most powerful clan among the troop's females and you wouldn't get away with picking a fight with one of their daughters, no matter how puny those daughters may be.

A little way off, two males are shoving at one another and bickering. The young female makes sure to keep well away from them but listens to their cries and barks. The fight ends with one of them shrieking and giving way while the other bellows in victory.

The baboons spread out across the bush on the hunt for food. Our female goes off on her own, which increases the chance she will be able to keep any food she finds. But that is not without its dangers, and it is vital not to lose track of the troop. She barks to make contact when she can no longer see them and is answered by several other females who are also roving around among the bushes within earshot. But when she barks again a while later there is no reply. She utters a series of loud "wah-hoooo wa-hooo" sounds and can soon hear a male she knows approaching and responding with his own "wa-hoo". Almost immediately she is back with the troop once again.

Together, the same troop finds a large fig tree with enough food for all of them. A band of vervet monkeys is occupying the top of the tree and picking figs, but there are a lot of windfalls on the ground that the baboons grab greedily. Ants and snails and other insects that have been attracted to the fruit also get devoured. But then one of the vervets utters a warning cry! The baboons know from experience that that particular cry means the vervet monkey has seen a leopard in the vicinity. All the vervets climb up the fig tree as high as they can and out onto the narrow branches that cannot take the weight of a leopard; the baboons are not far behind. The biggest baboons form a rearguard to protect the troop. After a minute or two a hissing sound can be heard from a thicket and the leopard peers out but when it realises all the baboons have climbed up the tree apart from the ones on guard it retreats – seven fully grown male baboons can be a real match for a leopard when they are prepared; the effort is not worth the leopard's while, as it can no longer reach the food on the tree.

\* \* \*

Our female baboon is having a perfectly normal day, interacting socially with the other members of her troop. She communicates with them while also listening to the exchanges she is not party to, and makes inferences based on what she can hear. She is particularly aware of the social interaction in the troop and of who is enjoying the highest status at that time. While she acts with a degree of self-interest, this takes place in a social context that she would absolutely refuse to do without. All this has a great deal in common with a normal day for you and me.

The fact that there is much about the daily life of this female

Two primates: a tarsier
and a human hand.

baboon we can relate to as human beings is really not that odd. We are primates ourselves, after all; humans are one of the roughly three hundred species of primate that currently inhabit our world. We and the other primates have a lot in common, both in terms of our anatomy and how we behave. What makes the monkey house at the zoo so popular is that it's like looking at yourself in a distorting mirror. Primates are sufficiently like us for us to be able to identify and empathise with them in a way we cannot quite manage with wolves or elks.

Despite his limited experience of other primates, Linnaeus rec-ognised these similarities as far back as the eighteenth century. In his major work *Systema Naturae* he decided to classify us together with the other apes in the group he referred to as Primates, from the Latin *primus* meaning "first" or "highest-ranking".

Linnaeus lived almost exactly one hundred years before Charles Darwin and, as far as we know, there is no concept of evolution underpinning his system of classification. The closest connection between the two is to be found in the fact that it was Charles Darwin's paternal grandfather who translated Linnaeus' work into

English. In his system, and with the aim of bringing order to the huge diversity of biological life and making communication between biologists easier, Linnaeus classified animals and plants into groups solely on the basis of the resemblances he could find between them. But Linnaeus' hierarchical system turned out to be well adapted to the evolutionary conception of the living world that would emerge during the nineteenth century. Although many of the specific groupings to which he assigned species have turned out to be incorrect, the system itself has survived the various biological revolutions – Darwin, Mendel and modern molecular biology – essentially intact. And the primates as a group have also survived, even if the line separating the primates from other animals has had to be adjusted since Linnaeus' time. It has now been established beyond all reasonable doubt that the human being, *Homo sapiens*,[10] is a primate that evolved from ancestors we would call apes if we could meet them face to face.

Today primates are social animals that communicate in various ways within their social groups. The female baboon in the introduction to this section is fairly typical – most primates have a comparable range of sounds even if the details vary. Many primates can use the sounds they make along with other signals to keep in touch, to warn and to inform each other about where food can be found and, above all, to interact socially within the troop. They possess signals for dominance and submission, for conflict and peace, for friendship and sex and many other social relations. All these signals constitute a system that allows primates to function

10 Some scientific terminology for identifying species is used in this book. Scientific names consist of two parts: the name of the genus which is spelled with a capital letter and the name of the species which has a small letter. Both names are always in italics. So we belong to the genus *Homo* along with various other extinct humans, and our particular species is called *sapiens*. The name for our genus is simply the Latin word for "man", while *sapiens* means wise or clever in the same language. I will occasionally refer to species with the whole of their double name, e.g. *Homo sapiens*, and sometimes just with one term. *Homo* refers to the entire genus of the various human species when used on its own, while *sapiens* with or without *Homo* in front of it refers to the species *Homo sapiens*.

in complex social situations in such a way that they can stay abreast of what is happening in the group and act tactically based on the information they possess. Some primates are perfectly capable of forming coalitions and alliances and conducting something that we would call politics if humans were doing it. Communication at this kind of level is so widespread among primates, including our closest relatives, that we can safely assume that our ape-like forebears must have communicated in similar ways.

*This provides us with a baseline for the evolution of language. Language evolved in a creature that already possessed both the intellectual and communicative abilities that chimps or baboons have today.*

I will occasionally refer back to this baseline. I will mostly be talking about chimps, both as our closest relatives and as the primate whose abilities we know most about. This should not be taken to mean that baboons or gorillas, or other primates for that matter, have been excluded from this baseline even though I may not refer to them as frequently.

## THE EVOLUTION OF THE PRIMATES

In order to place the origin of language within the correct context we need to know a good deal about the other primates and how they evolved. So at this point we are going to take a quick look at their evolutionary history.

Primates are divided into two main groups: a) the lemurs and their relatives and b) apes and monkeys proper. There is also a small third group, the tarsiers, which are related to the latter but are not usually counted as such. Lemurs and tarsiers have little to tell us about the origins of language so we can leave them aside. The other primates on the other hand, and apes in particular, are more interesting; they are our closest relatives and their evolutionary history and characteristics provide an essential background to the emergence of language.

Monkeys have existed for fifty million or so years. The evolution of the group of apes to which we belong began twenty million years ago. The most obvious difference between the apes and other primates is that apes lack tails. Another difference is the way they use their arms when climbing – apes have very long and flexible arms and will often grab hold of branches over their heads while most other monkeys are less flexible in the shoulders and move like quadrupeds along the branches. This mobility came in handy when our ancestors started using their hands for other purposes.

With one exception, apes currently consist of a few small and isolated species whose geographical distribution is very much restricted. The gibbons and the orang-utans live in Southeast Asia, while the chimps and gorillas are to be found in Central Africa. Most of these species are threatened with extinction. The rest of Africa and Asia is positively crawling with other kinds of primate, but apes disappeared from those regions five to ten million years ago.

The apes are all closely related, but differ in their way of life and in how they communicate. The gibbons also live in family groups and sing a bit like birds to mark their territory and keep the family together. Although orangutans usually live on their own, they stay in contact with their neighbours, occasionally using loud cries for this purpose that can be heard more than a kilometre away even in dense jungle. Gorillas usually live in harems made up of a male with several females and their young, while chimps live in troops that consist of many males and females.

Humans and chimps[11] are each other's closest relatives among the apes that currently exist. Gorillas are almost as closely related to us, while the orang-utans and gibbons are more distant cousins. Human beings are fundamentally African apes, and our evolutionary path diverged from that of the chimps less than ten, and maybe as little as five million years ago. That is not a very long time in

11 Here "chimps" includes both species: the common chimpanzee (*Pan troglodytes*) and the pygmy chimpanzee (the bonobo, *Pan paniscus*). This applies throughout this book unless otherwise indicated.

evolutionary terms. It is roughly five million years since horses and donkeys went their separate ways but they remain much alike, particularly to one another – they could hardly mate and produce mules otherwise. And in terms of our genes we are about as different from chimps as horses are from donkeys. Nevertheless, the risk of a human and a chimp falling so in love with each other that they would even consider producing ape-mules is virtually non-existent. So how is it that we look so different and that so much of the way our brains work is dissimilar – particularly in relation to language – despite the fact that we are closely related in evolutionary and genetic terms?

We do not know exactly what the common ancestor of chimps and humans looked like. There are some fossils from roughly the right period but it is very difficult to determine which of the species we have found, if any, is the real ancestor and which are just "great-uncles" to both us and the chimps. That common ancestor would certainly have been more like chimps than humans, simply because chimps, unlike us, are fairly typical apes. But fossils have also been discovered that are not that chimp-like, such as *Ardipithecus*, which some scientists think comes close to the common ancestor.

The exact time frame is also unclear, and it was no doubt a protracted divorce with some fraternisation between chimps and prospective human beings to begin with. It would have been barely possible to distinguish us, one from the other, in any case and the specimens who eventually became our ancestors would have ended up in the monkey house at the zoo if we found them alive today.

## BIPEDAL APES

The oldest fossil that we know with certainty came from the human branch of the family tree, once the chimps had gone their own way, belongs to the genus *Australopithecus*. This is a large and persistent genus whose most celebrated member is Lucy the skeleton. Lucy was a young and very small woman – just about a metre tall, like a five-year-old nowadays, despite the fact she was adult – who lived about 3.2 million years ago in what is now Ethiopia. Lucy's legs and hips clearly show that she normally walked on two legs just like we do.

Chimps and many other primates can walk on two legs if they want to, but it is uncomfortable for them and they will not do so unless it is essential, such as when they need to use their hands to do something else. The way the human hip is put together

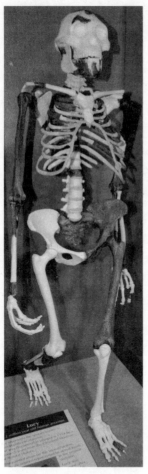

*Australopithecus afarensis,*
reconstruction of Lucy's
skeleton.

is different from theirs, however, which means that a bipedal posture is natural and comfortable for us and that change had already started with *Australopithecus.*

But apart from its bipedal gait, *Australopithecus* was to all intents and purposes still an ordinary primate. They did not possess markedly larger brains than chimps and there is no archaeological or other evidence that they could do anything chimps cannot, apart perhaps from the fact that they may have used flakes of stone as tools. There is therefore little to suggest that their intellect was markedly different from other apes, and that applies of course to linguistic ability. They would remain on the linguistic baseline.

The genus *Australopithecus* appeared about four million years ago, evolving perhaps from some species in the *Ardipithecus* genus, and died out two million years ago. In the course of that couple of million years different variants would spread across large parts of Africa from

Ethiopia to South Africa but no further. They gradually evolved a more human-like body but their brains remained ape-sized. Many different fossils of *Australopithecus* have been endowed with species names of their own by their discoverers. The process began with *Australopithecus africanus*, which was discovered in Taung in South Africa nearly a hundred years ago in the form of a skull belonging to a small child of pre-school age. But it took a long time before the researchers of the period were convinced that this really was a human ancestor; the idea that our ancestors might have had such small brains and lived in Africa besides came up against too many of the prejudices of the time.

## SHAPING STONE

Making and using tools is a skill that has long been considered a defining human attribute, even though it has been known since the nineteenth century that chimps can use them too. Nowadays we have realised that a great many different animals use tools and some can also make basic ones of their own. Chimps can shape sticks to fish for termites, and members of the crow family can be really inventive toolmakers, even using quite new materials in situations they have not previously encountered. It may even occur to them to bend a piece of wire to hook a piece of food out of a pipe.

But even if tools as such are not uniquely human, the diversity and complexity of human tools are exceptional, and this was the case in prehistoric times as well. That is why the first appearance of stone axes in the fossil record signals a milestone in human evolution. Making a good stone axe requires much more cognitive ability, skill and practice than making a good stick, and stone axes can therefore tell us something about the capacities of their creators.

Some researchers have even considered whether there may be a link of some kind between the cognitive ability required to make

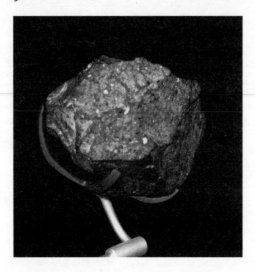

An early stone tool from
the Oldowan era, along
with a metal holder from
the post-industrial period.

stone axes and the cognitive ability needed for language. One of
them is the Canadian archaeologist Cory Stade who has found
support in her experiments for the notion that humans capable of
producing standardised stone axes would also have been capable
of using language. If this is true then the history of stone axes may
be a vital clue to the history of language.

\* \* \*

The oldest evidence of stone tools coincided for a long time with
the oldest traces of the human genus *Homo*, which is roughly
two million years old. But in recent years a number of discoveries
have been made – both of stone tools and animal bones that
someone has hacked at with some form of axe made from stone –
that are over three million years old. The only fossils of potential
toolmakers we have from that time are *Australopithecus*. Even
though their brains were no larger than that of a chimp, the notion
of how to make basic stone tools did apparently occur to them.
These are, of course, not very sophisticated axes, just a stone with
a pair of flakes chipped off so as to make a sharp edge, although
this is not that easy to achieve – try it yourself and see.

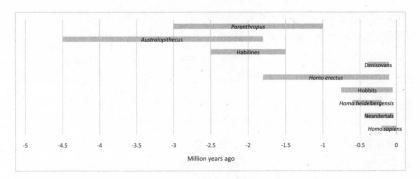

Timeline of when various fossil humans existed.

"Try it yourself" has actually become a fairly standard methodology in contemporary Stone Age archaeology. Archaeologists try to make copies of ancient stone tools in order to learn how this was achieved and to understand what cognitive abilities the stone axe maker must have possessed. Some experiments have also been done in which researchers have measured the brain activity of people making stone tools in order to see which part of the brain is most active at various points in the process of making different types of tool. More sophisticated tools involve more of the parts of the brain that do the planning and the assessing of alternatives.

As it turns out, stone axes were not all alike throughout the Stone Age. There is a considerable difference between the oldest tools, which were no more than a flake of stone with a sharp edge, and modern stone tools produced by the handful of Stone Age people who still exist today.[12] Modern Stone Age people know exactly what they are doing when producing a stone tool; they know which stones to use as raw material and they know how to shape it as they require. They are in total control of the process.

12 Apart from those peoples out of contact with the rest of the world, such as the Sentinelese, there are some groups, notably on New Guinea, who still habitually make and use stone tools, even though they have some access to metal through outside contacts. See e.g. https://www.jstor.org/stable/23273167?seq=1#metadata_info_tab_contents

This is far from simple, and it takes many years to become a skilled stone-axe maker, but the result is a tool of high quality.

Flaking stone would go through several different stages before arriving at this point. For a million years or so, stone tools remained just bits of stone with sharp edges whose shape was determined by chance. The prehumans of the time did become increasingly skilled at producing sharp edges efficiently, but that was as far as the process got while our ancestors had ape-sized brains.

Four trends become apparent in the evolution of stone tools over the millions of years. First, the toolmakers get better and better at selecting the appropriate stones as raw material. Second, production becomes better planned and more thoroughly designed, unlike the first tools which could look any old how. Third, the toolmakers learned how to get more and more tools out of the same quantity of stone; how to be economical, that is, with a raw material that might be scarce and hard to find. Fourth, the tools become ever more specialised, designed increasingly to suit different purposes.

The first stone tools that were clearly deliberately shaped begin to appear just over one and half million years ago. These are no longer simply stones with a sharp edge but deliberately fashioned

A hand axe with the characteristic symmetrical teardrop shape.

hand axes with a standard shape. No matter the shape and size of the original stone, it was knapped until it was a teardrop shape and just the right size to fit the hand. This became the standard tool that our ancestors would use for a very long time, from one and a half million years to half a million years ago. As such it is evidence of significant progress because a certain cognitive ability is required even to understand the notion of standardisation: to have a pattern in mind when making a stone axe.

Previous makers of stone tools had a function in mind when they flaked their stones – they wanted a sharp edge, but the overall shape did not matter. But the makers of hand axes did not simply have a function in mind, they must also have been able to imagine what its shape would be and able to visualise the ideal teardrop design as they struck flakes from the stone. They must have been able to deliberately plan the flaking process, and being able to calculate what to do based on a predetermined goal is not something many animals can achieve.

Santino at Furuvik Zoo in Sweden, 2012.

A male chimp by the name of Santino lives in the Furuvik zoo just outside Gävle in Sweden. Being in a zoo is pretty boring and not made any better by all the chatter on the part of the visitors who troop by and make stupid comments. So Santino does what he can to enliven things. His favourite pastime is to throw stones at the visitors.

Only the visitors failed to appreciate having stones thrown at them. People complained, and the zookeepers did their best to clear out of the chimp cage anything that could be used as a missile. This is where it becomes interesting, however, as the process turned into a battle of wits between Santino and his keepers. They did the cleaning out during the day, but when they were not working he would accumulate small stocks of stones he kept hidden. He dug out pebbles and broke off small bits of concrete from the walls and concealed his ammunition in a secure but easily accessible site. And when the zoo opened in the morning he was ready for a new round of sniping at that day's visitors.

Every evening Santino would prepare his missiles for the next day. He could hardly have done this if he lacked the capacity to imagine a goal. Or if he lacked the ability to plan how to achieve that goal, or the ability to carry out a plan with many steps before the goal could be reached.

There are animals that can make plans.

\* \* \*

Hand axes are the first solid piece of evidence for our ancestors' capacity to make plans; although, it has to be said, we have no reason to doubt that *Australopithecus* was able to plan at least as well as Santino.

Enormous quantities of hand axes have been found, primarily in Africa and Europe. These are the oldest archaeological discoveries that can currently be bought quite legally on the open market. All the really ancient finds are so rare and unique that they are reserved for museums and for researchers. There are more hand axes, however, than all the world's museums could ever display. For a couple of hundred pounds you can buy a hand axe and hold in your hand a tool that was fashioned by a distant ancestor or ancestress more than a million years ago.

## THE GENUS *HOMO*

The oldest fossils that can be assigned to our own genus *Homo* are just over two million years old. But these people were still not particularly human-like and differ in such a minor way from the species of the genus *Australopithecus* that some researchers think that is where they belong. There are a number of fossils from the same period, two million years ago, that have slightly larger brains and smaller teeth than *Australopithecus*, but they do not resemble one another to any great extent and can hardly belong to the same species. The first of these fossils to be discovered was named *Homo habilis* and, to avoid any fuss about which fossil species should be called what, this whole group of early humans is frequently referred to informally as habilines.

There was still very little about these early humans to suggest they would have been markedly more intelligent than chimpanzees. They lived in more open terrain and ate more meat than

*Homo habilis*, reconstructed face.

chimps usually do, and they used stone tools extensively. But they ranged no further than *Australopithecus* and there is no evidence they were any more successful.

A new kind of human emerged from these various species around 1.8 million years ago that was considerably more like us than its ancestors. It is from around this time that we find skeletons that really look like human skeletons. This new kind of human was an early form of *Homo erectus*, although it is sometimes considered to be a separate species, in which case it is referred to as *Homo ergaster*. The name *Homo erectus*, "the upright human", is in fact rather misleading: Lucy and her relatives walked upright a couple of million years before *erectus* did, but this was not known to Eugene Dubois in 1892 when he bestowed the scientific name on what had hitherto been called "Java man".

The brain of *Homo erectus* was smaller than a modern human's but it was twice as large as that of a chimp, as would become increasingly apparent. There are perfectly healthy humans alive today whose brains are no larger than that of the average *erectus* and who suffer from no apparent intellectual or linguistic deficiencies.[13] If a particular brain size is required to be able to use language, that limit had definitely been passed by *erectus*.

The tool most closely associated with the species *Homo erectus* is the hand axe referred to in the previous section. It proves that *Homo erectus* could make plans. The fact that the hand axes remained standardised for such a long period also proves that *Homo erectus* was capable of transferring knowledge in a stable and reliable fashion down the generations. The children must have learned how to make them from their elders as well as what a proper hand axe should look like, otherwise the axes would

13 The French writer Anatole France is a celebrated example. Despite his *erectus*-sized brain he had sufficient linguistic ability to be awarded the Nobel Prize in Literature in 1921. For that matter there are also humans alive today with brains no larger than a chimp's, but in these cases we are referring to deformities which entail serious functional impairment of the cognitive faculty.

have been much more varied in shape. Making a hand axe is not a simple matter either – modern humans need a great deal of training and patience to produce something that looks like a hand axe unless they have a very good teacher – and, for this reason too, *erectus* must have been able to transmit knowledge accurately.

It is true that young apes also learn from their elders, but that learning is not at all as reliable or as detailed, and chimps find it hard to keep traditions going over several generations.

*The stable transmission of knowledge across generations is an essential prerequisite for language. Otherwise, every new generation would need to reinvent it, which would mean language would never be able to evolve into the comprehensive and complex system we know today. Furthermore, language is a powerful tool for facilitating the transmission of knowledge. Would it be possible to learn how to make standardised hand axes without possessing a language, and what role might the teacher have played in the emergence of language?*

\* \* \*

The earliest memories I can put a date on are from when I had just turned three. Two events from that time are ingrained in my memory: my baby sister arrived and we moved to a new home. I have one or two mental images of our old flat and I can also remember the move itself quite clearly, and one episode in particular when Dad and I drove to the new house on our own in the car filled with our things.

\* \* \*

Unsurprisingly, remembering specific episodes from your life in that way is called episodic memory or autobiographical memory and is a normal and indispensable part of every person's life. But how does memory operate among other animals?

\* \* \*

The beautiful blue-grey bird flies out of a large oak with an acorn in its mouth. It lands beside a tuft of grass, scrapes away a bit of soil, shoves the acorn under the tuft and covers it. Then it flies back to the oak, fetches a fresh acorn and repeats the process at another tuft of grass. As it lifts off from the hiding place it takes a look around as usual and spots another bird like itself at the top of a nearby tree. Could it have seen the hiding place? The next day the bird comes back and just to be on the safe side moves yesterday's acorn to a new hiding place. Then it continues to hide acorns, one after the other. Towards the end of winter, food is getting thin on the ground. There are no acorns on the trees and not much else to eat either. So the bird flies from one hiding place to the next, digging out the acorns it had been saving up. This is how it manages both to survive the winter and still have some flesh on it when spring arrives, and with it the mating season.

* * *

The Florida scrub jay is a bird that lives in Florida, obviously. Though its body is grey, the plumage on its head, wings and tail is a lovely bright blue. As the name suggests, it is related to the jay familiar to Europeans and has a similar way of life. Just like the jay we know, it is accustomed to hiding nuts and other kinds of food to serve as a reserve for when times are hard. A single jay may hide several thousand nuts in different spots and remember where every nut is concealed. Researchers have been able to demonstrate that the birds not only remember a list of hiding places, they can also remember when they hid what where. They can keep tabs on the best-before date of their various concealed meals, so that when they are hungry they first search for the food that is about to expire. They can also remember particular events in relation to a particular act of concealment, such as whether another bird was nearby and could see something being hidden. In that case they make it a priority to return to the hiding spots that have been observed and either eat or relocate the nuts before the other bird can get them.

Does a Florida scrub jay have an episodic memory?

* * *

The fruit had been all but consumed on the tree they had been eating from for the last few hours, but the chimpanzees were still hungry. Some members of the troop began to grunt that it was time to move on. Down on the ground individual chimps set off in different directions, while also trying to persuade the others to follow them. In the end roughly half the troop banded together and wandered downstream in a single group. Last year the gigantic fig tree by the lake had borne copious amounts of fruit that the troop lived off for at least a week. When they passed it a couple of weeks ago the figs were not yet ripe but it might be worth taking another look now.

* * *

Both the ability to make plans and episodic memory are based on being able to shift mentally in time and space, either thinking your way back to something that happened earlier or forward to something you expect to happen in the future. These abilities depend on being able to think about events that are not occurring here and now: to the extent that you can play a little film in your mind that shows the scene you remember or are planning and in this way visualise something that is not in the here and now. This process is referred to as mental time travel. Maybe this will trigger an episodic memory you might have from when you read the section on Hockett's list of language features earlier in this book? One of those very features was the capacity of language to communicate about matters other than those in the here and now.

*A precondition for communicating about what is not here and now is being able to think about the kind of thing that is not here and now. Mental time travel is therefore a prerequisite for language in its current form.*

Human language in its fully developed modern form possesses a wealth of refinements for dealing with time and space. A good deal of the machinery of language, particularly in relation to verb forms, would appear to be (and actually is) tailor-made for dealing with mental time travel. We talk about what we are going to do, what we have done, what we had done before that, what we might have done, what we might have wished we were free to do, what we intend doing to ensure that our children will have the freedom to do it, and so on. By means of all these linguistic expressions we are able to criss-cross time and space, and travel between real, possible and imagined worlds.

Language need not have possessed all these refinements from the outset. But there has probably been some form of interplay throughout the history of its evolution between what we were able to think and what we were able to say. Fossil evidence for what we were able to think is therefore of relevance, albeit indirectly, when it comes to shedding light on that history.

Mental time travel, both the ability to make plans and episodic memory, is of major significance for human cognition as well as for being human. We are richly endowed with the capacity to travel in time. But how does that work in other animals? There are animals that can make plans, as we have just observed, and there are animals that have at least a limited form of episodic memory. This would suggest a certain capacity to make mental journeys in time. It is doubtful, however, that that capacity is as well developed and as non-specific as it is in humans. The birds referred to above, for example, possess a capacity that appears to have evolved for a very specific purpose and we have no evidence that they are particularly good at remembering anything other than hidden acorns. Chimps, on the other hand, seem to possess a more general capacity to remember and keep track of various events, and they are good at keeping tabs on things such as which fruits ripen in which season, and where there are useful trees of various kinds.

Like many other cognitive faculties that we think are typically human, the difference between us and other animals appears to be more a question of degree than of kind. Our capacity for mental time travel is no doubt more profound and more universal than that of the chimps, but there is no vast mental gulf between us in this respect either.

*The baseline for the origin of language therefore contains a basic, albeit limited, capacity for mental time travel, which would have been sufficient to get language started. Lack of mental time travel did not impede the emergence of language.*

\* \* \*

Returning to *Homo erectus*, this is the first human species that we know could make plans, and that we know could travel mentally in time, and the first human species that even came close to following the Biblical commandment to "fill the earth". Could there be a link between their ability to plan, their linguistic ability and their evident success?

The earlier prehumans had kept to eastern and southern Africa. But *erectus* quickly spread across all of Africa and tropical Asia as far away as what is now China ("Peking Man") and Indonesia ("Java Man") and eventually they found their way to Europe. They could not handle climates that were too cold; they got as far as the site of modern Beijing but no further. Even in Beijing the winters can be very harsh with snow and sub-zero temperatures, but that they could deal with. There are primates that can handle climates that are just as cold – in Japan, for example, which lies as far north as Beijing; but there are few such species and they have thick fur to keep them warm.

Did *Homo erectus* have fur? The short answer is that we do not know for sure. Both skin and hair have been preserved as fossils under exceptional circumstances but we have had no such luck in relation to any of the early human fossils. There are a good many different theories about why humans have such a different pattern of hair growth to our relatives but none of them are entirely convincing. What they have in common, however, is that we must have lost our hairy pelts in a hot and sunny climate – losing a fur coat in a cold climate would not be likely to confer an evolutionary advantage – and for that reason this ought to have happened when our ancestors were still in Africa. This means that any fur would have disappeared with those early humans about two million years ago at the latest and, in that case, *Homo erectus* would have had bare skin – and would therefore also have needed to cover himself with something to survive the winters in Beijing. But we have no direct evidence that they were bare skinned.

The climate was a good deal milder a little further south in Indonesia, where neither hairy skin nor clothes were necessary. It was here, though, that *erectus* would encounter other barriers to its journey. At that time the sea level was considerably lower than it is today – this was at the beginning of the Ice Age – so you could walk dry-shod to the larger Indonesian islands such as Sumatra and Java. Further east, however, there was still deep sea between the islands but *erectus* managed to reach them nonetheless. We have found hand axes from the *erectus* period on the island of Flores, which never had a land bridge to the continent. Could *Homo erectus* build boats and, if not, how did they get there? There is still much we do not know about what they were capable of achieving.

The French scientist Jean-Marie Hombert maintains that language is an essential requirement for being able to undertake long journeys by boat and colonise the other side of the ocean, because both the technology required for building a seaworthy boat and the large-scale planning needed for a journey of colonisation would have been impossible without it. He is mainly referring here to the journeys *Homo sapiens* would later make as part of

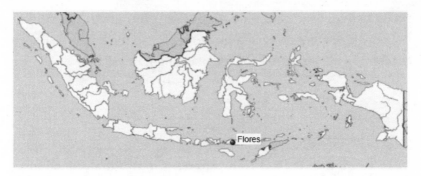

The island of Flores in Indonesia.

the colonisation of Australia. But if his argument is valid it could also apply to the colonisation of Flores by *erectus*, in which case *Homo erectus* must have possessed language.

\* \* \*

It is the end of the dry season in West Africa. On the savannah in Senegal the grass is yellowish brown and tinder dry. A troop of chimps is resting in the shade of a tree; they have spent most of the day searching for food without much success, and now the afternoon is too hot for them to move around in the sun. A thunder-cloud boils up in the sky above them, an omen of the monsoon to come. When the sun goes behind the clouds the chimps start moving around. They are still hungry. Not much rain descends from the cloud but there is thunder and lightning. A bolt of light-ning strikes a tree some way off. The tree catches fire; the sparks set light to the high grass as well and the fire spreads rapidly across the savannah. The chimps notice that something is burning, they can see the smoke mount towards the sky and soon enough a wall of flame is heading towards them. They are not seized with panic, however, but keep calmly moving sideways until they judge they are out of range of the fire. They know from experience how fire is spread by the wind and can predict where it will go.

Once the front of the fire has passed where the chimps were

sitting before, they make their way just as calmly back and search for food in the fire-ravaged area. With a bit of luck they will find another animal less good at understanding how fire works.

\* \* \*

Most wild animals are seized with panic when they come into contact with fire. But not chimpanzees. Chimps understand fire; they understand the way a fire burns and spreads and they know how to get to safety. Just like humans they are wary of fire but not afraid of it. That understanding is the first step towards learning to control it. Chimps in captivity can learn how to make a fire and tend it, but we have never seen wild chimpanzees do anything with it other than as described above.

\* \* \*

It is the end of the dry season just over a million years ago in what is now Israel. The grass on the slopes is yellowish brown and tinder-dry. A group of *Homo erectus* are resting in the shade of an overhanging rock; they have spent most of the day searching for food without much success and now the afternoon is too hot for them to move around in the sun. The only thing they have managed to collect are some very hard and bitter nuts, which are scarcely edible raw. A thundercloud boils up in the sky above them, an omen of the monsoon to come. When the sun goes behind the clouds the humans start moving around. They are still hungry. Not much rain descends from the cloud but there is thunder and lightning. A bolt of lightning strikes a tree some way off. The tree catches fire; the sparks set light to the high grass as well and the fire spreads rapidly across the hills. The humans notice that something is burning; they can see the smoke mount towards the sky and soon enough a wall of flame is heading towards them. They are not seized with panic, however, but keep calmly moving sideways until they judge they are out of range of the fire. They know from experience how fire is spread by the wind and can predict where it will go.

But they also know how useful fire can be. One of them speeds across just behind the front line of the fire and finds a branch that is still burning at one end. She carries the branch back to the group in triumph. The others quickly gather together sticks and grass and soon they have a campfire crackling merrily. They lay the nuts at the edge of the flames and let them bake there for a bit. They taste much better afterwards.

\* \* \*

Archaeologists have found traces of fire and what may have been crude hearths at several different sites that date from the period when *Homo erectus* existed. To what extent *erectus* really did master fire is, however, disputed. They could probably not make fire because most of their dwellings lack any sign of it, but it is quite possible that they could capture a flame that had occurred naturally and keep it going for a while. It is also conceivable, though by no means certain, that they understood how fire could be used to prepare food.

The British anthropologist Richard Wrangham argues that food preparation is the key to human evolution, and that it was when we discovered the trick of using fire to boil or roast food that we were able to evolve large brains and the accompanying cognitive and linguistic abilities.[14] His thesis is based on the fact that a large brain requires an enormous amount of energy on the one hand and, on the other, that we can derive more energy from cooked food than from raw. Raw vegetables are a very popular ingredient in weight-loss diets today whose aim is to make you feel full with the smallest number of calories. The same vegetables cooked are, however, less effective if you wish to lose weight.

14 See, for example, his book *Catching Fire: How Cooking Made Us Human* (2009).

Wrangham's argument is plausible in general but we have far too little evidence about when humans actually started cooking food. In order for his ideas to make sense, *erectus* would have had to be able to cook food, a notion few scientists find convincing.

## HUMAN DIVERSITY

*Homo erectus* was a remarkably successful species. It spread across a greater geographic range than any previous primate, and the species survived for more than a million years while giving rise to several new species in the course of its existence. By half a million years ago the fragmentation of *erectus* had been completed.

The species that evolved from *Homo erectus* are a miscellaneous collection. Some of them are very familiar to us, while there are others we know almost nothing about. The oddest of these is formally referred to as *Homo floresiensis* but known popularly as "hobbits" from the name of the halflings in Tolkien's books. The popular term refers to the fact that they were as small as Frodo and Sam. They were discovered on the same island, Flores in Indonesia, that *Homo erectus* somehow managed to cross the sea to reach much earlier on. What kind of creatures the hobbits really were and how they evolved is disputed, but it is reasonable to suppose that they are the descendants of *erectus* who were shipwrecked on this small island and then became evolutionarily adapted to a Robinson Crusoe existence by dwindling in size. Remarkably their brains also shrank to the same size as that of an *Australopithecus*. It is not an unbreakable law of nature that the brain has to grow larger as humans evolve.

The hobbits continued to exist on Flores until fairly recent times and were still there when modern humans first arrived on the island about 50,000 years ago or so. History fails to relate whether hobbits and humans had anything to with each other at the time.

The Denisovans are another descendant of *erectus* about whom we know even less than we do about the hobbits. The only fossils we have of Denisovans are a few teeth and bone fragments from the Denisova Cave in Central Asia, which fail to tell us anything at all about what the Denisovans looked like other than that they were broadly human; the fragments have more or less the same appearance as they would in our bodies. It is only because researchers have been able to extract D.N.A. from these tiny bits of bone that it is even possible to refer to the Denisovans as a separate species of human. The extracted D.N.A. shows that the Denisovans did not belong to any of the human species currently known to us. Among the very few other things we know about them is that they had intimate relations with modern humans at some point. The people whose descendants would become the aboriginals of Australia and New Guinea must have encountered the Denisovans on their way through Asia because they still have a percentage or two of Denisovan genes in their D.N.A.. This proves both that the Denisovans still existed less than 100,000 years ago, and that they were sufficiently human to have offspring with the modern humans who would subsequently become Australians. The

The Denisova Cave in Central Asia, close to the border between Russia and Kazakhstan.

Denisovans also had children with Neandertals; the fossil of a hybrid child of this kind was discovered only recently.

Both Neandertals and modern humans are the descendants of *Homo erectus* as well. There may even have been one or two intervening species – *Homo heidelbergensis* is a name often used for fossils that appear somewhere between *erectus* and us – but just how to classify these intervening fossils is a matter of dispute. And it really does not matter much what we call them because the evolution of *erectus* into modern humans in Africa was a gradual process, as was the evolution of *erectus* into the Neandertals in Europe, an evolutionary journey that in both cases began half a million years ago and was concluded about 200,000 years ago. While there were quite a few diversions and complications along the way – numerous fossils possess hybrid traits and are difficult to fit into any one group – the story is clear enough.

*The origin of language is hidden somewhere in this section. There is nothing to suggest that the habilines had any kind of language two million years ago, and yet there is plenty to indicate that the descendants of* erectus *could talk half a million years ago, as we shall soon see.*

But before we can get a real grasp on our subject, we need to take a few more excursions.

# Explaining the Characteristics of the Various Species and Languages

Why do elephants have such long trunks? Why do giraffes have such long necks? Why do humans have so many words? When we require an explanation for something, we usually want an answer to the question "why" – we want know what is the cause or the reason for the way things are. But that little word "why" is a tricky one and can be interpreted in many different ways.

In his time Aristotle described four different causes, four different answers to the question "why?"

- The material cause: what something is made out of
- The formal cause: what the form, e.g. shape, of something is
- The efficient cause: what brought something into being
- The final or purposive cause: what the purpose of something is

In 1963, the Dutch biologist Niko Tinbergen published an evolutionary version of the four causes that has become extremely influential.[15] In order to explain why an animal behaves in a particular way, or possesses a particular characteristic, the following four questions should be asked instead:

- Proximate cause – how does the mechanism behind the behaviour operate? Which neural pathways in the brain control the behaviour?

15 Tinbergen, Niko, "On Aims and Methods in Ethology", *Zeitschrift für Tierpsychologie* 20, 410–33 (1963).

- Ontogeny – how did the mechanism develop in the individual?
- Adaptive value – in what way does the behaviour confer an advantage on the individual through natural selection so that the predisposition for the behaviour spreads through the population and is retained?
- History – what is the historical origin of the behaviour and what is the nature of its evolutionary history? What intermediate forms have there been?

The language faculty of human beings emerged in the course of our evolution from ape-like ancestors. For that reason, Tinbergen's questions also apply to that faculty.

- Proximate cause – how do those parts of the brain that handle language operate, and how do our speech organs work, and so on?
- Ontogeny – how do children learn their mother tongue, and what is the developmental process of those parts in the brains of babies that the child subsequently uses to acquire language?
- Adaptive value – what advantage in Darwinian evolutionary terms does every human gain from their language faculty, and in what way does that faculty allow us to be better at surviving and reproducing?
- History – at what point in our evolutionary history did we acquire language, and what is the evolutionary origin of the vocal apparatus and all the other attributes we now use for language? Were there any half-evolved languages or precursors for language – protolanguages – that were used before fully formed human languages came into being?

Any satisfactory explanation of why human beings have language has to answer all four questions. And all four of them will be touched on in various chapters in this book, although more space will be devoted to the last couple than the first two.

In terms of how language came into being, our linguistic ability is not, however, alone in having gone through an evolutionary process. Language itself has evolved.

## THE EVOLUTION OF LANGUAGE

The formation of different languages and of distinct species, and the proofs that both have been developed through a gradual process, are curiously parallel.

Charles Darwin, *The Descent of Man,
and Selection in Relation to Sex* (1871)

Language is changing all the time, new words come into existence and are taken up and other words disappear. Why is that? What determines which words "survive" and which "die out"?

It may be fruitful at this point to remove the quotation marks from "survive" and "die out" and see words instead as a kind of creature that inhabits language. A word is born when someone coins and begins to use it. Words survive when they are used, and they reproduce when new people learn them. Words die when they stop being used and are forgotten. Changes in language then become a Darwinian process in which the words people like to learn and use live on, while other words are outperformed and disappear. This form of evolution among human ideas of various kinds is often referred to as cultural evolution. To all intents and purposes cultural evolution functions just like biological evolution, although some caution is warranted here as there are also crucial differences, particularly in how characteristics are inherited and spread.

Nowadays new words are coined because new events and concepts appear in our lives – new verbs such as to microwave and to text have been born in our lifetimes because we have begun microwaving food and messaging our friends. The appliances we microwave and text with did not exist fifty years ago, and so we had neither the concepts nor the words. Other verbs have disappeared at the same time because the corresponding activities have disappeared – very few people are skeining or tedding[16] these days.

But words can also be born and die for other reasons. Different languages influence each other and words get borrowed from all over the place. The Swedish language has been topped up in several rounds depending on which languages were more influential in the surrounding world. In the Middle Ages huge numbers of German words were borrowed; in the eighteenth century it was French words and in the twentieth, English ones in line with changes to the global cultural hegemony. English, like Swedish, also has a great many loan words from more exotic places – the phrase "to run amok" comes from Malay, and both "tomato" and "chocolate" were borrowed from Nahuatl which was spoken by the Aztecs in Central America.

Occasionally the fact that words come and go may be a matter of chance or the whims of fashion. It is difficult to find any more profound explanation for the alternation between violet, mauve, lilac, lavender, purple or magenta as names for the colour you get when you mix red and blue together.

Until now we have been looking only at words and how they change. But other aspects of language also change in similar ways; both sounds and grammar change over time. For example, the subjunctive endings have almost disappeared from Swedish in my lifetime, just as the plural endings of the verb disappeared a generation earlier, whereas the English-inspired plural formation with "s" has been added to the Swedish repertory. As another example, in Old English nouns were one of three genders, and until much more recently verbs were more inflected than they are now.[17]

16  To skein is to wind a ball of wool on a reel; to ted is to pile hay for drying.
17  As in, "Romeo, Romeo! Wherefore art thou Romeo?"

Counterparts to all these processes of linguistic change can be found in biological evolution. Animals that encounter something new in their environment can make biological adaptations to that change over time. Characteristics that no longer offer an advantage can disappear, as in all those cave-dwelling creatures that have lost both their pigmentation and their ability to see. It is very common for bacteria to borrow genes from one another in the same way that languages borrow words – this is one of the reasons resistance to antibiotics can spread so fast, the resistant genes get borrowed very quickly. And in biological evolution random factors can play a role as in the process biologists refer to as genetic drift.

So in many respects a language functions like an animal species, an animal species whose natural environment is human brains and human societies. Just as I have an intestinal flora made up of various species of bacteria resident in my gut, I have a linguistic flora of Swedish and English and several more languages living in my head. The bacteria help me to digest food; the languages help me communicate. What the bacteria get out of the arrangement is the fact that they have their food dished up in a protected environment and can spread every now and then via the drains and colonise the guts of other people. What languages get out of the whole thing is a similarly protected environment and the chance every so often to reproduce, as when my children learn their father tongue from me. When Cassandra and Faramir learned to speak Swedish at home two new individuals of the Swedish linguistic species were born, one in each of their heads, descendants of the Swedish in mine. Simultaneously their heads were also colonised by their mother's native tongue, Cebuano (a language in the Austronesian language family spoken by roughly twenty million people in the Philippines). So now Cassandra and Faramir both have two language individuals, one Swedish and one Cebuano, who have taken up residence in their heads, and those linguistic offspring are beginning to grow in Aina's head as well.

An individual "language animal" can therefore be said to live inside each individual human mind and reproduces when someone else learns that language from its host. Together all the various Swedish "language animals" that reside in all the Swedish-speaking heads form the "language species" called Swedish.

However, languages change over time as a result. The individual Swedish that lives in my head changes when I learn new words or adopt a new way of speaking, and the Swedish that my children are learning is not exactly identical to my Swedish. Swedish as a species is gradually changing as a result of all the changes occurring in Swedish individuals. If we consider English instead, it is very different today from how it was during the time of Henry VIII. The story of the Tower of Babel looked like this in Coverdale's 1535 translation of the Bible:

> Then came yᵉ LORDE downe, to ſe yᵉ cite & tower, yᵗ yᵉ childrē of mē had buylded. And yᵉ LORDE ſaide: Beholde, the people is one, & haue one maner of language amōge the all, & this haue they begonne to do, & wil not leaue of from all yᵗ they haue purpoſed to do. Come on, let vs go downe, & cōfounde their tonge euē there, yᵗ one vnderstonde not what another ſaieth. Thus yᵉ LORDE ſcatred thē frō thēce in all lōdes, so yᵗ they left of to buylde the cite. Therfore is it called Babell, because the LORDE cofounded there the language of all the worlde, and from thēce ſcatred them abrode in to all londes.

In the New English Translation (of the Bible) published in 2001 the same passage reads:

> But the LORD came down to see the city and the tower that the people had started building. And the LORD said, "If as one people all sharing a common language they have begun to do this, then nothing they plan to do will be beyond them. Come,

let's go down and confuse their language so they won't be able to understand each other."

So the LORD scattered them from there across the face of the entire earth, and they stopped building the city. That is why its name was called Babel – because there the LORD confused the language of the entire world, and from there the LORD scattered them across the face of the entire earth.

There are roughly five hundred years between these versions and they reflect what is a fairly normal rate of change for a written language. Nevertheless with a bit of application you can struggle through the early sixteenth-century version but it is no easy task and I certainly wouldn't say that I could understand every word without the modern version to refer to. If we go further back in time the passage soon becomes quite difficult to recognise as the same language. This is from the Wycliffe Bible from the late fourteenth century:

Forsothe the Lord cam down to se the citee and tour, which the sones of Adam bildiden. And he seide, Lo! the puple is oon, and o langage is to alle, and thei han bigunne to make this, nethir thei schulen ceesse of her thouytis, til thei fillen tho in werk; therfor come ye, go we doun, and scheende we there the tunge of hem, that ech man here not the voys of his neiybore. And so the Lord departide hem fro that place in to alle londis; and thei cessiden to bielde a cytee. And therfor the name therof was clepid Babel, for the langage of al erthe was confoundide there; and fro thennus the Lord scaterede hem on the face of alle cuntrees.

At the end of the tenth century English is all but incomprehensible to a layman. Here is the beginning of the Lord's Prayer in the Old English of the West Saxon gospels:

Fæder ure þu þe eart on heofonum, Si þin nama gehalgod. to becume þin rice, gewurþe ðin willa, on eorðan swa swa on heofonum. urne gedæghwamlican hlaf syle us todæg, and forgyf us ure gyltas, swa swa we forgyfað urum gyltendum. and ne gelæd þu us on costnunge, ac alys us of yfele. soþlice.[18]

Though should we really call this English? It is more properly referred to as Anglo-Saxon, one of the forerunners of the English language we know today.

A more modern English version reads like this:

Our Father in heaven, may your name be honoured, may your kingdom come,
may your will be done on earth as it is in heaven. Give us today our daily bread,
 and forgive us our debts, as we ourselves have forgiven our debtors.
 And do not lead us into temptation, but deliver us from the evil one.

Just as Anglo-Saxon and English have developed into new forms, identical processes have been at work in all the languages we have been able to track for long enough. We can trace the development of the Romance languages – Italian, French, Spanish and so on – as written languages from their beginnings in Latin through gradual changes all the way to the forms they have today. In this respect ancient manuscripts and inscriptions fill the same function as fossils do in the biological context: they provide robust evidence of what previous developmental stages looked like.

Historical linguists have developed systematic methods for tracing the evolutionary history of languages far back in time before there were written sources. As a result of their work we

18  http://www.bibleresearcher.com/anglosaxon.html

know that both Swedish and the Romance languages, along with most of the other languages in Europe including English and a number of languages in southern Asia – Persian, Hindi, Pashto and their relatives – all belong to the Indo-European language family. The common ancestor of these languages is called Proto-Indo-European and was spoken some five to six thousand years ago somewhere on the border between Europe and Asia. The language is completely extinct today and no written records exist, but it has proved possible nonetheless to reconstruct large parts of its vocabulary, quite enough to compose short passages. This is what a story in Proto-Indo-European might have sounded like:

*h₂áu̯ei̯ h₁i̯osméi̯ h₂u̯l̥h₁náh₂ né h₁ést, só h₁ék̑u̯oms derk̑t. só gʷr̥h̥úm u̯óg̑ʰom u̯eg̑ʰed; só mégh₂m̥ bʰórom; só dʰg̑ʰémonm̥ h₂ók̑u bʰered. h₂óu̯is h₁ék̑ʷoi̯bʰi̯os u̯eu̯ked: "dʰg̑ʰémonm̥ spék̑i̯oh₂ h₁ék̑u̯oms-kʷe h₂áageti, k̑ḗr moi̯ ag̑ʰnutor". h₁ék̑u̯ōs tu u̯eu̯kond: "k̑ludʰí, h₂ou̯ei̯! tód spék̑i̯omes, n̥sméi̯ ag̑ʰnutór k̑ḗr: dʰg̑ʰémō, pótis, sē h₂áu̯i̯es h₂u̯l̥h₁náh₂, gʷʰérmom u̯éstrom u̯ept, h₂áu̯ibʰi̯os tu h₂u̯l̥h₁náh₂ né h₁esti. tód k̑ek̑lu̯u̯ós h₂óu̯is h₂ag̑róm bʰuged.*

In English this would be:

A sheep that had no wool saw horses, one of them pulling a heavy wagon, one carrying a big load, and one carrying a man quickly. The sheep said to the horses: "My heart pains me, seeing a man driving horses." The horses said: "Listen, sheep, our hearts pain us when we see this: a man, the master, makes the wool of the sheep into a warm garment for himself. And the sheep has no wool." Having heard this, the sheep fled into the plain.[19]

19  https://www.archaeology.org/exclusives/articles/1302-proto-indo-european-schleichers-fable

Both Swedish and English are the evolutionary offspring of Proto-Indo-European and yet there is almost nothing here I can recognise. The Proto-Indo-European text is completely incomprehensible unless you are an expert linguist. Most linguists, however, refuse to try and reconstruct anything that is even further back in time. The uncertainty is too great; the languages have changed too much for any sensible conclusions to be drawn as to what even older languages would have been like. But 5,000 years ago is still only a tiny fraction of the overall history of human language – it is merely the most recent 1 per cent of that history and because that is all we have been able to reconstruct we will never know what the first spoken language sounded like.

Nor will we ever know what kind of grammar languages had hundreds of thousands of years ago, other than that they probably met most of the universal criteria we discussed in a previous chapter. As can be seen in the examples from earlier kinds of English, grammar has changed rather remarkably in just a millennium.

Although there have been attempts to trace back the history of language further than the last 5,000 years, the results have not been generally accepted by linguists. Several experts have tried to connect the Indo-European languages with other families of languages, most frequently into a grouping referred to as the Nostratic languages. In addition to the Indo-European languages, the Nostratic languages would also include the Uralic (Finnish, Sami and their relatives), the Altaic languages (such as Turkish and Uzbek), Afroasiatic languages (such as Arabic, Hebrew, Somali, Hausa) and the Dravidian languages (Tamil and so on), as well as a number of minor language families. Together these languages are spoken by a majority of the population of the world and cover an unbroken geographic expanse comprising virtually all of Europe, the western half of Asia and the northern half of Africa. The Nostratic hypothesis has been the object of extensive research but no consensus has been reached. There may have been a Proto-Nostratic language spoken ten to fifteen thousand years ago that was the forerunner of all the language families under discussion, but this is disputed.

Even more controversial is the hypothesis of the American linguist Merritt Ruhlen that it should be possible to reconstruct a protolanguage that would have been the common ancestor of all existing languages.[20] Ruhlen has constructed his theory using a different method to the prevailing norm in historical linguistics. Instead of making detailed comparisons between pairs of languages and finding corresponding systematic patterns in their sound systems and vocabulary so as to build a family tree from the bottom up, Ruhlen chooses to work both statistically and in an overarching manner by looking for matching patterns in the vocabularies on a very broad front across many different languages at the same time. This method of mass comparison is rejected by most linguists.

But by using his method Ruhlen does manage to find patterns. He has discovered a number of words he maintains are to be found in similar form across a large number of language families from all over the world. Water is called something like "akwa" in a great many different languages from Latin to various American aboriginal languages and the female genitals are called something like "but-" or "put-" in numerous languages around the world. But his detractors call these patterns matters of chance and ascribe them to wishful thinking.

Whatever the truth of Ruhlen's patterns, it is highly likely that the languages of today really do have a common origin dating from 100,000 years ago, but it is far from certain that it would ever be possible to reconstruct it. And even if that were possible we would still not have got much closer to the very beginnings of language – the very first protolanguage would be so much older than anything even Ruhlen could dream of reconstructing.

20 Ruhlen, Merritt, *The Origin of Language: Tracing the Evolution of the Mother Tongue* (1994).

The language Ruhlen is attempting to reconstruct – "Proto-Sapiens" as he sometimes refers to it – is not the *first* language but the *last* language that all the languages of the world could be derived from. There were certainly many other languages in the world being spoken both at the same time as Proto-Sapiens and before it. But all the others died out when the current language families expanded geographically, and they left no descendants behind. This does not necessarily mean, however, that those languages were in any linguistic sense inferior: the fact they became extinct could be down to pure chance, or that the speakers of Proto-Sapiens were more aggressive and eager for conquest than others, or to some other more or less irrelevant factor. In any case those languages have vanished without a trace and I cannot see any way of gaining access to them without a time machine.

* * *

A question that surfaces every so often has to do with the direction of linguistic change and, above all, with whether languages gradually become worse over time. It is a fairly common notion that language used to be superior, the longer ago the better, and that the language used by today's young people is both sloppy and impoverished. As long ago as the fifth century BCE Socrates was appalled by the youth of his day, and it is worth bearing in mind that the "youth of his day" included writers such as Aristophanes and Plato.

What we do see happening over time is that although every language steadily continues to change, the expressiveness and accuracy of each language remains more or less unchanged. Anything you could say in Latin you can say in French, but it will be said in a different way and using different grammatical tools. If there are any long-term trends in the changes taking place in grammar they are cyclical. There is a tendency for grammatical endings to weaken and vanish over time. In contemporary spoken

Swedish, for example, it is very common for the verb endings that mark the past (*–de*, like the English "–ed",) to be barely pronounced. *Vi pratade* (we talked) is pronounced by many Swedes as *Vi prata* with the *–de* ending dropped. In all likelihood that *–de* ending will eventually fade away entirely just as the plural endings of the verb have already done. And then the next stage in the cycle will be reached. If it is no longer clear from the form of the verb that the past tense is being referred to, some other time marker will have to be inserted into the sentence. It might become more or less mandatory, for example, to include the word *innan* (before) when the past is being referred to: *Vi prata' innan* (we talked before). The step after that in the cycle would be for the obligatory time marker to merge with the verb. If the same word always occurs when the past tense is being used, that word will increasingly be pronounced together with the verb as a single unit and will eventually become part of the verb as a new ending: *Vi pratinn*, to indicate an action in the past. And the cycle has come full circle.[21]

Whether Swedish will actually develop along those lines is a matter of speculation and, of course, remains to be seen. But the process as such is a real one, and each step in that process has been observed in one language or another. Several Romance languages have gone through the same cycle in terms of how the future is expressed. Classical Latin had a verb ending to show the future: *portō* (I carry) became *portābō* (I will carry). That ending gradually disappeared and in the Latin dialect that would become French an auxiliary verb began to be used instead to mark the future – *portare habeo* (I have to/I shall carry). That auxiliary verb would then coalesce with the main verb and become an ending of

---

21 An English example coud be the loss of both "thou" and second-person verb endings, and the consequent ambiguity as to whether "you" refers to just one person or several. There are now a number of dialectal forms emerging to resurrect the distinction, e.g. "youse", "y'all", etc. I expect that one of them will become standard eventually.

its own in modern French – *porterai*. That "new" ending, however, is used mostly in formal French – in the colloquial language it is usually dropped in favour of using a new auxiliary verb in front of the main one – just not the same auxiliary that was used in the previous round – *je vais porter* (I am going to carry). In another thousand years the current ending will probably have disappeared and the new auxiliary will have become a new ending.

If we consider the same process from the point of view of a single word – the word that will eventually become both an auxiliary verb and an ending – it will have begun as a content word with its own complete and autonomous meaning. The French verb that has started to mark the future means "to go". It is still being used as a trusty old main verb to say you will be going somewhere, which is precisely how it came to be a marker of the future – if you say you are going somewhere to do something you are indirectly saying that that something is in the future as you have not yet arrived. From there it is only a short step to marking the future tense by inserting a variant of "go" in the sentence even when you are not actually going anywhere. In English, the verb "to go" can be used in a very similar fashion, as is clear from the example above, while Swedish can use the verb *komma* (to come) in much the same way.

When a main verb such as "go" or "come" has become an auxiliary, it will subsequently lose its original meaning; when used too often in its new function it will become "semantically bleached". The more you use "go" to express something other than actual movement, the more the verb "go" will lose its meaning of to move. When the auxiliary verb eventually becomes an ending, semantic bleaching will normally have been completed; it will no longer occur to anyone that the ending once had a separate meaning of its own. An autonomous content word has developed into a purely grammatical marker.

This process is called grammaticalisation. Normally it only works in one direction: it almost never happens that an ending is reborn and reacquires its semantic lustre as a content word. Instead, the speakers of the language coin new words to fill the gap that has arisen. And the cycle can start all over again.

Function words and endings – in all the languages whose history we can trace back far enough in time – have developed out of content words in roughly this way. When humans invent new words it is content words they come up with. It is extremely unusual for anyone to invent a grammatical ending, precisely because grammatical markers of various kinds are invariably content words that have been or are being recycled through grammaticalisation.

*Grammaticalisation is an important process and one that means we can avoid a good deal of confusion when we come to explain the origin of grammar at the end of this book. It represents a form of evolution, but now we are in a position to see that the evolution of language is not identical to the process animal species undergo. Biological evolution does not go round in circles that way. The evolution of language also differs from that of animals in a number of other ways.*

One of those differences is that in biology practically all mutations occur entirely by chance. Species do not change according to some plan but because whatever mutations happen to occur offer an advantage. In contrast the linguistic counterpart to those mutations is frequently intentional, particularly when it comes to new words. An individual usually coins a new word deliberately – words rarely just pop up by themselves. However, it then becomes a Darwinian struggle between the words of the language that determines whether a new word will gain traction and spread.

Many attempts have been made nonetheless to direct the evolution of language from on high. Academies and organisations charged with maintaining linguistic standards and public bodies in different countries have frequently tried to determine how a language should change – albeit with very mixed results. The changes that *do* occur in language reflect how the people who speak the language actually use it. Academies that lay down the law have no immediate effect unless people pay attention to them and make a determined effort to adapt to their dictates, which they very rarely do.

Another difference from biology is that the transfer of material between unrelated languages is much more common than between unrelated biological species. Languages readily borrow words here and there, and sometimes even borrow sounds and grammatical features, although the latter occurs much more rarely.

What also happens every now and then in the linguistic realm is that languages from distinct lineages merge completely and form a new language with roots in both predecessors. This is how a *creole* is formed. And the process usually involves colonised or in some other way oppressed ethnic groups that develop a new language so the members can communicate with each other as well as with their colonial masters. A creole frequently derives much of its vocabulary from the ruling class, while the sound system tends to be characterised more by the original languages of the oppressed. The grammar, on the other hand, is often distinctive and need not resemble any of the languages of the groups involved.

Creole and other hybrid languages are relatively common in the linguistic realm; there are a hundred or so whose recent origins mean that their history is clearly evident. Hybridisation occurs in biology as well, but then it virtually always involves very close relatives. In contrast, the various parents of a creole language are normally not related at all, while hybridisation that does *not* involve closely related family members is something that occurs only extremely rarely in biological evolution.[22]

So, as we have seen, there are both similarities and dissimilarities between linguistic and biological evolution. Darwin's natural

---

22 The closest in that regard would be the handful of cases of endosymbiosis to be found in the history of the eukaryotes, when one organism has devoured another and the latter has survived inside its devourer and is then reproduced with it. The mitochondria in our cells are the result of an event of this kind two billion years or so ago.

selection is an active principle in the world of language as well, and a Darwinist perspective is fruitful when pondering the history of language change, but parallels with the evolution of animals should not be taken too far.

\* \* \*

When taking a slightly longer view, we will need to consider the interaction between the evolution of language and the biological evolution of human beings. Language pervades all human societies today, and that has been the case for many thousands of years. Anyone who cannot master the language of the society around them will encounter great difficulties in everyday life and is likely to fall short in purely Darwinian terms.

In a community that has language, natural selection will therefore favour individuals who can quickly and easily acquire it in the course of growing up, the earlier the better. Almost all children do so now – very few cannot speak their mother tongue fluently by four or five years of age. Children learn language much more easily than they learn a lot of other things, though that has not necessarily always been the case. We were probably not as good at learning language when it was new to us as a species. Language is actually rather complicated, at least as complicated as algebra, for example. It may have cost our ancestors as much time and effort to learn to talk as it costs us to learn algebra. The task facing the apes we have tried to teach language to is far from easy, and it took them many hours of training to build the rather limited vocabulary that some of them eventually mastered.

Our ancestors' capacity to learn languages was probably at the same modest level as that of chimps today when language was entirely new. In the course of the millennia, evolution has refined our capacity to acquire language in childhood and nowadays we can do it quickly.

The other side of that coin is that natural selection among

languages will also favour languages that are easy to learn. Languages reproduce through being learned by new human beings. A language someone cannot learn will rapidly become extinct. The languages in a human society will therefore evolve very quickly – compared with the slow pace of biological evolution – towards becoming more easily learned.

* * *

In a laboratory in Edinburgh a young student is trying to learn a simple artificial language. He is shown different images on a screen: a rectangle or a circle or triangle in various bright colours can be seen moving across the display in different directions while a word is pronounced for each moving image – a term from the artificial language that describes what is being shown. The word "bigato" means that a blue rectangle moves round and round. The word "kosami" indicates that the same blue rectangle moves diagonally across the screen instead. And so on for a variety of combinations of shapes, colours and movements.

Having heard a large number of words and been shown what they are supposed to mean, the student has to demonstrate how much he remembers by saying the right word when a particular moving image is shown on screen. This does not go particularly well: there is no pattern to the words and each one has to be memorised without any kind of reference to the others.

What he comes up with is recorded and then used as a language lesson for the next student, who performs the same experiment once the first student has finished and left. The answers to the second student's quiz then become the lesson for student number three. And so on down a long chain of student volunteers.

The task is much easier for student number ten than it was for the first one. While the latter was provided with an entirely arbitrary language without any patterns, the language the tenth student encounters is almost entirely regular. The first syllable in each word indicates which colour the shape had; words for "blue" scenes always begin with "ko" while red scenes begin with "gi". The second syllable shows the shape: if a rectangle is involved this was always "mi". And the final syllable describes the movement: if the shape moves round and round the last syllable is always "to". Learning a regularly structured language of this kind poses few difficulties and student number ten gets almost all the answers right.

And that brought the experiment to an end: it was not about the capacity of the students to learn but about the capacity of language to evolve "learnability". When the students early in the chain tried to recall those unfamiliar words, they made many mistakes, but their mistakes were mostly consistent; they produced more regular forms that were easier for the next student to learn. And the next one remembered the regular ones but made mistakes with the forms that were still irregular. Without any conscious design the language spontaneously evolved to become increasingly easy to learn, evolving from chaos to order as it acquired patterns and a basic grammar. This is essentially the same process as when a young child says "goed" instead of "went".

\* \* \*

Several variants of the above experiment have been conducted by Jim Hurford's research team in Edinburgh, and the results are unambiguous.[23] In only a few "generations", or cycles of learning, language adapts to become easier to learn. The rough edges are quickly rubbed off, and the artificial language becomes more like a standard human language.

This process is not just something that occurs in laboratories. The same thing happens with newly formed languages "in the wild". Pidgins are languages that come into being when people

23 This particular variant was conducted by Hannah Cornish as part of her doctoral dissertation (2011). https://www.era.lib.ed.ac.uk/handle/1842/5603

without a shared language knock something up between them that is good enough to serve as a means of communication. These languages often have an unusual structure and lack some expressive possibilities. But as soon as the speakers of pidgins have children together, and the children learn the pidgins as their mother tongue, then the languages will be shaped by the children acquiring them and within a few generations they will closely resemble standard languages. The result is the kind of creole we referred to a couple of pages earlier.

A few examples of sign languages that have arisen relatively recently among groups of deaf people can also be found. Until the 1970s, there was no established sign language in Nicaragua or any systematic teaching of deaf children. But in 1977 a special school for deaf youth was opened in the capital Managua. The teachers tried to teach the students normal spoken Spanish, with no great success. Instead, the young people developed a sign language entirely of their own during the breaks: a newly created language without any roots in an existing one. Like pidgin languages, this form of signing was pretty awkward to begin with and offered only limited expressive possibilities, but once younger children started learning the language from their older classmates at the school, it would be further refined by the new arrivals and, within a decade, had evolved to become like any other natural language.

This all serves to illustrate the fact that the evolution of language takes place much more quickly than human biological evolution. Languages, no matter how they initially appear, adapt to the learning capacity and expressive needs of human children in only a few linguistic generations. The languages we use today are eminently well adapted to being learned by people and are spoken by humans who have become good at learning well-adapted languages. A large part of the explanation of the universal patterns in the structure of different languages can probably be found in the way that language adapts to us.

The birth of these sign languages also demonstrates how languages do not arise fully formed but develop in several stages. Even if the development takes no more than a few years, we are clearly not talking about a linguistic version of the Big Bang here. The version of the language that is spoken by the first generation might better be described as a protolanguage; in every instance it will be much more basic and less structured grammatically than a mature human language. Each new generation of children will then take the language another step along its evolutionary path.

And yet here we are referring to contemporary children who already possess a fully developed linguistic ability and capacity to learn languages. They can quickly refine a language with rough edges to create something flexible that can be more readily acquired. When it comes to our earliest predecessors who were capable of language, it must have taken longer for children and the language to adapt to each other, particularly in relation to the ability of the children to make refinements.

*Once our ancestors actually spoke some kind of protolanguage, this would have quickly led to their children evolving into better and better learners of language. In parallel with the children's efforts, the protolanguage would have adapted even more quickly to become more easily learned.*

## DARWIN AND THE DIVERSITY OF LANGUAGES

Noam Chomsky poses two key questions about the origin of language: "Why does language exist at all?" and "Why are there so many different languages?" While most of this book consists in an attempt to answer the first question, we need to consider the second as well. In most animals the sounds they make are more or less innate and basically identical among all members of the same species. The way cats in all countries meow is roughly the same, while dogs bark alike all over the world. Why is human language not similarly innate, so that we all speak the same way? Just think how much easier that would be – no language barriers between all the peoples of the earth. The answer to this question offers clues to how language arose and why it exists. If the only point of language were to transfer information between human beings in a clear and comprehensible way, we would not have 7,000 different ones.

A comparison can be drawn here with the programming languages of computers. By now there are quite a lot of them as well – nearly a thousand different languages, plus numerous dialects[24] – and we know much more about how they came into being than we do about the origins of ordinary human tongues. All these programming languages have been designed for a particular purpose. This design process will very often involve an individual or a group who is dissatisfied with the existing computer languages and thinks they could do the job much better. They then construct a new language that offers some improvement when doing whatever it was that the people who created it were frustrated by in the language they were already using.

But could this really be the way human languages are born – by someone deciding to design a new language? There are, in fact, a few languages that were produced in that way and that do have an identifiable creator, but they are very much the exception. The best-known designed language would have to be Esperanto, although there are a handful of others that came about in similar fashion and with the same goal. These were all constructed to serve as international auxiliary languages: Ido, Interlingua, Lojban, Novial, Volapük and one or two others. They differ from ordinary spoken languages in several respects, primarily by being deliberately designed to be easy to learn: with simple rules and no

24   See e.g. https://en.wikipedia.org/wiki/List_of_programming_languages

irregular forms or exceptions. Both Esperanto and a couple of the others were taken up to some degree – there are supposed to be several million people today who can speak Esperanto. Even though the language is entirely artificial, there are something like a thousand people who speak it as a mother tongue: children who grew up in homes where the parents spoke Esperanto to each other. These children have learned Esperanto in the same way that other children learn ordinary languages. The process has worked perfectly well and there is nothing odd about the linguistic development of these children. This means that the human faculty for language is perfectly able to handle artificial languages, not to mention that the language in question will be adapted and refined by the children in the same way that the sign and pidgin languages we referred to previously were.

There are also languages designed for purposes other than international communication. A number of languages have been created in various fictional realms so that the imaginary beings who inhabit them are not obliged to speak English or any other human language. Klingon, Quenya and Dothraki are just a few examples. All three are languages that function well enough, and you can take courses in them. The language Láadan is slightly different; it was constructed as a feminist experiment by the linguist and science-fiction author Suzanne Haden Elgin. The idea behind Láadan is that standard human languages are too steeped in the patriarchal power structures of society, and that a gender-equal language, designed for and by women, would need to be different.

Written languages are often designed. There are instances of decisions being implemented by individuals or groups about the way a language should be spelled. The differences in the way American and British English are spelled, for example, are largely the work of Noah Webster, who published a highly influential dictionary in 1828 in which he deliberately simplified some spellings, replacing "plough" for instance with "plow". Written Swedish today is to a great extent the result of the spelling reform of 1906 in which old spellings such as *hvad* (what) and *hvirfve* (whirlwind) were changed to *vad* and *virvel*. In contrast with Noah Webster's individual design of American-English spelling, the Swedish reform was a top-down process based on the work of a committee of inquiry, followed by legislation that would then be implemented in the way Swedish was taught in schools.

In contrast, ordinary spoken language is rarely the result of conscious design as we have already observed. Most of the features of spoken languages develop out of an interaction of all the speakers of the language, unconsciously for the most part.

All languages gradually change over time. What also happens occasionally is that what was once a single language splits into several others that are no longer mutually comprehensible. This is a lengthy process, however, and takes a millennium at least. The existence of 7,000 languages today tells us that this process has been going on for a long time: for tens of thousands of years at the very least. But why does one language split into several others? Why do dialects tend to grow further apart with the passage of time and eventually become mutually incomprehensible? There are three different parts – if not more – to the answer to that question.

The first part mainly involves what happens when a group that shared the same language from the outset suddenly splits, and the two halves have little or no subsequent contact. Their ways of talking will then change irrespective of each other. Differences will arise purely as a matter of chance, but these linguistic changes will fail to be synchronised by the two new groups and instead keep piling up. With the passage of time so many minor differences between the ways they speak will have arisen that they can no longer understand one another and two new languages will have been born. This is very similar to the way new species arise as a result of biological evolution.

The second component of the answer relates to the fact that

various elements within a social group may maintain different external contacts with other groups that speak other languages. One part of the group may be trading with people who speak an entirely different language and end up borrowing a great many words from the latter's language to facilitate commerce, while a different part of the population has their land conquered by yet another ethnic group, and the original language becomes influenced by the language of their new overlords. After a long enough interval and under various forms of external influence the tongues spoken by the different parts of the population may have diverged so much that they can no longer understand each other.

The first two components involve different parts of the same language developing in different directions independently of one another, as a result of a variety of driving forces. The third component is quite different in kind, however, and has to do with the fact that human beings like to use language to signal their affiliation. Groups that want to accentuate their particular identity while distinguishing themselves from another group may often deliberately magnify any existing linguistic differences. They may adopt a divergent pronunciation or use their own special words or in some other way make the language of their particular group differ from that of the society around them.

It is fairly common in our large modern societies for various subcultures to adopt their own linguistic peculiarities in order to distinguish themselves from the majority and in order to be able to recognise other members of the same subculture. Speaking the correct variant of the language thus becomes a shibboleth for the group, of the same kind as the Biblical language test I mentioned at the beginning of this book.

In ancient times, before the advent of agriculture, communities were rarely large enough to encompass subcultures. It might then have been more a case of two neighbouring tribes becoming enemies and using language as one of the various means at their disposal to distinguish Us from Them. Perhaps the dialect differences that already existed were amplified in order to make the linguistic variants more distinct, and gradually – over a sufficient number of generations of enmity – they were no longer able to understand each other's speech at all. Two new languages had come into being that may have preserved their individual identities by literally applying the Biblical shibboleth-test.

A more recent phenomenon that can also influence linguistic separation in a similar way is, paradoxically, the trend towards the creation of standardised national languages that appeared when nationalism emerged as a political movement at the end of the eighteenth century. Countries such as France and Sweden tried with varying degrees of success to introduce a national form of French or Swedish as the common language of the nation, using the nascent forms of state education as their tool. This may have been important with regard to creating a sense of national unity and facilitating communication within the country, but it also tended to drive a wedge between the dialects spoken at its borders. An evident political ambition was (and frequently still is) to create sharply defined linguistic borders to replace the dialect continuum that had always existed.

Things become more complicated when nationalism collides with linguistic diversity in countries that have not been dominated by a single language. Even though there were many different dialects in countries such as France and Sweden, it could plausibly be argued that they were all the same language, with the result that a national language could be introduced without anyone being forced to change their own. Of course, a decision was also taken in Paris and Stockholm to simply ignore the fact that Basque and Sami, along with other minority languages, were also spoken within the national borders. Respect for the rights of minorities has never been a high priority for nationalists.

Very few countries in the world have, however, been as close to "monolingual" as Sweden and France. In most countries there are a number of indigenous languages spoken in addition to all the languages introduced by the various waves of migration. Creating a list of countries in which more than a hundred different indigenous languages exist is an easy task. Attempting to impose a national language on countries of this kind cannot be achieved without friction.

Throughout the ages, conquerors and imperialists have brought their own languages with them to subjugated and colonised regions. Frequently the language of empire succeeded in suppressing the local languages – sometimes as a matter of deliberate policy, sometimes simply by being the language of power, the language one has to master to have any success in life. Latin spread across half of Europe in this way, as did Arabic across the Middle East and North Africa; Spanish and Portuguese in South America; English in North America, and countless other tongues in empires large and small. All these imperial languages rode roughshod over a vast range of indigenous ones, which either became extinct, like Etruscan under Latin, or survived on the margins of society, like Basque under Latin and its descendants.

Global linguistic diversity has thus been rapidly diminishing ever since our societies developed to the point at which large-scale military conquest became possible, and several languages still become extinct each year. There are striking similarities here with what has been happening during the same period to global biological diversity. And while it is true that new languages and new species are coming into being,[25] in both instances that process takes place much more slowly than extinction.

The other side of the coin is that the 7,000 or so languages that exist today are little more than a pale shadow of the diversity that must have existed in prehistoric times. When you consider the few regions on the planet that have not been linguistically overrun by one or more empires, they are positively teeming with different languages. Just over a tenth of all the languages on earth are

25 Esperanto, Montenegrin and Nicaraguan sign language are three different examples of newborn languages.

spoken by various tribes on New Guinea; there is roughly one language for every thousand square kilometres in that country. If Sweden had the same linguistic density as can be found on New Guinea, it would have four hundred different languages, while the United Kingdom would have nearly two hundred and fifty, the United States 8,000, and the world as a whole would have 150,000. New Guinea may be an extreme example, but it is highly probable nonetheless that linguistic diversity on the planet was once at least a whole order of magnitude greater than it is today.

And as if having fewer languages were not enough, the languages that remain to us may well resemble each other more closely than the languages they have replaced. Half of all the languages on earth belong to one of only a handful of different language families, and the languages within each family all work more or less the same way.

People who spread across the globe normally take with them various animals and plants. If we are going to colonise an island somewhere we will deliberately take pigs with us and, unintentionally, rats as well. Both rats and pigs like to spread out and will eat absolutely anything at all, which often has devastating consequences for the local fauna and flora. Vast numbers of animal species have disappeared in this way over time.

What happens linguistically when a certain culture spreads across the world is almost identical. The colonisers bring with them both rats and languages, and the language of empire has just as devastating effect on linguistic diversity as the rats do on the biological kind.

This process has occurred repeatedly throughout history, and most parts of the world have been affected. The Proto-Indo-European language referred to in the previous section became the ancestor of most of the European and South Asian languages today because the people who spoke Proto-Indo-European were successful at conquering large swathes of land, introducing their language wherever they went. With speakers all the way from the

Atlantic coast to the Bay of Bengal, more localised dialects soon developed that would, in turn, become ancestors of the Indo-European languages we know today, from Portuguese to Bengali. During the heyday of imperialism, various modern Indo-European languages spread to other continents, crushing the local languages more or less brutally, and there is no continent on earth today where a significant part of the population does not speak an Indo-European language.

The Austronesian languages did the same thing in South-east Asia and Oceania. A small tribe from Taiwan managed to colonise almost all the islands in the Pacific and Indian oceans, over-running whatever local populations existed there before. Today, closely related languages are spoken on thousands of islands, from Hawaii all the way to Madagascar. Only the highlands of New Guinea were able to resist the assault.

In Africa it was the Bantu languages that expanded south of the Sahara, while the Semitic languages moved to occupy the vast area north of the desert. The outcome was, however, the same as usual: a rapid loss of linguistic diversity.

The question then arises as to how many radically different languages were lost when Indo-European, Austronesian and other languages stamped out the diversity that in all likelihood existed before they spread across the world. Presumably we will never know the answer.

We can reliably conclude all the same that the human linguistic faculty has the capacity to cope with not just the 7,000 languages of today, but at least ten times that number and with a much greater range of variation. Some researchers estimate that as many as a half a million different languages in total may have been spoken through the ages.

*The nature of the origin of language was such that it prompted the evolution of a very flexible linguistic faculty.*

## EXPLAINING THE FEATURES OF LANGUAGE

So there are a number of consistent features – universals – in all languages, as well as a great many patterns that recur in their grammars.

Different theories of language, as well as different theories about the origin of language, explain these universals and recurring patterns in various ways. If it is the case that the core of grammar is innate, the explanation will be rather straightforward: the patterns in languages reflect the structure of that innate grammar. But in that case one would have expected more patterns and fewer exceptions. Besides, that still leaves unexplained the nature of innate grammar and how it could have evolved.

An alternative explanation would be that the different languages are all used in similar ways and that there are purely functional and practical explanations for why the languages have the structure they do. On one level this seems plausible, inasmuch as everyday conversation in most cultures revolves around similar themes: normally these are the social relations within a particular group, gossip about who is doing what and with whom and the telling of stories that are more or less truthful. And it is only logical that all languages possess the grammatical tools needed to be able to clearly express who is doing what to whom and to ensure that a story is coherent. These tools look very different in different languages, however, and it is by no means obvious that the actual functioning of the patterns that do exist can be explained in any straightforward fashion.

In this section I will be talking a good deal about the various possible ways in which grammar works. This is a key question both because it serves as a dividing line between paradigms and because it is of major importance for explaining the origin of language. The very name of the functionalist theories of language tells us that language, including grammar, is supposed to be functional and explanations of the features of language will involve function and benefit. Explanations of the origin of language will also therefore be based on what the protolanguage was used for and what benefit or advantage we derived from it.

Generative grammar, in contrast, is careful to avoid any question to do with function, and generativists can sometimes sound almost derisive about functional issues, particularly in relation to the origin of language. In the generative paradigm (see p. 47), grammar is sufficient unto itself and the possible functions of language are largely ignored. Grammatical rules are explained instead in terms of more abstract principles and generativists would, in the final analysis, prefer to explain all grammar as a consequence of mathematical structures and logical necessity. In a number of different contexts, Chomsky has likened language to a snowflake that acquires its particular form as a result of the operation of basic natural laws without either its function or evolution being involved at all. This serves to dissociate the origin of language from whatever advantage our ancestors may have gained from it.

The functional issue has additional significance in relation to the origin of language because it sheds light on what natural selection may have had to work with when language was evolving. Biological traits adapt to become better at operating the function they express, better, that is, at providing their bearers with a selective advantage. What the language faculty is good at providing will therefore furnish us with a vital clue as to how it evolved and what function it was adapted for. Chomsky gets round that argument, however, by introducing his snowflake – if the language faculty arose suddenly, without any process of adaptation, function is irrelevant.

The vast majority of people would agree that, overall, language is of benefit to us. A person without language would have enormous difficulties surviving in a human society in which language is the foundation of all communication and social relations. Language as a whole may therefore have an evolutionary value, and it is reasonable to assume that the advantages conferred by the language faculty in general may be selected for the advantages it confers.

And how does this relate to the various features and components of language? What about whatever advantages they provide? And what about the various stages that may have occurred during the evolution of language? If language did evolve over many stages, can we identify the particular advantage conferred by each stage; identify, that is, an evolutionary advantage which meant that a particular stage was favoured over its predecessors by natural selection? We will be returning to an evolutionary ladder of this kind in a later chapter.

But let us look first at the patterns to be found in language today and see if we can identify any function they express, any advantage that may have favoured those patterns in the course of our evolutionary history.

Spoken languages always have both consonants and vowels, for the simple reason that the right mixture of vowels and consonants is easier to pronounce and easier to understand. Words made up solely of consonants soon become hard work – try saying "krkgt-vrvmbstkpkt" without the odd vowel stealing in here and there – and ones consisting only of vowels are difficult to pronounce distinctly enough to be comprehensible – try saying "eiouäaeeåiöuaea" quickly without it all merging into a shapeless mess – and such words would become very long because our speech organs cannot produce an enormous number of distinct vowels. There are, however, several languages that have the odd short word made up solely of consonants or vowels. More extreme examples are "aueue" from Hawaiian and "clhp'xwltlhplhhskwts"[26] from the Nuxalk language spoken in western Canada, but words like these are the exceptions among the languages of the world. The normal

26 "then he had had in his possession a bunchberry plant" (https://en.wikipedia.org/wiki/Nuxalk_language)

combination of speech sounds is not that hard to explain in functional terms.

The fact that languages are open and flexible systems also has a plausible functional explanation; otherwise, neither the expressiveness nor the capacity to couch every thought in words – something that characterises human languages and forms the foundation of the benefit language confers – would be possible.

The hierarchical structure of language is also functional and it, too, is connected with the infinite expressiveness that we have already discussed in relation to Hockett's list of the design features of language.

*Language must be capable of being pronounced by a human throat – or being signed by a human hand – and language must be capable of being housed in a human brain and of being learned by human children in a reasonable period of time. All these factors impose functional limitations on the structure and form of language and explain a great many of the really universal characteristics of human languages.*

But function does not necessarily explain everything. Grammatical patterns – above and beyond the fact that languages possess a structured grammar – are not so easily explained. How much of grammar may have a functional explanation – and what functions are involved in that case – is a controversial issue among linguists. Proponents of generative grammar frequently dismiss functional explanations and tend to assert the impractical and non-functional aspects of grammatical subtleties, while functionalists naturally adopt the opposite perspective.

One example of a grammatical pattern whose functionality has been questioned relates to what one can and cannot ask about in a sentence. Most languages can make a question of a statement by replacing what one wants to ask about with a question word. In a sentence like "He bought a book in Stockholm", one can either create a question about the buyer – "Who bought a book in Stockholm?" – or create a question about what was bought "What did he buy in Stockholm?" – or a question about the place "Where did he buy a book?" In Swedish and English, as in many other languages (although not all), the question word is placed first in the sentence and the slot normally filled by what is being asked about is left vacant.

All languages with this kind of question construction impose limits on what can be asked about. English and Swedish are fairly liberal in this regard and allow various types of question that other languages do not permit. In the sentence "He thought that she had bought a desert rat despite her mother's protests and her father's anger", you cannot just ask about the mother's protests directly. Questions such as "Despite her mother's what and her father's anger did he think she had bought a desert rat?" or "Whose protests did he think she had bought a desert rat despite and her father's anger?" do not work. You can of course extract the entire inserted clause and then ask: "Despite what, besides her father's anger, did he think she had bought a desert rat?" or create other paraphrases, but it is not possible to create questions about simply anything and in any way at all.

Could there be a functional reason why some types of questions work and others do not? To discover a possible function for grammatical subtleties of this kind is no easy matter. Part of the problem is that functionality can exist at various levels. There may be a function to the grammatical rule as such, or the functionality may be found in some more wide-ranging grammatical principle so that the limitations on questions become a side-effect of the latter.

From a functional perspective the notion that there should be some form of "complexity limit" in language seems plausible. It is harder for the speaker to pronounce difficult words when the grammar is complicated, and even harder for the listener to interpret a sentence that has become too complex. Something else that sets limits on complexity is that language has to be "learnable" by children. The prohibited kinds of question are also more complicated than the permitted kinds, so it seems reasonable, at first sight, to assume that it is complexity that sets the limit. But that cannot be the entire explanation because sentences can be constructed that are very difficult to comprehend, but when analysed carefully turn out to follow all the grammatical rules – and, vice versa, there are sentences that are easy to understand but which break those rules. For example, one of the rules of written English is that every sentence must have a verb and a subject in its main clause, but in our use of everyday language, not to mention in texts and such like, we often leave out one or both when it is clear from the context what the issue is. I might very well text my wife: "Driving to fetch kids now. Home in an hour", even though neither sentence is grammatical, formally speaking, according to the grammar of the written language at least. Both lack a subject and the second lacks a verb as well.

"The rat the cat the dog the man the woman shoved released hunted bit screamed" sounds at first sight completely nonsensical and most of us would spontaneously say that it must be much more ungrammatical than "Home in an hour". But, technically, the "rat" sentence is grammatical; all the rules have been followed. In English you can insert a relative clause directly after the subject in a sentence: "The rat that the cat bit screamed." In most cases you can leave out the subordinate clause marker "that" as well: "The rat the cat bit screamed." Then all you need to do is apply this same grammatical rule four times over so that subordinate clauses are inserted after the subjects of the subordinate clauses as well.[27]

Does a peculiar sentence like that really belong to the English

27 To spell it out in full:
"The rat screamed."
"The rat, that the cat bit, screamed."
"The rat, that the cat, that the dog hunted, bit, screamed."
"The rat, that the cat, that the dog, that the man released, hunted, bit, screamed."
"The rat, that the cat, that the dog, that the man, that the woman shoved, released, hunted, bit, screamed."
. . . And then if we delete all the "that"s and the commas:
"The rat the cat the dog the man the woman shoved released hunted bit screamed."

language? I doubt anyone would ever say or write anything like it, other than as an example in a book like this; a fact that has been confirmed by the Finnish scientist Fred Karlsson who has searched through vast amounts of text from books and periodicals without finding a single sentence that actually has more than four layers of embedded subordinate clauses. Sentences that have more subordinate clauses *can* be found, but in that case they have been tacked on at the end, like this: "He thought she wanted him to sell the bike he never used because the chain kept coming off." This sentence has just as many layers as the sentence involving the rat, the cat, the dog and so on but can be said much more plausibly. The odd sentence with several layers can be found in Karlsson's findings but more than three layers is extremely rare in writing, and never occurs in natural spoken language.[28] But even sentences that are not obviously peculiar can become so long that our brains cannot handle them. In principle we can tack on as many relative clauses as we like at the end of a sentence, but in practice we tend to get lost pretty quickly. We might be able to deal with four subordinate clauses at the end and even one or two more if they are simple and we have a chance to think about it. Written language is easier because we can go back and check if we lose the thread. But after ten it becomes difficult to follow, even in writing: "He thought she wanted him to sell the bike he never used and that stood outside the garage because there wasn't room inside the garage in winter when the car was kept in there because it was so cold outside that the car wouldn't start if it was left out in the cold this winter which was more bitter than anyone could remember." And in that case what about sentences with hundreds of subordinate clauses? Or thousands? It is possible to construct

28   Here is one of the few examples in Karlsson's findings that approaches the complexity of the "rat" sentence: ". . . and the councillors of state, who, in the hope that henceforth, with the King away in Poland, they would be able to rule Sweden themselves, had furthered Sigismund's departure, now became objects of persecution and the targets of Johan's wrath." (Yrjö Koskinen, *Lärobok i Finlands historia*, Helsinki, 1860–80).

them – or to generate them in a generative grammar – but could a sentence no human being could utter, much less understand, really be considered to be part of language?

Whether peculiar sentences that cannot be used in practice actually form part of the language is a question that will get a different answer from each of the various grammatical paradigms we have already referred to. Generative grammar answers the question very definitely in the affirmative; generativists define language as the entirety of sentences that can be generated by the rules of grammar, no matter how improbable it may be that anyone would ever use them. Other paradigms stay closer to language as it is actually used in everyday life, with all our human limitations and imperfections. Which language faculty are we supposed to explain the origin of exactly – the ability to come out with hundreds of layers of rats and cats, or a more limited faculty that can only handle sentences we actually use?

There is a link here to a question we discussed earlier: whether it is spoken or written language that grammar should describe and explain. Written language likes long complicated sentences and is more rule-governed, whereas spoken language has shorter and simpler sentences and is more free-form. Which kind of language should we be explaining? When it comes to how it all began we have already answered that question: only spoken language is relevant to the origin of language.

\* \* \*

Another issue related to these peculiar sentences is whether language is finite or infinite. Everyone is more or less agreed that language is limitless in the practical sense that a speaker will never encounter limits that are purely linguistic. You can, as a speaker of language, basically invent sentences that are as long and as complicated as you like – your inner grammar will not stop you; there is no grammatical rule that says "a maximum of seven subordinate clauses and not a single one more". What would bring you to a halt, instead, is the capacity of your memory and other practical considerations – you would simply be unable to keep track of all the component elements of the sentence once there were too many of those clauses, and you would become tangled up in your own complexity if you tried. So while language is finite in practical terms, it is not grammar as such that imposes those limitations.

In the generative paradigm, all such practical matters and human shortcomings are situated outside language itself. The underlying theoretical language faculty is considered to exist separately from any kind of restriction, and the language it can generate is therefore seen as infinite. The other paradigms do not see language as divisible in that way; our practical limitations form part of the language faculty instead, and it is therefore not considered to be limitless as it is by the generativists.

The issue of whether language is infinite or not has a bearing on the origin of language because the generativists occasionally put forward an argument that goes something like this:

- Premise 1: Language is essentially infinite.
- Premise 2: The difference between finite and infinite is a difference in kind and not a matter of degree.
- Conclusion 1: It is not possible to get from finite to infinite in many small gradual evolutionary steps; there are no "semi-infinite" intermediate forms.
- Conclusion 2: Language must have arisen suddenly, at a single stroke.

The logic of this process of deduction is valid as it stands, but is based on the premise that language really is infinite, not just unlimited in practical terms but infinite in the strict mathematical sense. It also depends on the tacit premise that infinity is an essential and defining quality of language, one that language cannot do without.

Other paradigms, which consider the linguistic faculty to be limited to what can actually and practically be said and which do not define language on the basis of a single attribute, do not share the conclusion that the origin of language must have been sudden. We will be returning to whether the origin of language was gradual or sudden once we have considered some more of the evidence from prehistoric times.

* * *

To return to those notions of function and advantage, we have already observed that the concept of advantage is crucial to Darwinian evolution. It is important, however, to distinguish the biological evolution of the innate language faculty of human beings, whatever its actual nature, from the cultural evolution of language as such. Conferring an advantage means different things in biological and cultural evolution. In terms of human biological evolution, an advantage means the kind of thing that favours the survival and reproduction of the individual (or the individual's genes, strictly speaking). An advantage in terms of the cultural evolution of language itself would be the kind of thing that favours the spread of language features and language elements as such, both between individuals and to future generations. The features that are biologically advantageous need not be the same as those that are culturally advantageous.

A human being's biological language faculty – that is, the innate attributes we possess that mean we are capable of learning languages – needs to offer an advantage in biological terms in order to evolve; those attributes must also favour our survival and reproduction – unless we want to postulate that it was just a matter of luck that we ended up having language. But those aspects of language that are not innate need not be advantageous in Darwinian terms at all. How much of language is innate, and in what form, is therefore of decisive importance in explaining the origin of language.

*Everyone is, however, agreed that some form of innate language faculty exists: there is something innate that distinguishes a human baby from an infant chimp, and which means that the former can learn language with ease while growing up but not the latter. This something requires a biological explanation.*

The principles behind this explanation are to be found in the work of Darwin.

# Darwin's Explanation

Darwinian evolution by natural selection has been the premise implicit in much of the first half of this chapter, but now it is time for us to get down to the nitty-gritty of the theory.

In 1859, Darwin presented his explanation of the characteristics of different species in a theory of evolution by natural selection; this is the account that forms the basis of Tinbergen's third question about adaptation – how did a behaviour benefit the individual so as to cause the predisposition for the behaviour to spread through the population by natural selection? Darwin was not the first person to speculate on evolutionary ideas, nor was he the only proponent of the idea of natural selection – Erasmus Darwin, Charles' grandfather, had written about evolution two generations before, and Alfred Russel Wallace discovered natural selection at the same time as Darwin himself.

But Charles Darwin was the first to succeed in putting forward convincing arguments that evolution had, in fact, taken place while presenting a tenable explanation in the same work of how it had occurred. What his grandfather Erasmus had done was, for the most part, simply to speculate, whereas Wallace would fail even to begin to match the detailed arguments supported by a wealth of data that Charles Darwin published. As a result it was Darwin's version of evolution that carried the day and revolutionised biology.

The core of Darwin's argument still holds today, even though the theory has been embellished with many variants and become more complicated during the 160 years that have elapsed since.

Charles Darwin.

Charles Darwin's
(1809–1882)
theory of evolution
by natural selection
laid the foundations
of both modern
biology and our
understanding of
our own origins.

Evolution remains the crucial explanatory model in modern biology. As the biologist Theodosius Dobzhansky put it: "Nothing in
biology makes sense except in the light of evolution."[29] And human
beings are no exception: like all other living creatures we are the
fruit of millions of years of evolution.

Evolution is fundamentally a very simple idea. Only three
things are required for evolution to take place within a species:
variation, reproduction and heredity. Variation means that the
individual animals are not identical but differ in various ways.
Reproduction means that the animals mate and have young, but
not all of them reproduce to the same extent and some individuals
have more offspring than others. And, finally, heredity means
that the young are like their parents to some degree. If variation,
reproduction and heredity as described above are present in a

29  Dobzhansky, Theodosius, "Nothing in Biology Makes Sense Except in the Light
of Evolution", *American Biology Teacher* 35 (3): 125–9 (1973).

species, then, in the next generation of that species, there will be more animals that are the offspring of the individuals who had many young, and fewer that are the offspring of the individuals who did not do as well at reproducing themselves, or who died before they could reproduce. And if traits are inherited then the characteristics that are connected with surviving and having many young will become more and more common with every succeeding generation. Those traits that are connected with dying young or not having offspring will not be reproduced and will therefore become increasingly rare.

This applies irrespective of what it is that causes the differences in how many young an animal produces. Where differences exist, their impact will be felt in the next generation. Or, to put it another way: until very recently it was more the rule than the exception in most human societies that a large proportion of all children never became adults but died in infancy. As much perhaps as half of all children never reached puberty. But if you think about it for a bit, you will realise that this does not apply to your ancestors; it simply cannot be the case that half of your ancestors died in infancy. Your grandfather did not die as an infant or he would never have become your grandfather. Every ancestor to every one of us must come from that other half: the people who actually reached puberty. We are not the descendants of a random selection of the people of past ages. We are all the descendants of a very special group instead – we are the descendants of the survivors, of those who managed to survive all the dangers and illnesses they faced in childhood.

Why this particular group managed to survive is another question. They may have been more resistant to disease or starvation, or so irresistible they were not exposed on a hillside, or they may simply have been lucky. No matter the reason, the fact that they survived has left its mark on future generations.

Some of Darwin's ideas on evolution were inspired by the way humans breed domestic animals. It has been known for millennia that desired traits in animals and plants can be bred for by control-ling which individuals in each generation are allowed to reproduce. If a farmer wants sheep that produce more wool, he allows the sheep who produce the most wool to breed, while the sheep that provide less wool are turned into roast lamb instead. As a result, the next generation of lambs will be the offspring of sheep that produced a lot of wool and will presumably produce a lot of wool themselves. And farmers have continued this form of selective breeding over many generations of sheep. The animals that are from the farmer's point of view best are allowed to breed, while unprofitable animals are ruthlessly culled.

In nature there is no farmer to do the selecting – other traits operate instead to favour reproduction. Wild sheep have enough wool to keep warm, but nothing like the several-inch-thick layer that insulates a farmed specimen. Wild sheep have longer legs and larger horns than their domesticated counterparts, and also profit from other and very different options for escaping predators – because all wild sheep are the offspring of sheep who were *not* taken by wolves before they could reproduce. The animals that are the least good from the wolves' perspective – the ones that are hardest to catch – survive and have lambs, while the slower and more defenceless animals will be culled.

Many of the more subtle aspects of evolution relate to factors that result in particular animals having more young than others. The selection process practised by the farmer is based on deliber-ately favouring animals with "good" traits while culling those with "bad" ones. Darwin's theory of evolution by natural selection is based instead on the fact that particular individuals, with particu-lar traits, are simply better than others at surviving and reproducing and actually prove more successful at doing so. What constitutes a "good" trait in the Darwinian sense need not have anything to do with what we think ought to be good but is simply a trait that, in the environment the animal finds itself in at the time, increases the probability it will survive and have young. In many instances this will obviously be about being the biggest, the best or the most beautiful, but entirely different traits than these may also confer an advantage and spread to future generations.

A distinction is frequently drawn between traits that help an animal to survive and ones that help an animal to reproduce. The latter were grouped together by Darwin under the term "sexual selection". Standard natural selection involves being good at getting food and avoiding becoming food so that you can reach sexual maturity and, in theory at least, enjoy the possibility of becoming a parent. Sexual selection has to do with being good at attracting a partner so you can actually become a parent.

Something worth considering while we examine these two kinds of selection is whether language mainly helps us to survive, whether it helps us to reproduce or whether it does not help us at all in Darwinian terms – and what that would then tell us about the origin of language.

## NATURAL SELECTION

Natural selection in the standard version is often very straightforward to understand. Hares can move swiftly in order not to become food for foxes, and foxes can move fast so hares can be their food. Hares have the right kind of teeth to nibble on carrots, and foxes have the right kind of teeth for nibbling on hares. Nothing too difficult thus far. But it can be a more subtle business on occasion and there are frequent compromises. Every animal is fundamentally a compromise between a set of different demands – a hare has to be good at finding carrots, good at keeping warm in winter, good at running away from foxes, good at spotting foxes so it gets the chance to run and good at hiding in order not to have to run – while remaining cheap to fuel so it doesn't need too much food, and able to grow up fast so it has time to reproduce before it becomes the fox's dinner. Being able to run extremely fast might mean that the hare never got caught by a fox but being able to run that fast would require such an uncompromising adaptation of the body that the hare would not be good at anything else and would also require so much food that it would starve. That is why hares can run fast enough to get away most of the time and no faster.

Fundamentally these are the same sorts of compromise as when people design a car, for example. As someone buying a car you would ideally want a car that can go as fast as you like, with space for as big a load as possible while only needing the odd drop of petrol and never breaking down or wearing out and that costs less than the price of a cup of tea. But cars like that don't exist. Every ordinary car is a compromise, just like every normal animal.

When it comes to our bodies, human beings are also a compromise in most respects. But we have one trait that has been prioritised without compromise: our large brains. Other apes have larger brains than the average mammal as well, but we humans are at the extreme end of the spectrum with brains that are three to four times larger than the average brain of an ape of the same body size. It is as though a car designer decided to put a Ferrari engine in the chassis of an ordinary family car. This makes for an extremely costly design – the brain is hideously expensive both to construct and to maintain, just like a Ferrari engine – that would have been eliminated by natural selection unless we gained such enormous advantages from our huge brain that it outweighed the cost. Humans have proved successful in evolutionary terms; we have survived to fill the earth after all, so we quite evidently gained enough of an advantage from those brains of ours. The precise nature of that advantage is a key question in the study of human evolution and one to which there is no obvious and simple answer. *The relationship between the brain and language should also be considered in the light of the Ferrari engine.*

## SEXUAL SELECTION

It is a morning in early spring; the sun is just about to rise above the moors in northern Sweden. The blackcocks are in full courting mode with ten or so of them cooing and leaping about and trying to impress the females that are watching from a secluded spot. Several of the male blackcocks start fighting and the defeated are forced to withdraw. Which of the males will be allowed to mate and which will have to leave on their own? Eventually the females allow the victors to approach them.

\* \* \*

It is an early summer morning, the sun is just about to rise above Piccadilly Circus/Times Square. The nightclubs are about to close, the last round of the human mating ritual is in full fling. Who will be allowed to mate and who will be going home on their own?

Both the mating rituals of the blackcocks and the city dwellers are about sexual selection. Everyone involved has already survived to a fertile age – but which of them will become parents to the next generation, and which will not? From the point of view of evolution, surviving without producing children is just as bad as dying young – your genes are permanently taken out of circulation and will not be passed on to the next generation. Seen from a genetic and evolutionary perspective, sexual selection is just as much of a life or death struggle as natural selection.

Sexual selection is often expressed in a way that is blatantly impractical: in peacock fans, deer antlers, nightingale song and Porsche 911s, but every now and then it can be a more subtle process. The females of some species of fruit fly, for example, may mate with several males and then choose whose sperm of those onboard will be allowed to fertilise her eggs.

There are important biological reasons why it is usually the males in sexual selection who do battle while the females get to choose, and this is related to the factors that determine the reproductive options available to males and females. In the case of a typical mammal the contribution made by the male to the offspring is limited to a few minutes and some sperm, after which the female has to manage on her own. This means that the number of offspring a female can have during her lifetime is limited by how many pregnancies she has the endurance for and how many young she is capable of providing for. Enticing a male every now and then poses little difficulty. Males face the opposite problem: they have little difficulty maintaining a few minutes of intercourse with as many females as they can, but finding willing females is the rub. Ultimately reproduction is limited for females by access to food, whereas for males the constraint is access to females. This is why it is the males who put on the display in species of this kind and the females who are picky about selecting the best partner.

But not all species work that way. In many species the males and females work together to feed the young, and in that case sexual selection is usually a more symmetrical process in which both sexes choose each other. This is how it operates in many bird species. There are also a few animal species, including the sea horse, where the males are in charge of "the pregnancy" – and here sexual selection works differently again. In many primates such as baboons and chimps, sexual selection usually has more to do with politics than sex – both the males and females try to attain a high rank in the troop; an elevated status will then give them advantages when choosing a partner. Higher social status may also have its advantages in Piccadilly Circus.

Sexual selection in humans is special in a number of ways, and there is a considerable degree of variation between individuals in particular. Many people are monogamous: with the mother and father remaining together all their lives and raising the children together. Many others, however, are not monogamous; quite a few of them may spend a large part of their lives on the prowl, attempting to find a new partner every night with varying degrees of success. And it is not at all rare, among both men and women, to try and have your cake and eat it: to have a family with a steady partner while trying to find further opportunities for mating on the side. This makes human sexual selection complicated for both genders in tactical terms, with a wide range of options available.

What kind of role does language play in human sexual selection? Being a smooth talker is of course an advantage in Piccadilly Circus – could that provide a possible explanation for why human beings have language?

Probably not. While it is obviously true that language plays a considerable role in human flirting, this does not, of itself, prove language arose through sexual selection. On the contrary: language is nothing like the traits that sexual selection usually produces. After all, sexual selection typically results in spectacular but clearly impractical behaviours in one sex but not in the other. Language may, of course, be considered spectacular on occasion, but it is also extremely practical and usable – and, even more significantly, the distribution of the human language faculty is strikingly equal between men and women. People speak more or less equally well irrespective of gender. The small difference that can be found in average linguistic ability favours women, but it is an extremely modest difference and depends on how the ability is measured – the variation within each gender is much greater than the difference in the mean value between the sexes.

The fact that the language faculty is so gender-equal means that explanations of the origin of language based on sexual selection, or on something that is mainly the province of one gender alone, should be taken with a pinch of salt. What the gender equality of our language faculty indicates instead is that both sexes participated in the evolution of language and on equal terms.

*Whatever the first conversation was about, it must have been about something that concerned every person present, no matter their gender.*

## LANGUAGE AND NATURAL SELECTION

The third of Tinbergen's four questions, with which we began the previous chapter, the one that relates to adaptation, asks in what way language provides an advantage in natural selection. But before we tackle that question, we need to consider whether the human language faculty did in fact evolve through natural selection, or if we possess language through some other means. This is a contentious issue among researchers working in the field. So what possible explanations other than natural selection could there be for an innate language faculty and the other biological traits displayed by human beings?

From the outset this question bears on the relationship between heredity, environment and culture. Anything that is not based on heredity in some form cannot be the object of natural selection. But even if we disregard that and consider only the heredity-based aspects of our language faculty, it is by no means obvious what role natural selection played in its origin.

Human evolution as such is not a matter of dispute; it is perfectly obvious that we evolved from ape-like ancestors. But even if we and all other living creatures have come into being through an evolutionary process, this need not mean that every trait exhibited by every creature is the result of that particular attribute being selected for. There is a great deal of room in evolution for acts of chance – many mutations make no difference at all to survival, and in that case it is pure chance whether they spread or not. This means that there are very many minor details of our traits that are not the result of natural selection – they just turned out that way.

It is also rather common for a species to possess a particular trait, not because that trait is favoured by natural selection here and now, but because it happened to occur in an ancestor for whom it may have been advantageous. As long as the trait does not cause any significant harm, a rudiment of this kind, as it is called, may persist in the evolutionary process for a long time after it has ceased to confer any advantage. There are many rudiments in human beings, two well-known examples being the coccyx and the appendix. Another example that may be less obvious is that we get goose bumps when it is cold. An animal with fur or hair can frequently ruffle its fur when it is cold to make its coat thicker and better able to keep the animal warm. Goose bumps are the result of our bare skin attempting to erect hairs that no longer exist. Entirely pointless, but completely harmless as well. But because language is not a trait that existed among our distant much hairier ancestors, language can hardly be an evolutionary vestige of the same kind as goose bumps.

Numerous traits can also be considered to be by-products, the unintended consequences of some other evolutionary change. The fact that we have a navel is not something that of itself gives us any advantage through natural selection; it is simply a by-product of our being attached by an umbilical cord before birth. While the umbilical cord has an obvious and very considerable evolutionary value, we just happened to acquire navels as part of the process.

It is also fairly common for traits that initially appeared as a by-product, or by chance, to subsequently offer an advantage and to have evolutionary value. Equally common is the incidence of traits that evolved for a particular purpose but then turned out to be useful for something else. Our lungs, for example, have the same origins as the swim bladders of fish, whose purpose had nothing to do with breathing but served to keep the fish afloat.

Could language have arisen as a result of something of this kind, a recycling of traits that did not evolve for linguistic purposes? In terms of our language faculty as a whole this is a matter of dispute. But everyone is agreed that we possess numerous traits that are of great benefit to us in contexts of language, although they could clearly not have arisen for linguistic purposes because the traits existed long before language appeared. Our ears and our vocal chords are two obvious examples. What is so controversial instead is the nature of the very core of our language faculty, the capacity of our brains to handle all the component parts of language: words, grammar and so on.

* * *

In 2002 Marc Hauser, Noam Chomsky and Tecumseh Fitch published an article in which they discussed the content and origin of the language faculty.[30] The article attracted attention both because of its occasionally controversial message and because of the particular combination of authors. The scientists in question constituted a rather odd trio. All three of them were leading figures within their respective fields, but they came from entirely different scientific backgrounds and had not previously shown any sign of sharing either interests or views. At the time Marc Hauser was seen as one of the world's leading authorities on the ability of animals to think, although his reputation would lose much of its gloss when he was found guilty of research misconduct in 2010. We have already become acquainted with Noam Chomsky, the world-famous linguist. And, lastly, Tecumseh Fitch is a biologist and expert on the evolution of the vocal organs.

Apart from its combination of authors, the article is best known for two things. One is that the authors explicitly drew the distinction referred to briefly above between the core of the linguistic faculty and the diverse traits that we use for language (but which have different origins), and they gave names to the two parts. These are referred to in the article as "the Faculty of Language Narrow Sense" (F.L.N.) and "the Faculty of Language Broad Sense" (F.L.B.), respectively. This is a distinction many researchers regard as sensible and useful, even though views may differ as to how

30 Hauser, Chomsky & Fitch, "The faculty of language: What is it, who has it, and how did it evolve?" *Science* 298: 1565–6 http://science.sciencemag.org/content/298/5598/1569.lon (2002).

clear-cut the dividing line between the two parts really is, and where that boundary actually runs.

The article is also famous for something more controversial. The authors maintain that the core of the language faculty is made up of a single component, namely recursion. Everything else is deemed to lie outside the core and, as a result, must have evolved for other purposes, apart from the connections that exist between the core and the rest. This is closely related to Chomsky's efforts to narrow and focus his theories on what, according to him, is really the innermost core of language and which he refers to as the Merge operation.

Recursion means that something is defined in terms of itself, or that it can refer to itself. Recursion is fairly common in computing contexts, where being able to call up a function in a computer program from within the function itself is often useful. In linguistic contexts, the term recursion refers to the capacity of language to contain layer upon layer of the same sort of components. A sentence can contain a subordinate clause, that contains a second subordinate clause, that contains a third subordinate clause, that contains . . . and so on.[31] In a computer program a structure of this kind would normally be handled through recursion, so to assume that our language faculty also makes use of recursion does not seem like such a huge leap. According to Hauser, Chomsky and Fitch this would be the only new thing to have occurred in the evolution of language: recursion plus whatever is required to link the machinery of recursion with the rest of the brain. We simply

31 Here is one of my favourite examples, from "On Poetry: A Rhapsody" by
    Jonathan Swift (1733):
> The Vermin only teaze and pinch
> Their Foes superior by an Inch.
> So, Nat'ralists observe, a Flea
> Hath smaller Fleas that on him prey,
> And these have smaller yet to bite 'em,
> And so proceed *ad infinitum*:
> Thus ev'ry Poet, in his Kind
> Is bit by him that comes behind.

got language into the bargain once the human brain became capable of handling recursion, or that is what this trio asserts.

Recursion would also automatically mean that language was infinite from the outset, because recursion has no natural limit. If Hauser, Chomsky and Fitch are right about recursion we end up with the argument discussed earlier, that gradual language evolution is incompatible with language being infinite.

Different grammatical paradigms adopt different views on the status of recursion. It plays a vital role in generative grammar, whereas connectionism excludes the possibility of genuine recursion. A connectionist grammar (see p. 49) can handle simple recursion-like structures, albeit ones that are restricted to only a few levels – which is roughly what we find in natural spoken language – whereas construction grammar (see p. 51) has no difficulty making use of recursion while failing to assign to it the key role the generativists accord it.

* * *

The different ways of producing a new trait in an animal other than by natural selection have in common that they work best for relatively small and simple evolutionary changes. If all that is necessary is to piece together and recycle existing parts, or if a single mutation is sufficient, then acts of chance or luck may provide an adequate explanation for the appearance of a new trait. If the origin of language is that simple it could be pure luck that we possess language – and sheer bad luck that the chimps do not.

Another aspect of this process is that these simple changes that can occur without natural selection are so basic that they can appear at a single stroke, without any intermediate evolutionary forms along the way. There would never have been any kind of protolanguage, in that case, or any simpler varieties of language to serve as intermediate forms between nothing and a fully developed language. But is human language sufficiently simple to have emerged at a single stroke?

In contrast, complex traits that are based on many different interacting components are very difficult to produce without natural selection being involved in some way. These traits do not arise out of nowhere, and a number of intermediate forms and half-finished variants can always be found in their evolutionary history. Our eyes are an obvious example; the eye began its history as a tiny light-sensitive patch a couple of billion years or so ago, and the various other components involved have appeared since then and been gradually refined in a process involving many different stages, each of which has led to improved vision.

The issue of the role played by natural selection in the origin of language must also, therefore, take into account the complexity of the human faculty for language. Were that faculty to consist solely of a single component – recursion or something else – then it would be worth considering non-adaptive explanations – explanations without natural selection. If the language faculty, on the other hand, is based on the interaction between a number of different components that have been adapted to each other and for linguistic purposes, which it is, then the only plausible explanation is that natural selection has played a crucial role in the origin of language.

On this point the different grammar paradigms touched on in the previous chapter can be divided into two groups. On the one side we have generative grammar with its indivisible language module, and on the other are all the rest.

The language module of generative grammar is supposed to be an indivisible whole and would therefore exclude evolutionary intermediate forms. Those generativists who are even willing to consider the origin of language are keen to suggest therefore that language arose as a result of a single mutation, without involving any gradual evolution through natural selection. And yet it is difficult to envisage the emergence of the grammar module as the kind of fundamentally minor change that may occur as a matter of chance. Proposing that the module is able to work together with the rest of the brain as part of the same change is not any easier to accept. The supermutation required goes far beyond what is biologically plausible.

The other theories of grammar are more open to gradual changes that take place in many small steps. The networks of connectionism can be freely expanded and while they work to some extent when small, they operate better and better the more neurons are added on. So starting on a small scale would fit in quite well here. And in most variants of the functionalist paradigm (see p. 50) it is also possible to start at a modest level that would be within the purchase of our ape-like ancestors, and then add on more and more sophisticated functions. This might not be perfectly smooth and gradual, but it does not require anything even remotely resembling the leap made by generative grammar: from nothing to a fully formed grammar module.

None of the alternatives to natural selection that we have surveyed can explain ability to use language.

*So natural selection must have played a crucial role in the evolution of the biological components of the human language faculty.*

# Heredity, Environment and Language

Tragic examples can be found of children being forced to grow up in isolation from any human contact. The most famous case is a girl known as Genie, who was tied up in a locked room and left completely alone. Her parents had confined her when she was very small before she started talking. They gave her food, but she had no other contact with the outside world and never heard anyone talk. She was punished if she made any sound. She was discovered when she was thirteen and could not speak at all at that point. She received extensive training afterwards but never really learned to speak properly.

In families with deaf children and in which the parents do not have a good command of sign language, a communication system made up of simple gestures often develops on its own, but if the children do not come into contact with sign language at a fairly early age their linguistic development may be permanently hampered.

The cases of both Genie and the deaf children show us that language is not purely hereditary, and that there needs to be language in their environment if children are to develop it. Which language, what kind of language, or how many languages there are in the environment does not seem to matter – children learn the languages on offer no matter what they are, and they have no difficulty learning two or three or even more if that is the nature of the linguistic environment they share. Nor does it make any difference whether the language is signed or spoken, as long as the children have functioning sense organs of the right kind. Hearing children born to deaf parents are perfectly able to learn sign language as their mother tongue.

Furthermore, we know that children adopted as infants have no difficulty learning the language of their adoptive parents, no matter what language their biological parents speak. A Chinese infant adopted in Sweden will learn perfect Swedish and vice versa. This tells us that there is nothing hereditary about the specific language we speak – it is purely a matter of environment. All humans, no matter their biological origin, can learn to speak any human language at all like a native, just as long as they come into contact with the language at an early enough age.

The environment is therefore of decisive importance for language. But how important is heredity?

We know that there must be an hereditary component to our ability to learn languages. This was clearly demonstrated by experiments that involved people adopting young chimps and bringing them up in a human environment surrounded by spoken language. Those young chimps could learn to understand some of what their adoptive parents were saying, but they could not learn to speak. That difference between humans and chimps must be a matter of genetic inheritance.

Ten years or so ago, the FOXP2 gene attracted a great deal of attention and was embraced by the uncritical media as heralding the discovery of "the language gene". Although the articles were exaggerating, what the researchers had discovered was rather interesting – people with damage to the FOXP2 gene also had damage to their language faculty, damage that could be passed on to their children.

So is the origin of language a matter of heredity or environment? To answer that question we first need to delve more deeply into how the relationship between heredity and the environment actually works.

## HEREDITY OR ENVIRONMENT?

The various social sciences devoted much of the twentieth century to the battle between heredity and the environment, often referred to as "Nature versus Nurture". Are a person's characteristics decided by the individual's genetic make-up, or are they shaped by the environment they grow up in? The debate also encompassed the human traits to do with language: are the linguistic differences between human beings to do with nature or nurture? The answer to this question is of major importance for any explanation of the origin of language.

Fundamentally, though, the whole question of nature versus nurture is flawed; it is perfectly obvious that the reality cannot be either/or. Neither of the extreme positions is scientifically plausible in relation to the non-trivial human traits, including language. But the issue can still provoke powerful feelings.

The question is also politically loaded. Are there group-specific traits that are naturally associated with a particular nationality or gender, or are group traits (and the groups involved) no more than simply social constructs that could potentially be put together in an entirely different way. Historically, both extremes have been fraught with ideological abuse. Evolution plays a rather odd and paradoxical role in these overly dogmatic ramblings. A key idea in evolution is, after all, that species, including human beings, are changeable over time and their form is malleable as a result. This makes it rather peculiar that Darwin's ideas were dismissed in Stalin's Soviet Union, despite the fact that the Communists chose to believe in a human being who could be moulded for ideological reasons, whereas a distorted version of evolution was adopted by Nazi Germany despite the Nazis' belief in the unchanging nature of the ethnic characteristics of human beings.

In any case this political dimension means that the issue of nature versus nurture is even more of a poisoned chalice than would be warranted by the disputes that take place solely within the scientific world. For this reason discretion is required when trying to write something sensible about the scientific foundations that actually underpin the issue of nature versus nurture in order to avoid both causing offence, and leading the reader to jump to conclusions about my own political leanings.

\* \* \*

Let us start with the extreme positions: it is quite obvious that a person's traits are not solely the product of heredity. In an environment without food your heredity makes no difference; the only trait you will develop is being dead. On the other hand, it is equally obvious that a person's characteristics cannot be the product of environment alone. If your inherited genes include a mutation that means that some vital bodily function does not work, then it makes no difference what environment you are in. Again, the only trait you will develop is being dead.

If you grow up in an environment with less food than you need, you will be short in stature no matter your genetic inheritance. In an environment with enough to eat, however, not all human beings will be tall. What enough food makes possible instead is for everyone to reach the height determined by their heredity, and that height can vary a great deal. An adequate supply of food is the normal state of affairs in Sweden, but just how much our environment can affect our height struck me very forcibly when I visited the Philippines for the first time. You could see the difference between rich and poor by noticing how tall people were. When I, a Swede of average height, visited the slums and walked between the shacks I was a head taller than everyone who lived there and had to watch out that I didn't bang my head against projecting roofs. But I did not stand out at all in that regard in the better-off areas. The class divide in the Philippines leads to an environmental disparity that results in a difference in height of between ten and twenty centimetres.

To take another example of the importance of environment, monozygotic twins – those who come from the same egg and have the same genes – are not completely identical as individuals. They may be very similar to one another in appearance, but their personalities can differ to a considerable degree. This tells us that personality does not depend solely on heredity. On the other hand, the fact that monozygotic twins are so alike in terms of appearance, much more than ordinary siblings, tells us that appearance is largely dependent on heredity and not the environment.

The fact that heredity plays a role in appearance is not particularly controversial; it is sufficiently apparent that children resemble their parents by and large, and that adopted children resemble their biological parents more than their adoptive ones. But the idea that personal characteristics may have a hereditary component is much more controversial, and the debate can become really toxic when it touches on cognitive features as well as gender identity and sexual inclination. I intend to keep well away from the latter two but the human faculty for language is a cognitive feature and there is no avoiding its possible heritability in a book about the origin of language.

But first I will examine how nature and nurture work in purely practical terms, and how they interact from an evolutionary perspective.

## HOW DOES HEREDITY WORK?

In this context heredity refers to the biological inheritance that we get from our parents in the form of D.N.A. D.N.A. is a molecule that comes in four variants; these molecules can build long chains, and the position of the different variants along the chain forms a code that can be read and interpreted inside our cells. Heredity lies in that code and its most important part consists of instructions to make proteins.

Put simply, a gene is a piece of a D.N.A. chain that contains the code for making a particular protein from start to finish. There are many complications in practice but they are not that relevant here. A great deal of our D.N.A. does not, however, consist of genes. Around each gene are special codes that are used to control exactly when and where in the body a particular gene should be read and a protein produced. These special codes are vitally important and serve as switches to turn production of a particular protein on and off. We will return to them.

Sometimes there are errors in a D.N.A. sequence; this is known as a mutation, a change to heredity. Mutations occur fairly frequently; you are bound to have a number of mutations in your D.N.A. that your parents did not. For the most part mutations do not matter very much, but on occasion they can actually change what protein a particular gene will form, or change when and where the protein is produced. A change of this kind is rarely beneficial; only very occasionally does it improve the way a protein works. Improvements of this kind are the raw material of evolution.

## WHAT KIND OF INFLUENCE DOES THE ENVIRONMENT EXERT?

The genes in our D.N.A. are sometimes likened to a blueprint of how the body is supposed to work. But that is not a good simile. The genes work more like a recipe than a blueprint. It is a very complicated recipe with many parallel processes occurring in the body at the same time, like a master chef simultaneously preparing a dozen different dishes in a dozen different saucepans. Timing is the key to success for a master chef: the exact moment the heat beneath a pan should be lowered, the exact moment butter has to be added to another pan and how to synchronise the preparation in two different pans so that both are ready to go on the plate at the same moment, and so on.

Timing is also a vital factor when our bodies are being formed. The process is set in motion when an egg is fertilised. Fertilisation activates a number of genes, and production starts on their proteins. Some of these proteins start work on the construction of the body: they stimulate cell division and so on. Many of the proteins are also used to activate the switches in the D.N.A. that turn on and off the production of other proteins. It is these control proteins that play the role of the chef in the process and make sure that the right gene is activated at the right time and in the right place.

But all these are fundamentally straightforward chemical reactions and, just like other chemical reactions, this protein-making machinery can be affected by external factors: by the environment in and around the body. Some environmental effects are unintentional, while others are deliberate – part of the recipe.

This is typical of the way the body develops: there is a constant interplay between heredity and the environment. One recurrent pattern in this process is that while heredity lays down a basic functionality, it also provides a mechanism for picking up the signals from the environment so that the body can react appropriately to it. For this reason it is misleading to talk about heredity *or* environment.

Genie and the young chimps we began this chapter with prove that this applies to language as well.

*It is pointless debating whether language is a result of heredity or environment. The more relevant question has to do instead with the interaction between the two, both in relation to the development of language in the individual and to its emergence in the human species.*

## THE NATURAL, THE GOOD AND THE RIGHT?

A further complication that needs to be considered in relation to heredity and the environment is the all too prevalent confusion of how things actually are with how they ought to be. The former is a matter of objective fact – how things are in reality – while the latter is a value judgement – how we think they ought to be.

For centuries the relationship between *is* and *ought* has been raised over and over again by moral philosophers. The Scottish philosopher David Hume (1711–76) established the principle, subsequently known as Hume's guillotine, that says that an *ought* cannot be derived from an *is*. The English philosopher G.E. Moore (1873–1958) elaborated on Hume's work and coined the term "the naturalistic fallacy" to describe the faulty reasoning that leads from what *is* to what *ought* to be. After Hume and Moore it was no longer possible to maintain that values can simply be derived from facts. But that has not stopped people doing it, unfortunately.

In recent years the word "natural" has taken on a strongly positive connotation. We would like to live a natural life and eat natural food, and many people believe that anything that is natural is automatically beneficial and good. Regrettably this has made it even easier to slip into the naturalistic fallacy, because the word "natural" can also be used purely descriptively without any implied value judgement. In descriptions of the lives of animals there will usually be repeated reference to the animal's natural environment, the natural behaviour of the species and so on. Most of the time there is no value judgement being made at all in a description of this kind; it is simply an observation about which environment the animals are to be found in, and how the animals actually behave in day-to-day life. But this sort of description of what is natural is frequently misconstrued as being about values, as though the writer were insisting on natural behaviour as morally right.

In this book I will also have reason every now and then to write about how both humans and other primates behave in their natural state when that behaviour is relevant to the origin of language. Gender roles in traditional societies will be touched on a couple of times, for example. Please do not read any value judgements into these descriptions.

## LANGUAGE INSTINCTS

There is no real reason to believe that heredity and the environment function differently in relation to the behaviours or the cognitive faculties of animals than they do in relation to their physical characteristics. There are behaviours, particularly in less complex animals, that are controlled purely by heredity, but they are the exception. In general, animals should be able to react to what is happening and do different things in different situations, that is to say, respond to environmental factors.

Our language ability is a cognitive faculty that governs our linguistic behaviour in turn. What we know about how other behaviours and faculties have evolved can therefore be used to shed light on the evolution of language.

Behaviours are governed by the nervous system of an animal. The nervous system, in turn, is constructed in the same way as the rest of the body by an interaction between genes and environmental factors. Genes can control the repertoire of behaviours an animal may possess, but events in the environment decide which behaviours actually come into play.

Specifying the nature of the entire nervous system through the genes works for the simplest animals. But it does not work for more complex ones and fails completely for human beings who have around 80 to 100 billion neurons in their brains; the slightly more than 20,000 genes we possess are not enough. The detailed nature of our nervous systems, and therefore our behaviours, cannot possibly be governed by our genes.

The overall growth of the brain and its basic structure in more complex animals are genetically determined, as are the inner workings of each neuron. Where the nerves to and from the rest of the body connect with the brain is also genetically determined. But what has made the evolution of larger brains possible is the emergence of mechanisms that allow the connections between nerve cells to be affected by the environment. To make a long and complicated story very short and simple, a great many of the nerve cells in the brain are genetically programmed to do two things: (1) to set up huge numbers of connections to other neurons in the brain more or less at random,[32] and (2) to detect how much the various connections are being used and what effect they are having, and then prune the connections that are not doing anything useful. What happens in stage 2 will depend on what input the brain gets from the environment. The system is set up to be self-programming so that the network of connections in the brain adapts itself to do something useful with the input the brain actually receives from the environment. As a result of this self-programming the brain becomes an incredibly powerful tool that can develop and adapt behaviours flexibly to the environment the animal finds itself in.

This is, in essence, the same kind of arrangement we referred to earlier in this chapter – heredity sets up a mechanism in order for there to be an appropriate reaction to the environment and the outcome is the product of the interaction between that mechanism and the actual environment.

Early in life the brain is extremely flexible and can reorganise itself entirely in order to adapt to the input it receives. In adults, however, the self-programming capacity of the brain is more reduced, and major changes are no longer possible. And, despite

32   There are control signals that tell the neurons in roughly what direction they should look for connections, and what type of neurons they should link up to, but it is chance that determines which particular neuron that is. The control signals are different for different parts of the brain so the resulting patterns of connections differ as well.

that flexibility, most of us end up behaving according to similar patterns.

The same flexibility also applies to language. There are a number of tragic cases of children who are born with one side of the brain so incurably damaged it has be surgically removed. Although these children grow up with only half a brain, they often manage remarkably well. If the half of the brain that is normally used for language is surgically removed from very small children who have not yet learned to talk, they will learn language nonetheless, but it will be handled by whichever half of the brain they still have. Much of the brain is flexible in this way – but not all of it. There are a great many behaviours in animals that are based on a mechanism set up by the genes that is triggered by some environmental factor. When the mechanism in the brain is activated, it sets a pre-programmed default behaviour in motion as a response to environmental stimulus. These default behaviours are what we usually call instincts. Instincts cannot be the product of a largely flexible brain, but need to be specified in a more detailed way by our genes, even if those details are often difficult to work out.

Human beings possess some instincts. When a new-born baby senses that it has been laid against something that resembles mother's breast, the child will instinctively search for an object to suck on. This is not a behaviour the child could plausibly have learned from the environment during the few minutes it has been outside the womb and therefore it must be pre-programmed. In evolutionary terms this is a highly appropriate instinct – it is absolutely vital for a baby to be able to quickly find its way to its mother's breast and the food it contains; having to wait for an environmental stimulus would not work as it would take too long. Natural selection has therefore endowed young mammals with an instinct to immediately find their maternal food source.

It is typical of instincts that they are standardised (innate behaviours are rigid and predictable) and not particularly flexible.

When they are triggered, the behaviour is carried out even if this happens to occur in the wrong situation. When my daughter Aina was born I was in a position to notice that the instinct to find the breast was also triggered by being laid on Dad's hairy chest. She found her way to the right spot and nuzzled at it, even though it was not what was required on that particular occasion.

Apart from that, pure instincts are not particularly common in human beings and other creatures with large brains. Instead a large brain makes flexible behaviour possible that can be adapted to an understanding of the actual situation. A large brain can solve the problems it is confronted with on its own without recourse to an inborn solution in the form of instincts, and this means it has a range of options for tackling new problems in new environments. It is not the case, however, that the human brain is an entirely impartial problem solver that operates like a computer. It differs from that model in several ways:

- Our senses are systematically programmed to prioritise certain kinds of sensory input. Our eyes do not operate like unbiased cameras, nor our ears as neutral microphones. Some input is highlighted and flagged as important and attracts our attention, while other data is allowed to pass unnoticed. Of particular relevance to language is the fact that our hearing is tuned to filter out other sounds in favour of human ones, and other human sounds in favour of speech. The latter part of that filtering system probably arose in tandem with the evolution of language, and because the filter is already active in newborn babies, it must also be innate.
- We are much better at solving social rather than abstract problems (if problems of the same underlying complexity are being compared), and when something happens we try to identify intent before we look for natural causes.
- We are much better at learning language than we are at

other skills that are not actually more complicated, such as solving differential equations.

These aspects of human cognition are not bugs in the system but sensible adaptations to the kinds of problem that have proved important for us to solve during our evolutionary history. The price we pay is that we are slightly less good at solving some abstract problems than we might have been. But being able to spot malicious intent, or to learn languages quickly, turned out to be sufficiently important in evolutionary terms to make that a price worth paying.

* * *

Bears will eat anything, from elks to blueberries. A common Swedish bear in its normal Swedish habitat has a varied diet depending on what is available and in season and would not ordinarily specialise in a particular kind of food. As a result its biological adaptations are a compromise: it has teeth that can both chew elk flesh and blueberries and much else besides, even though they are not the perfect tools for chewing either elks or blueberries.

Now assume an ice age is dawning. The glaciers have come creeping down from the mountains, and a group of bears has been cut off at the coast and cannot escape across country. Soon there are no more elks or blueberries to consume; the only food they can find instead are seals out to sea. So the bears become full-time seal hunters. An ordinary bear is capable of catching seals but it is not particularly good at it. So if seals are the only food available then the bears who are slightly better genetically equipped for seal hunting will be the first to survive and have offspring, and natural selection will subsequently favour the genetic adaptations that turn bears into better seal hunters. Their fur will become whiter to provide better camouflage against the pack ice and water-repellent into the bargain; their bodies will slim down and become more supple and their teeth will become more like those of a pure carni-vore. The brown bear has adapted genetically to its new life, very swiftly by evolutionary standards, and become a polar bear.

\* \* \*

This is roughly what happened when polar bears evolved from brown bears during the last ice age in the regions around the Bering Strait. Note the sequence: the bears adapted their behav-iour *first*, they began by hunting seals, and *then* they adapted genetically over several millennia to become better suited to the new way of life they were already leading. This is perfectly normal among animals with a flexible repertoire of behaviours. The be-havioural flexibility that many animals have evolved means that some behaviours can be changed in advance with the genetic adaptations following on behind.

This aspect of behavioural flexibility applies to human beings in particular. The Inuit live in the same regions as the polar bear and have a similar diet – and the Inuit have also adapted genetic-ally to this state of affairs, mainly by various minor changes to their bodily proportions and other physical attributes in order to better handle the cold. Here too the sequence is the same: they moved into the Arctic first and then adapted genetically over many generations once they were there.

Changes in behaviour often come first, triggered by the environment, and the evolutionary adaptation of heredity comes afterwards. *Language too – a basic protolanguage at least – may have preceded the adaptations we have evolved that allow us to speak. We will be returning later to how that might have occurred.*

Our language faculty is underpinned to some extent by a genetic component. But does that mean we have a language instinct in any more specific sense? Steven Pinker even called his bestseller *The Language Instinct* and maintained that that is what our language faculty is: an instinct, just like the ability of birds to fly or the ability of beavers to build dams. There is, however, no agreement among scientists as to whether there are reasonable grounds for assuming such an instinct exists, and even less of a consensus about what it consists of if it does.

An important dividing line that exists between researchers has to do with how much of our language faculty is innate, and, if so, what that innate quality would be. Another dividing line is whether the innate faculties we use for language evolved purely for the sake of language, or whether these are more general faculties that we use both for language and for other purposes. A third and related divide has to do with the chicken or the egg – did the biological language faculty need to be in place before we could utter a word or is it a subsequent evolutionary adaptation in humans who were already speaking, just like the example of the polar bear above?

One difficulty that needs to be considered in relation to the language instinct is that the location of language in the brain is not fixed. As we noted in the previous section, children can learn a language even when the part of the brain that normally handles language has been surgically removed in infancy. And yet an innate language instinct would have to have a home somewhere in the brain; instincts must be made up of physical networks of neurons that control instinctive behaviour. The fact that language can be managed by several different sites indicates both that it does not require there to be any finished language-specific networks in place, and that it can make use of more general neural structures that are distributed in many different locations in the brain. This argues against the existence of a more wide-ranging specifically linguistic and innate language instinct.

In respect of the innate language faculty, it is quite obvious on one level that it must exist – there is *something* in the biology of human beings that allows us to learn language quickly and effortlessly at an early age, something that distinguishes us from all other animals. Some linguists, including Noam Chomsky, think that this inborn something is grammar and, if that is the case, then we are born with a built-in grammar module in our heads, built-in structures in our brain, to carry out grammatical analyses according to the general rules common to human languages. Language would not be possible from this point of view without the existence of an innate grammar; it must therefore have been in place before language.

But other researchers, those within the functionalist paradigm in particular, have very different perspectives on the biological foundation of the human language faculty. They do not consider grammar as the core component of language in the same way that Chomsky does, but focus more on language as a social system that is used for communication and social interaction and that children learn in a social context. An innate grammar, in the strict sense, cannot therefore exist within the functionalist paradigm. Instead, language is assumed to be based on general cognitive and social faculties that may in their turn be wholly or partially innate. These faculties are, however, used for all kinds of things, not just for language, and did not evolve specifically for language. They do not therefore constitute a form of language instinct.

If language instincts, which most linguists agree exist, are to be identified, then we need to turn to small children and examine how they begin learning language. Very young children have several language-relevant faculties that appear to be inborn. From the moment of birth they can distinguish speech from other sounds and they devote more attention to it than to the other noises they can hear. They apparently began listening to languages inside the womb because they can distinguish their mother's tongue – even when someone other than the mother is speaking that language – from other languages immediately after birth. This seems to involve an instinct to gather input in order to learn their native language.

Babbling also appears to be an instinct whose purpose is to practise how to make speech sounds. Six-month-old babies babble and listen to their own babbling in order to fine-tune their capacity to articulate appropriate speech sounds. Initially they babble every kind of sound, but their babbling will then narrow down to the speech sounds of their mother tongue. Babies that are born deaf babble as well, in two different ways even. A deaf baby begins to babble using its voice roughly like a hearing baby, but because it cannot hear its own babbling no fine-tuning of the sounds takes place, and the babbling fails to develop further. If the parents speak sign language with the baby it begins to babble instead with its hands, practising just as hearing babies do with speech sounds but using the hand shapes of sign language.

Infants also appear to have a number of specifically human social instincts that make it easier for them to initiate social interaction, which makes language learning easier in turn. Newborns learn almost immediately to recognise their mother's face and they recognise her voice from their time in the womb. They can also identify human social expressions from day one and tell smiley faces from non-smiling ones. An instinct of a slightly different kind has been called "the interactional instinct" by the American linguist John Schumann. This has to do with motivation rather than ability: human infants instinctively *want* to interact socially with parents and other people in their environment.

Babies start making eye contact and imitating others as soon as they have the motor skills required, and social turn-taking appears early on as well. Chimps and other apes do not display the same level of social interaction with their newborns that we do and the difference may be explained as a combination of social instincts in the human child and social initiatives on the part of human parents.

Overall this constitutes a complete package of instincts that provide newborn humans with a fast track to social interaction. The various components in the package both facilitate the making of social connections and motivate the baby to take an active part in its growing social network. The fast track to social interaction then becomes a fast track to language.

One early social ability that is particularly important for language is known as "joint attention" and involves two individuals jointly directing their attention towards the same thing. This is something we do all the time without thinking about it in any significant way. Adult chimps can handle joint attention with a bit of application, but it does not come particularly naturally to them and they do not spend anywhere near as much time on it as we do. Nor do adult chimps practise it with their young to any great extent.

And yet it is hard to imagine how children could start using language without being able to manage joint attention with their parents and the other people around them. A human child devotes a lot of effort during its early years to learning all the words in its language. In order to achieve this, children need to hear a great many words, they need to hear language being used (or to see language, if it is being signed) and they need to be able to participate in forms of linguistic interaction. In that interplay they use what language they have already acquired in order to work out what the new words mean. But at the very start, when the child is not yet familiar with many words, it finds itself confronted with what is known as the "gavagai" problem.

Gavagai is a word invented in 1960 by the American philosopher W.V. Quine. If someone who speaks a language that is completely unknown to you says "gavagai" when a rabbit hops past, how can you know what the speaker is referring to? Can you take for granted that "gavagai" means "rabbit", or could it mean "food" or "let's hunt" or "rabbit ears" or "mammal" or something else entirely that has nothing at all to do with the rabbit?

There are two parts to the way the child solves the gavagai problem. One part is joint attention – if the child and the speaker have jointly noticed something, the child can safely assume that the something is what the speaker is referring to. The second has to do with the conceptual level. Everything and anything can be referred to on a variety of different levels. Is that an animal, a vertebrate, a mammal, a lagomorph, a rabbit, a wild European rabbit, a Swedish male rabbit, or a specific individual – Bobby? On a different tack one could also envisage an entire ecosystem, or all herbivores, or a colony of rabbits, or a rabbit, or rabbit ears, rabbit inner ears or rabbit ossicles. The word "gavagai" – or the word "rabbit" to a one-year-old – could in theory refer to any level at all in these hierarchies. But children all over the world will make specific assumptions about which level is being referred to, and adults adapt to the assumptions their children make when they name things to them. Children normally opt for a middle level from the hierarchy when they hear a new word at the same time as joint attention is being directed towards a new object. They also start from the premise that the new word is aimed at a whole individual and not a group or a part. This is the level that corresponds in both cases to the word "rabbit" in the lists above.

The fact that children and adults agree on which level things should be named first might just be the result of mutual adaptation – but the level they agree about is strikingly uniform in different cultures all over the world, which raises the question of whether we are dealing with something innate here.

Once children have learned the word for the starting level they can go on to learn words that apply on other levels, both the parts of rabbits and more wide-ranging group terms. In general, when a child already knows the word for certain aspects of what is being jointly attended to, the child will assume that a new word has to do with a new aspect or new level not covered by the words it is already familiar with.

So a child possesses very effective tools for solving the gavagai problem, tools that are probably at least partially innate although that may be difficult to prove. The ability to participate in joint attention is a key that unlocks a great deal of the understanding of language. But joint attention is not something specific to language; it is used in all forms of human collaboration. If I need help lifting something heavy and you are standing beside me, it will frequently suffice for me to establish joint attention towards the heavy object for you to give me a hand entirely without any verbal communication. The best place to find the roots of joint attention are therefore among the roots of human helpfulness.

* * *

In order to speak and understand its mother tongue fully, a child needs to know both words and grammar. The gavagai tools explain how children can learn words, and words are needed in turn for children to be able to tackle grammar. It is not, however, self-evident how these tools then help the child to analyse the structure and rules of the grammar of its mother tongue.

One argument for a more language-specific language instinct that could be factored in here is a principle known as the "poverty of the stimulus". In order to learn their mother tongue children need to hear a sufficient amount of that language to provide them with the evidence required to work out all the rules and peculiarities of its grammar. According to the poverty-of-the-stimulus argument, the linguistic evidence that the child actually hears during normal growing up is both insufficient and of too poor a quality to derive the grammar of its mother tongue from. But because children manage to learn that grammar nonetheless, according to the same argument they must have been provided with its nucleus for free as part of an innate faculty for language.

The relative importance assigned to this line of reasoning depends on which language paradigm you adopt, which depends in turn on the different views that the various paradigms espouse on what the child is actually learning when it learns its mother tongue. According to the generative paradigm, it is the formal structure and rules of grammar that are the nucleus of language, and the child's task is to identify the correct grammar for its mother tongue amidst a myriad of fundamentally different possible grammatical structures. Considered as an abstract mathematical problem, deriving any kind of structure from the data supplied would be an impossible task to solve with the limited evidence that the child possesses. If this is really what children do, then part of the solution must be innate.

In the connectionist paradigm, the task facing the child is to train the neural networks in its brain instead, so that the output from those networks is close enough to that produced by the networks of all the other speakers of its mother tongue. This is a completely different kind of undertaking to that of the generative paradigm and does not make the same formal demands on either the evidence or the outcome. It also makes the child's task much simpler and there is no need for any specific language instinct. Connectionist learning works for small and simple examples, but it remains to be shown whether it is sufficient for learning a complete language under realistic conditions. The types of networks that have been experimented with up to this point are probably not adequate.

In the various functionalist theories about language, the child's task is to put together a working language that is good enough to communicate with other speakers. Exactly how this is supposed to happen differs a great deal between theories but, on the whole, the task is more limited and more achievable than the mathematical problem that confronts the generative child. The functionalist child gradually develops a language that works, picking out fragments large and small from everything that is said around it and experimenting with different constructions and combinations until its message can be transmitted. In this instance, too, there is no need for any more wide-ranging or specific language instinct, nor an innate grammar.

* * *

Irrespective of the language paradigm that a particular scientist or researcher subscribes to, there is a great deal everyone can agree on in terms of what is *not* innate about language. Because all children can learn any language at all, what distinguishes one language from another cannot be innate. An inborn grammar could therefore only help with what is universal, common to all languages, and that as we have seen is a short list.

Every language has its own vocabulary and its own grammatical features, and all that has to be learned by children the hard way. But the process happens very quickly: children learn several words a day during their entire childhood. By the time they start school they can understand close to 10,000 different words in their mother tongue, yet a seven-year-old will have been living with language for only just over 2,000 days – that makes five new words a day, seven days a week, year after year. On top of that there is all the language-specific grammar and so on that has to be learned as well. Multilingual children also manage to learn all these thousands of words and rules in each of the languages they speak, while also learning to keep them separate. Children must therefore have especially powerful learning tools in order to acquire the linguistic knowledge that we generally accept is not innate.

Joint attention will take the learner quite a long way in relation to non-abstract words whose referents can be attended to jointly. But children also apply a great many statistical patterns to their learning, particularly to work out the grammar and in order to associate specific words with word classes. Initially, statistical patterns are also used to identify what speech elements in an utterance are words, and several experiments have shown that even very young infants can recognise patterns of this kind. Even if word classes such as nouns and verbs are innate as concepts – which is disputed – the assignment of words to classes, that is, which word goes into which class, cannot possibly be innate. Nor can the way a stream of sounds is divided up into words and sentences be innate, because this is accomplished by different means in different languages – and all the mental effort that has gone into getting computers to understand human language has shown that distinguishing words one from another is by no means a simple problem, even if it is one children solve pretty quickly.

* * *

So is there some kind of language instinct, and what can the answer to that question tell us about the origin of language? On the one hand everyone agrees that human children possess a number of specific adaptations that together make it possible for them to begin to learn languages – selective hearing, babble, joint attention, and a number of other social instincts along with an understanding of concepts. Several of these, however, are not language-specific but general social instincts that allow babies to participate in human social interaction and cognitive activities as a whole. Babble and selective hearing are language-specific but would constitute a rather modest language instinct that could hardly present any insurmountable hurdles to evolution.

There is a great deal of consensus as well that children are remarkably good at learning words, so good that it is tempting to postulate a specifically innate mechanism that facilitates the acquisition of language, even if we cannot imagine how that might work. Children are also good at statistical patterns, but it is unclear whether that ability is general or specific to language.

There is, however, no agreement at all about the innate grammar that generativists consider to be the key element in our language instinct. The debate has been raging for most of my lifetime and shows no signs of flagging or reaching any kind of consensus. This is troubling for those of us researching the origin of language because the "to be or not to be" of innate grammar is of crucial importance to what the nature of that original language might have been.

The few language universals to be found are, of course, easier to explain if an innate grammar does exist, but, if that is so, one has to wonder why so few universals really are universal – if everyone has the same grammar module built into their heads. There are also patterns to the mistakes that children make – and to the ones they do not make, in particular – when learning their mother tongue that are difficult to account for unless there is something innate that sets limits to how much children experiment with the structure of language.

One particularly thorny problem in relation to the language instinct that we have already alluded to is the actual nature of the task that confronts children when they learn their mother tongue. The kind of mathematical problem-solving that the generative paradigm relies on so heavily does not resemble the way we learn other skills: it is function that matters for everything else. The poverty-of-the-stimulus argument, on the other hand, is based on the mathematical view of language acquisition and diminishes in strength when other assumptions are made about what and how children learn.

Evolving an innate monolithic grammar module gradually by means of natural selection is extremely difficult. A few years ago the Irish linguist Anna Kinsella demonstrated in her doctoral thesis that gradual Darwinian evolution simply does not work for the minimalist calculating module which is currently the leading model in the generative paradigm.[33] Noam Chomsky has indirectly admitted that this is true by postulating that innate grammar did not develop gradually, but appeared as a result of a supermutation. But given that we know human beings as a species have evolved gradually over a long time, Kinsella's results have proved an embarrassment for the concept of an innate grammar.

Even if the grammar module as envisaged by Chomsky is not "evolvable", other kinds of innate support for the child's

33 Parker, Anna, *Evolution as a constraint on theories of syntax: The case against minimalism* (2006), University of Edinburgh. https://pdfs.semanticscholar.org/52d6/c086ac935a-7099fedc95d5f70a86d1a7a446.pdf (she changed her surname from Parker to Kinsella shortly after submitting her thesis, which was then turned into a book with the title *Language Evolution and Syntactic Theory*).

acquisition of grammar can be envisaged, something like the tools children use to solve the gavagai problem, perhaps, and it is by no means unlikely that something along those lines is a component of our language faculty. But we do not know whether that is so and the toxic debate around innate grammar makes the question a difficult one to tackle.

The fact that language can be repositioned in the brain would also argue against innate grammar. An innate grammar module ought in all probability to be situated in those parts of the brain that normally deal with grammar and should therefore disappear when those parts are surgically removed. But babies that have been operated on in this way can nevertheless learn their mother tongue.

*We know that human beings evolved from ancestors without language. This means our language faculty must have evolved and it must therefore be capable of evolving. The innate grammar module the generativists propose is not "evolvable" and poses other problems besides, and cannot therefore be part of our language faculty.*

*On the other hand, there probably are language instincts linked to babbling, selective hearing and the learning of words. Language is also based on a range of social instincts but these are not language-specific.*

## LANGUAGE GENES

Having an innate biological language faculty, although perhaps not a language instinct the way Pinker envisages, means that there must be a number of genes that control the development of that faculty. The evolution of the language faculty would then consist of changes to D.N.A. in and around these genes. The D.N.A. changes would affect how the embryonic brain develops new connections in such a way that the pattern of those connections lays the foundation for the language faculty. However, we have no clear understanding of exactly how this takes place – the fraction of the process we have been able to chart merely demonstrates that it is a long and complicated story.

The evolution of the language faculty proceeds from changes to D.N.A., via changes to the development of the embryonic brain, to changes to the brain's ultimate pattern of connections and to our cognitive faculty as a result. This fact applies no matter which grammar paradigm we adopt. Both a generativist and connectionist can reach agreement at this abstract level, even though they take a completely different view of which patterns of connections are being developed.

A great deal of research has been carried out into the genetics of language. In essence, all human beings possess a basic language faculty that makes it possible for us to use our mother tongues. However, there are differences as to how talented we will prove to be at language – some people find it easier than others to learn new words or new languages. While these differences depend for the most part on what kind of linguistic environment one has grown up in, some of them may also be linked to genetic differences.

There are also more subtle relationships between genetic differences and different languages. Some genetic variations are, for example, more common in those ethnic groups that speak tonal languages (languages in which pitch plays a role) while others occur more frequently among populations that speak languages with many different consonants. We actually have no idea at all why certain genetic variations are associated with particular kinds of language, but it probably has to do with small differences in the ability of individuals to learn to produce tones or consonants. These differences are so tiny that they play barely any role as far as the individual is concerned, and they cannot be measured in the laboratory, but the way language itself evolves can magnify tiny differences of this kind with the result that additional consonants find it easier to survive in the linguistic struggle for existence among speakers who are just a tiny bit better at learning that kind of speech sound.

We have not been able to find any genetic links at all for the vast majority of differences between languages, however. And those differences are very small: every healthy baby can still learn absolutely any language at all, even languages they have the "wrong" genes for.

In contrast, the role played by heredity becomes clearer when studying human beings who fail to acquire a complete language in childhood, despite growing up in a normal linguistic environment. "Specific language impairment", as it is known, involves language problems that cannot be traced back to some external cause or some other functional variation. What the genetic studies of children with specific language impairment have demonstrated is that there is a considerable inherited component in our language faculty, but that this inherited component is extremely complicated, with a wealth of different genes involved in one way or another.

At the beginning of this chapter I referred to the FOXP2 gene, which attracted a great deal of publicity some years ago and was referred to in the less scrupulous media as "the gene for language". What had actually been discovered was that a mutation which makes that gene stop working was sufficient to cause specific language impairment. The mutation was detected in a familial lineage, many of whose members were affected by specific language impairment. The vast majority of cases of specific language impairment have very different causes, however, so this gene is not in any way the key to language. It is one of the many genes needed to produce a normal language faculty.

The FOXP2 gene is interesting in evolutionary terms inasmuch as it occurs in all vertebrates and appears to be identical in most mammals. At some point in the course of human evolution, however, one little detail of the gene changed with the result that it does not do exactly the same thing in humans as it does in other mammals. Exactly what this gene does is a long story. FOXP2 affects the body indirectly by controlling and blocking the activities of other genes. It is active at various different locations in the body including sites that very obviously have nothing to do with language. In the brain the gene appears to reduce the activity of several other genes that affect yet more genes in their turn, and so on, in a cascade that results in an increase in flexibility in certain kinds of nerve cells. When this cascade does not function as it should, the language faculty is affected, though it is still unclear how or why.

Ever since it was discovered that FOXP2 has something to do with language, a great deal of research has been carried out on it. Bats and whales, in which the gene operates slightly differently, have been studied in particular. Both bats and whales include many species that use sound to navigate with, and this probably makes great demands on the animals' ability to produce and perceive patterns of sounds. FOXP2 is also active in songbirds. Experiments have been conducted in which the activity of the gene has been blocked in young songbirds, with the result that they fail to properly learn their own song. In other experiments mice have had their own version of the FOXP2 gene replaced using gene modification with the human variety. While this did not lead to talking mice, it did affect the rodents' behaviour in several other ways, including how they used their normal sounds. The opposite has also been tested, sabotaging the FOXP2 gene in mice in the same way as in the family with specific language impairment in whom the gene was discovered. Mice babies with a sabotaged FOXP2 gene are affected by a specific impairment to their squeak, and they squeak much less often than ordinary mice. What has become clear is that in a large number of animal species the FOXP2 gene affects the ability to use sounds. And FOXP2 particularly affects the ability to learn new sounds, in the case of those species that can do so.

It is worth noting that both Neandertals and Denisovans possessed the human version of FOXP2. The mutation that altered the gene must therefore have occurred before our path diverged from theirs about half a million years ago. The D.N.A. that exists around the site of the mutation in modern humans shows clear signs of being favoured by natural selection, which means that it would have spread rapidly in the populations where it occurred. It seems that the human version of FOXP2 gave our ancestors a distinct evolutionary advantage. Although we do not know with certainty that the advantage in question had anything to do with language, that would be a reasonable guess nonetheless.

Even though it is very far from being "the language gene", FOXP2 is a fascinating gene overall. We know that a great many other genes are also involved in language in one way or another, and yet we know far too little about how the entire pattern of gene activity and environmental factors interacts to construct the human language faculty. What we definitely have not found is one particular "language gene" that can turn the whole language apparatus on or off – it is just not that simple. Nor have we found any genes that can be linked in a straightforward way to a specific aspect of language. Instead, all the genetic effects on language we have been able to identify are diffuse with broad effects across several language domains.

*We can therefore conclude that the language faculty evolved gradually by means of many small adaptive improvements over a very long period and that it did not occur as the result of a single supermutation.*

One question we have to ask is whether the genetic adaptations to language occurred before or after language came into existence. As we have seen, animals capable of flexible behaviours will frequently initiate a new behaviour first and then, when that behaviour has become sufficiently important to the animal, an evolutionary adaptation will occur at the genetic level that improves the performance of that behaviour. So how much language instinct would have been required by the very first language? Could it be the case that we were already able to start a simple protolanguage using the cognitive abilities we had evolved for other purposes without possessing a true biological language faculty, and that the particular genetic adaptations to language we observe today arose afterwards and made more advanced language use possible?

If a fully fledged language faculty with all the genetic adaptations already in place is required before language can get going, we are faced with an evolutionary dilemma. Without language, the genetic adaptations offer no apparent evolutionary advantage – but without the genetic adaptations there can be no language.

*It is therefore more plausible in genetic terms that language and the language faculty evolved in parallel, so that the very first protolanguage provided the impetus for genetic adaptations that would, in turn, make more powerful languages possible, which, in their turn, prompted further genetic adaptations and so on in a dialectical interplay between genes and language, between heredity and the language environment.*

# The Language-Ready Brain

The human brain is the organ that differs most from that of the other primates, and it is also the organ that manages the larger part of everything related to language in our lives. So the evolution of the brain plays a crucial role in the evolution of language.

The expression "the language-ready brain" was coined by the British scientist Michael Arbib and serves to highlight the difference between possessing a brain that is capable of handling language and one that actually uses that capacity.

So what is the difference between having a brain that can handle language and one that cannot? The short answer is that we do not know. The location of the language faculty in an adult brain can be identified to some extent; we can point to roughly what part of the brain does what. Scientists could actually do that as early as the nineteenth century by studying people who had lost their language faculty as a result of head trauma or a stroke. In 1861, Paul Broca was able to identify what has come to be known as Broca's area, usually on the left side of the brain and quite far forward, roughly halfway between the eye and the ear. Patients who had suffered damage to Broca's area had difficulties in both speaking fluently and adhering to grammar. They could still speak, but only slowly, and all the little words and endings that make language coherent were missing. Wernicke's area, slightly further back just inwards from the ear and on the left side too, was similarly named in 1874 after Carl Wernicke had observed that damage to this area led to people speaking fluently, but without making sense – they had apparently lost the connection between words and what they mean.

Nowadays we have been able to map the location of language in the brain in greater detail, using both Broca's and Wernicke's methods as well as modern ones such as M.R.I. scanners that allow us to measure what is going on in a healthy and awake brain while it is actually being used for language. We also know now that while Broca and Wernicke were on the right track, the real state of affairs is considerably more complicated. Many more parts of the brain are involved in language in a variety of different ways, and the division of roles between these parts is not at all as simple as Broca and Wernicke envisaged: with grammar appearing to be situated in Broca's area, while semantics was in Wernicke's. Hierarchical structures in language, and perhaps in contexts other than language as well, are still managed primarily in and around Broca's area. Semantics, however, is much more widely distributed than Wernicke imagined.

But it is much harder to pinpoint whatever it is in a newborn's brain that allows the child to learn language. What distinguishes a human baby's brain from that of a baby chimp and means that the human but not the chimp will eventually learn to talk? Everything we touched on in relation to our language instincts needs to be underpinned by structures of some kind in the brain, but we do not know exactly what these are.

The size of the brain differs, of course, between humans and other primates: the brain of a human is three to four times bigger than that of a chimp. When an infant starts talking at around the age of one its brain is already twice the size of that of an adult chimp. But it cannot only be the size of the brain that the language faculty is dependent on. There are several animals that have bigger brains than humans – both elephants and most whales have brains that are at least twice the size of ours without their being particularly talkative as a result. Dolphins have brains that are almost as large as the human brain in proportion to their body size. If dolphins do not have a language, it cannot be for lack of brain cells.

## OUTSIDE RIGHT, INSIDE LEFT

Human beings and most animals are roughly symmetrical, with the result that the right and left sides of the body look almost identical and function almost identically. But only almost. Most of us have one hand that is more dextrous than the other, and that is usually the right hand. Conversely, in most of us the heart is on the left side (anatomically at least if not necessarily politically). The brain, too, is roughly but not exactly symmetrical and the right and left sides of the brain do not deal with exactly the same things. That applies to human beings and to many other animals as well.

The differences between the two hemispheres are not unduly great, however, and in almost all the things we undertake the left and right halves of the brain work together and jointly determine the way we think. An idea popular some years ago was that certain people thought mostly with the left half, while others thought mostly with the right; this was supposed to explain why some people were more analytical and others more intuitive. This notion lacks any scientific foundation and is derived from both over-interpretation and a misinterpretation of research findings.

But some differences between the hemispheres do have a firm foundation, particularly in relation to language. Most of us have language on the left side of the brain – as Broca and Wernicke had previously observed and about which they turned out to be correct, at least in relation to basic linguistic functions involving words and grammar. There are also aspects of language that are wholly or partially managed by the right side of the brain, includ-ing prosody. Prosody is to do with the melody of language and is managed naturally enough by parts of the brain that are close to the areas that handle the melodies of music.

Experiments on people who have had the connection between the two hemispheres of the brain surgically severed for medical reasons – this is sometimes carried out to treat severe epilepsy – have shown that while the right half of the brain understands language fairly well on its own, only the left hemisphere can actually produce language. The right hemisphere can listen but not talk, while the left one can do both.

Not that the situation is as simple as all human beings having language situated in the same places in their brains. While around 80 to 90 per cent of us manage language with the left hemisphere, a small percentage have language distributed on both sides and another few per cent manage it using the right side of the brain. Interestingly there is a connection here to which is our dominant hand: right-handed people almost always have language in their left hemisphere, while left-handed people are often language-righties.

One peculiar aspect of the way the brain is connected to the body is that everything is linked transversely, or contralaterally. The right half of the brain rules the left side of the body and vice versa. This applies to both incoming and outgoing signals. Nerve signals from the fingertips of your right hand are sent to a small part of the left hemisphere and another small part of the same half of the brain sends the signals back to the right hand and tells it what to do. This contralateral connectivity may seem almost ridiculous in relation to hearing because signals from the right ear end up after various detours in the left hearing area which is just above the *left* ear, and vice versa.

Contralaterality makes no great difference in a healthy brain; both halves have so many neural connections across the divide between them that the right hand can normally keep track of what the left is doing. And sensory data from the right and left ears, like the right and left eyes, are correlated at an early stage so that an integrated sound image is delivered to your awareness.

The cross-connection between brain and body is very ancient in evolutionary terms – all vertebrates have the same kind of contralateral organisation.

This form of connectivity between the brain and the body means that in a right-handed person the dominant hand is controlled by the left hemisphere, and vice versa. For most of us, therefore, language and the dominant hand are governed by the same side of the brain. That may seem a bit odd because both language and handedness are particularly important functions that make considerable demands on brain capacity. It would have been easier to fit everything in if they had been located in opposite hemispheres. The fact that they are on the same side, however, raises the question of whether there is some kind of link between language and our hands.

Handedness as such is actually not unique to human beings. Most apes also have a dominant hand they are better at using. However, being left- or right-handed is more or less equally distributed among the other apes. There is a lively and occasionally rancorous scientific debate about the handedness of chimps – some researchers maintain that the distribution is perfectly equal, while others report that there is a slight preponderance of right-handed chimps. Both sides agree, however, that any conceivable left–right difference among chimps is at a very modest level, with a maximum of 60 per cent of chimps being right-handed. The patterns for other primates are roughly the same in as far as this has actually been checked.

Among humans, however, the imbalance in distribution is striking. Right-handed people are much more numerous than left-handed ones in all cultures. A typical distribution would be 90 per cent right-handed and 10 per cent left-handed. This imbalance is sufficiently universal among humans, and handedness is sufficient hereditary to establish that its origin must be biological and genetic, even though the genetic details have not yet been determined. This imbalance evidently arose at some point in the course of human evolution once our path had diverged from the other primates.

We do not know why right-handedness became so dominant among humans. Handedness has its benefits, but whether it is the left or right hand that is dominant cannot conceivably make a difference to dexterity. But it is suggestive that a proverbial toss of the coin decides the matter among chimps, who lack language, whereas in humans who are endowed with language, the dominant hand is systematically governed by the brain hemisphere that also determines language.

The two hemispheres are roughly the same size in a human being but their shape is slightly different. There is considerable variation among individuals, but the statistical patterns that have been discovered indicate that the parts of the brain that control language are quite clearly more asymmetrical in people than the corresponding parts of the brain in chimps. There is a degree of asymmetry in chimps as well, however, but if you go further afield in the family tree the asymmetry disappears; in rhesus monkeys, for example, the two hemispheres are entirely symmetrical.

*The asymmetry of our hands and the asymmetry of the brain appear to be related, in which case the hands may provide us with a clue to the nature of language.*

## FOSSIL BRAINS

Brains are rarely found as fossils, for obvious reasons. They consist of soft matter that rots easily. On the other hand the brain is contained in a skull made of hard bone that exactly encloses it. The inside of a fossil skull can therefore provide an accurate picture of both the size and shape of the brain that once resided within, even though the brain itself disappeared long ago. Even details such as the folds and wrinkles of the brain, or the blood vessels that supplied it, can leave an impression on the inside of the skull that can be seen in well-preserved fossils. As a result we possess a considerable body of knowledge as to how the size and shape of the brain evolved in our fossil ancestors.

On rare occasions an archaeologist is lucky enough to find a fossilised brain preserved. The first *Australopithecus* fossil to be

The Taung child, a skull of an *Australopithecus africanus* discovered in Taung in South Africa in 1924. It belonged to a child who died at the age of four or five just over two million years ago. The rear half of the skull is missing, and this is where the petrified brain can be seen.

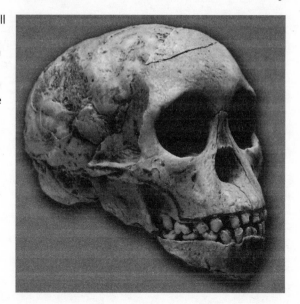

discovered almost one hundred years ago had a petrified brain of this kind inside the skull, as seen here.

The brain of an *Australopithecus* is, however, not noticeably different from that of an ape, neither bigger nor differently shaped nor remarkable in any other way. For several million years our ancestors were just two-legged apes who ran around Africa making monkeys of themselves.

The growth in size of the human brain occurred in two fairly distinct stages, one roughly two million years ago and the second half a million years ago. The volume of the brain doubled during the first stage from an ape-sized brain to roughly that of a two- to three-year-old today. In the second stage the full human size was reached.

Both stages coincide with periods when there were several kinds of humans in circulation. This is probably not an accident but the pattern is hard to interpret. In any case these are two periods that show a great deal of evolutionary activity. There may be a connection with the climate. The ice ages really got going roughly half a million years ago, following a gradual deterioration

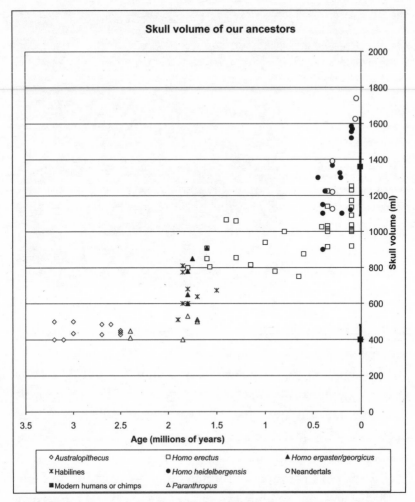

The evolution of brain size in fossil pre-humans by age and group. Each symbol shows an individual skull. Different symbols refer to different groups in accordance with the key. The long black strokes along the right edge show normal variation among modern humans and chimps. The vertical axis shows the internal volume of the skull in millilitres.

of the climate which began just over two million years ago. While the climate was getting colder in the north, it was getting drier in large parts of Asia and Africa, and a landscape of wide grassy savannahs and steppes gradually expanded. During a period around two million years ago you could walk on a virtually unbroken swathe of grass all the way from South Africa to China.

That is probably the route by which *Homo erectus* spread throughout that entire area. It would get even more dry later on, and the grass was replaced by desert in several regions of North Africa, the Middle East and Central Asia, which may have isolated different groups of *erectus* from each other. This could have led to the evolution of several kinds of human beings.

The technical development of stone tools also shows an obvious connection with the various stages of brain size. Before the first stage, only very simple tools were made among the variants of *Australopithecus* with ape-sized brains: stone flakes with a sharp edge but without any particular shape. After this, and during the very long plateau in brain size from one and a half to half a million years ago, enormous quantities of standardised hand axes were produced that were more or less identical. Following the second stage half a million years ago, technical change accelerated in a way it had not done before. Although still not rapid by modern standards it was beginning to take off. Innovations appear in archaeological findings, a profusion of differently shaped tools along with different methods for making them. Stone axes, stone knives and other stone tools in a wealth of different varieties, of course, but our relatives did not only work stone – the oldest wooden spears found date from this time, as does the first evidence that handles had been attached to stone axes.

The shape of the brain would also change in the course of this journey, although this is difficult to measure from fossil evidence. It is rare to find old skulls that are fully intact; usually they are so shattered or deformed that it is difficult to be sure whether small changes in the shape of the skull really occurred while the owner of the skull was still alive, or when the skull was buried deep in a cave somewhere instead. We must therefore be cautious about drawing conclusions based on minor changes in shape, particularly in relation to the symmetry of the brain.

There is, however, one change that is obvious: modern humans possess noticeably rounder brains than our ancestors and cousins did. Our brains are rather tall and narrow which gives us our high foreheads and a skull whose broadest point is slightly above the ears. In all the other human species, including the Neandertals (who had brains as big as ours), the shape is flatter and more oblong. A Neandertal had a low brow, but also a considerable protuberance at the back of the neck that contained as much brain volume as our high foreheads. The broadest point on a Neandertal skull was also lower down, roughly level with the ears.

Some scientists, notably Cedric Boeckx of the Universitat de Barcelona in Catalonia, believe that this change in shape is linked to language. The idea is roughly that the rounder shape of the human brain made possible shorter connections between its different parts, and this allowed us to think more effectively, which was what got our ancestors started using language. According to this model, language would have arisen very late in our evolution because the brain did not take on this more rounded shape until relatively recently, just 200,000 years ago. If a round brain is key to language, then other kinds of humans would not have had language, including the Neandertals.

But we shouldn't be too swift to dismiss the notion of Neander-talkers.

* * *

Let us return to our hands at this point. If right-handedness has something to do with language, then it would be interesting to discover how far back in time the human pattern of handedness extends. There are various different ways of determining whether fossil humans were right- or left-handed. We can examine stone tools – when you knap a flint axe, slightly different patterns of flaking occur depending on whether you knap with the right or left hand. But a more reliable technique is to examine the front teeth in ancient skulls. Just like us, our ancestors often used their teeth as an extra hand with which to hold something firmly. A common working method when you were cutting off a strip of meat, for example, would be to hold one end of the meat between your teeth, the other end in one of your hands and a flint knife to cut with in the other. Naturally you held the knife in your dominant hand. And if you sawed away with the flint knife near your teeth tiny scratches could easily be made on your front teeth if the knife happened to scrape them. These scratches were made in different directions depending on whether you sawed from the right or left. Examining scratches of this kind on the front teeth allows us to determine therefore whether the owner of the teeth was right- or left-handed.

What researchers have discovered in fossil front teeth is that right-handedness can be traced very far back in time. We have definitely been right-handed for half a million years, since the second brain expansion, and right-handedness may even go as far back as the first expansion in the size of the brain two million years ago.

*This shows that our brains have been asymmetrically organised in the human fashion for a very long time. This provides us with another clue to consider in our search for the origin of language.*

## THE CONNECTED BRAIN

The changes that make a brain language-ready, or ready for human thinking in general for that matter, are not in fact very much to do with the brain's average size and shape. Instead the crucial thing is the way the brain is connected up: the wiring of the circuits and networks that are formed by the neurons. But the details are difficult to examine at this level even in living brains, and all but impossible to detect in fossils. For this reason, research into the evolution of the brain has primarily examined shape and size, not because that is actually the most interesting aspect, but because that is the spot under the street light where the light is brightest.

There are a small number of obvious differences in brain

circuitry between humans and other primates that are related to language in various ways. The bow-shaped or *arcuate fasciculus* is an association tract or "cable" made up of nerve fibres connecting Broca's area with that of Wernicke. The fact that it connects these two areas in particular indicates that it is important for language, and an examination of patients that have suffered damage to this cable has confirmed that suspicion. Several different aspects of language are affected when the cable is damaged, and these range from the ability to name objects to the ability to articulate speech sounds.

A similar cable can be found in the other primates as well, but there it is much thinner. It is the connection to Wernicke's area that has been most actively developed in the course of human evolution. The nerve cable is also larger in humans on the side of the brain that we use for language.

It seems rather obvious that this cable has something to do with language. But which is the chicken and which the egg here? Did the cable thicken on its own and thus make language possible – or did language appear first, and we then made such demands on the neural connections that a thicker cable evolved? The latter is more plausible in evolutionary terms, but it presupposes that a thinner cable would have been adequate for a basic protolanguage. Making an existing cable thicker would not in any case be much of a problem for evolution.

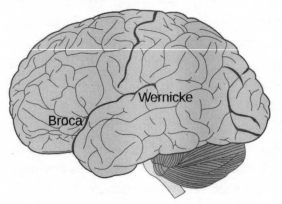

Model of human brain seen from the left. The forehead is on the left of the image and the back of the neck on the right. The bow-shaped association tract runs from Broca's area to that of Wernicke just above the ear.

Another important difference in brain wiring concerns the control of the vocal tract. Primates are completely incapable of imitating sounds, and this prevents them from talking. This is largely because they have only indirect control of their vocal tract. In mammals these organs are normally controlled by a particular little brain module, deep down in the older parts of the brain. That module is pre-programmed with the normal sounds of the animal and affords no scope for making new sounds. The only thing the animal can do at a more conscious level is to send signals to this sound module telling it to produce one of the pre-programmed sounds.

A basic pre-programmed module of this kind would be completely useless for language. In people – and in songbirds and other animals that need to use sounds creatively as well – new ways of producing sounds have developed as a result. Instead of allowing everything to pass through the sound module in the human brain, there are a number of nerve cables that circumvent the sound module and link the conscious brain and the vocal organs together directly.

You could liken this to an old computer equipped with a very basic sound card that can only produce a number of standard sounds. It might seem as though the obvious thing to do when better sound control is required would be to upgrade to a better sound card with greater range. What evolution has managed instead, in both humans and songbirds, is to let the old sound card remain in place while running cables past the sound card directly from the C.P.U. to the speaker outlet.

The old sound card in our brains is still connected up and working. It is what handles laughter and similar emotional sounds, all those noises we make that we feel we do not have complete control over. That is why it is so much harder to stop laughing than to stop talking and why laughter can occasionally erupt in the middle of continuous speech. Spoken language circumvents the sound card entirely, however, and makes no use of it at all.

The direct circuit that is used to bypass the sound card is absolutely essential for spoken language. We could not therefore have had any spoken language before that connection was in place. But the question is, what can have prompted the evolution of that additional connection, if we had no spoken language while it was evolving? So once again we find ourselves asking which came first: the chicken or the egg? A reasonable solution for getting past the chicken is to start with the egg – the circuit – because the ability to freely produce a huge range of different sounds that it makes possible may be useful for purposes other than language. An ability to imitate different sounds may have provided an evolutionary benefit even before we had spoken language and an ability of that kind may have evolved and been refined in a gradual process. Imitation might, for example, have been useful for hunting, as previously suggested. If language began as a form of signing, then imitating noises might have been useful as a means of supplementing the signs with the kind of meanings that are more easily conveyed by sounds.

Both the arcuate association tract and the direct wiring to the vocal tract are already formed in newborn babies and are, to all appearances, innate adaptations to language, part of the hardware underpinning our language instincts. Neither of them can be seen, however, in the fossil evidence, and as a result we have no direct proof of when they evolved. The direct connection has been set up in the great apes: they possess a few thin nerve conductors along the right lines, but their function is unclear. It is entirely absent in the other primates.

## Mirror Neurons

One form of neural connection that has attracted a great deal of attention in debates on the origin of language are the mirror neurons. These are neurons that are connected in such a way that they emit a nerve signal both when the owner of the cell does something, and when that owner sees someone else doing the same thing.

Several varieties of these neurons that respond to different kinds of action have been directly observed in various primate species. We do not know for certain whether there are mirror neurons in humans, as they have not been directly observed in our brains – the experiments conducted to identify them in primates are not considered ethically acceptable when performed on humans – but there is indirect evidence that we possess something similar, and if various other primates have them it would be odd if we did not, although not all researchers are agreed on that point.

We do not know very much about how these mirror neurons actually work. They probably have a comprehensive network of brain circuits behind them which is capable, first, of reverse-engineering an observed action in the other animal to determine the muscle signals that must have given rise to it and, second, of connecting the result with the pattern of muscle signals produced by the action of the observer.

In the absence of detailed knowledge about the way mirror neurons work, there is a comprehensive literature that consists in speculation as to what they are for. This is a long list, because it is not difficult to come up with applications for neurons that can connect together the observer's actions with those of others. Understanding the intentions, thoughts and feelings of others comes high up that list, as does the ability to imitate others and to learn from what others do. It is probable that the function of the mirror neurons in primates in which they have been detected lies somewhere along those lines because it is, of course, important for primates to understand what other primates are up to and even to "ape" them. The fact that primates rarely imitate other primates would, however, seem to undermine many ideas about the function of mirror neurons.

There has also been a lot of speculation about whether mirror neurons may provide a key to the origin of language, particularly by the same Michael Arbib I borrowed the title of this chapter from: "The Language-Ready Brain". In his book *How the Brain Got Language* he devotes many pages to mirror neurons and how they are supposed to be essential to making the brain language-ready. Arbib mostly uses mirror neurons as a springboard for the evolution of the human ability to imitate the actions of others. This mimetic ability could then be decoupled from its original function and operate instead as "going through the motions", like a pantomime, which would then have led on to language.

It is nevertheless rather odd that, as one of the supposed keys to language, mirror neurons have been proved to exist in primates that do not possess language, and have not definitively been found in humans who do. While the evolutionary process Arbib proposes is not implausible, mirror neurons per se offer no obvious help in providing that key.

## THE LANGUAGE-READY MIND

We use language to express our thoughts to a great extent, and vice versa: to use language in a meaningful way, we need to be able to think the corresponding thoughts. In order to use a word meaningfully we also need to understand the concept the word refers to.

The concept of "a concept" is not an entirely trivial matter, however. A concept is something that lives in our thoughts, but that is connected at the same time to something in the external world. Concepts are tools that we use to think about the kind of things that exist and occur in the world around us. Every concept can be considered as a mental representation of some aspect of our environment. And above all we need concepts when conducting a more general argument about matters both abstract and concrete that are more than simply mental representations of specific objects; we also need concepts for categories of objects and classes of events. Every concept of this kind connects a mental structure with a structure that we perceive in (or impose upon) the world around us.

When we then make the link to language, each concept becomes a tripartite connection. Connected to each concept is not just a structure in the world but a word, a label for that structure as well. This is, in essence, the same as the mental lexicon we discussed earlier, but seen from the perspective of cognition rather than language. In this sense a word becomes a symbol for that which the concept refers to.

Children develop concepts and language in parallel as they are acquiring their mother tongue. Their first words normally refer to concepts that already exist in their mental universe (mummy, daddy) but soon there is an interplay between language and concept and environment as they learn a word and then test the conceptual boundaries for when that word can be used. A child who has learned a new word often uses the word in ways that seem odd to an adult listener, a one-year-old who has just learned the word "doggie" may either use the word too broadly and call the neighbour's cat "doggie" as well, or conversely too narrowly and only use the word for the family's miniature poodle and possibly other poodles but not for the neighbour's Alsatian. This is how children learn the boundaries and the range of meaning of words: by experimenting and seeing what happens, by noticing how adults react to their attempts and, of course, by listening to how adults use the words. But at the same time they are also learning a productive conceptual structure for the world around them – they are learning that the structure of the surrounding world is better captured by a word that bundles together poodles and Alsatians rather than one that lumps together poodles and cats.

What kind of words children pick up and where they explore those boundaries is closely connected to the kind of world around them and thus to the surrounding conceptual world. "Doggie" probably appears considerably earlier in the vocabulary of the children of dog-owners than in that of children who have never seen a live pooch. And trying to teach that same one-year-old what an okapi is will probably be doomed to failure – not many European one-year-olds have even seen an okapi, and even fewer have had an opportunity to explore the boundaries of the concept of "an okapi". They might learn to repeat the word but it will not "stick" and will not become a real part of their language unless it can be linked to a concept.

Similarly, unless you as an adult speaker are knowledgeable about the conceptual world of string theory it would be virtually meaningless for you to learn words like "dilaton" or "brane" or terms such as "tachyon condensation". They cannot become a living part of your language until you are familiar with string theory – on the other hand you cannot learn string theory without acquiring the vocabulary that is used for the concepts of that theory. This has to be a dialectical process in which language and mind expand together.

Normally, however, concepts are one step ahead in the process. It is rare that we behave the same way as Pippi Longstocking does with the "spink": first she invents a new word and then she spends a whole chapter searching for a concept to match the word. Instead, it is the concept that is formed first – and thus the need for a word – and the word comes after.

The same applies to grammatical concepts. If you cannot handle time travel in your mind, there is no point having tense endings on verbs – but those journeys in time will be much easier to manage cognitively when you have a language that can express temporal states. Once more this is a positive spiral that begins with the concept but is reinforced and expanded by language.

*With regard to the origin of language we must therefore assume that the first simple words had a conceptual basis, that the first speaker already possessed a living conceptual world. As is the case with a young child, the first words spoken by the first speaker would have been about*

*things that the first speaker already had concepts for, things that were*
*already present in the everyday reality of the first speaker.*

No doubt some of these concepts would have had to do with making their livelihood as hunter-gatherers – "hunting", "gathering", "hand axe" and a number of different prey animals and edible plants – but just as certainly they would have included a range of concepts to do with human relationships – "mother", "child", "friend", "enemy" and so on – and a lot of other day-to-day stuff such as concepts to do with day and night, weather and wind, life and death. Although this cognitive world would then be able to expand and develop using language as a tool, a basic ability to handle concepts would be required for language to take off. Most of these first words were what we would we nowadays call nouns or verbs, even if it would have been pointless at the time to distinguish between word classes.

As noted in the section on animals that learn languages, there are a lot of language-related abilities that are latent in our closest relatives and that were therefore probably present among our common ancestors five to ten million years ago. This applies in particular to the language-ready mind as it exists in the animal kingdom and in which concepts can be well developed, too. Some animals employ very sophisticated concepts that accurately capture structures in the external world and make it possible for the animal to think about what is happening and make more or less well-founded decisions. What is evident in particular is that a great many animals have mental representations of things that are not in the here and now, as revealed by the fact that their mental representations persist even though the object of representation has been absent for months or years. A dog can remember an owner who has been gone for years on end. Our closest relatives, too, can keep what is absent alive in their thoughts.

These representations of what is absent can be considered as a kind of precursor to what is called "off-line thinking", which involves the capacity to think thoughts that are completely disconnected from what is happening in the here and now. Human beings use off-line thinking almost all the time, when we are planning or day-dreaming or in some other way living in our own mental worlds, somewhere else than the present, that is. Off-line thinking requires more than just the capacity to sustain mental representations of the kind of thing one has seen but can no longer see; it also requires an ability to construct concepts and putative relationships between them out of thin air, without any previous experience to attach our thoughts to.

Two researchers, Derek Bickerton and Denis Bouchard, have each published books that contain very different ideas about the origin of language but both give particular emphasis to off-line thinking as a uniquely human ability and one of the keys to language.[34] Bouchard also maintains that off-line thinking requires special systems of neurons in our brains, Offline Brain Systems, and that language is a by-product of the evolution of these systems. It should be noted, however, that some other animals at least are actually capable of planning for the future – remember Santino, the stone-throwing chimp? – and ought therefore to possess at least a basic level of off-line thinking. As things stand, chimps and other apes would appear to have a fairly well-developed conceptual apparatus in their heads that should serve as a good foundation to language. And while their conceptual world may not be as complex and many-faceted as ours, it should be good enough to get things up and running. Most of the concepts I have just attributed to the first speaker ought to be present in chimps as well.

In order for a protolanguage to develop, concepts need to be connected to labels: to something that can be expressed by a person and comprehended by another in the kind of triangular setup I referred to above. This far from simple step has been put forward by researchers, including Bouchard, as a key to the evolution of language. And yet the experiments on teaching language

34 Bickerton, Derek, *More than Nature Needs* (2014); Bouchard, Denis, *The Nature and Origin of Language* (2013).

to apes demonstrated that they were able to learn that particular connection at least, the link, that is, between concept and label. This is not something they do spontaneously in the wild, but when taught with sufficient patience by humans, many apes can grasp the point of the label and learn quite a few of them.

When we subsequently progressed to develop more advanced forms of language, an ability to handle more complex concepts would also have been required along with a semantic ability to put together those same concepts into chains of events. But by this point our ancestors already possessed a protolanguage that could help them with the necessary dialectic between language and mind.

Even if apes already possess concepts aplenty, what is striking is the contrast offered by how little both primates and other animals make use of their concepts when communicating with each other. Primate communication rarely reaches the level of abstraction that their internal conceptual systems operate at. They can communicate about specific things, but even then this is frequently a purely dyadic (two-handed) exchange. They do not discuss abstract or general matters with each other even though their minds are fully capable of handling abstract and general ideas. And although being able to connect labels to concepts is evidently within the reach of chimps, they do not use that ability in everyday life. We need to consider why our own ancestors began communicating their ideas and why other primates do not do so. Is it the ability or the will that they lack?

*As far as concepts as such are concerned, chimp minds are language-ready; the first protolanguage could have managed fine with chimp-concepts.*

# The Cooperative Ape

Aina, whom we met at the beginning of this book, has reached the age of two while I've been writing it and is now talking non-stop. One lovely summer's day Aina and I were out walking in the woods. I was pushing her in the buggy but she refused to sit still; she wanted to get out and walk on her own so she could discover exciting things.

A blackbird flew past. "Look, bird . . . Daddy, look!" "Yes, Aina, that is a blackbird. A blackbird." "Blabud?" "That's right, a blackbird." We continued on our walk. "Daddy. Hungry. Want biscuit." My eyes moved to the box beneath the buggy with the biscuits in. Aina rushed over to the buggy and searched right where Dad was looking and got out the pack of biscuits. "Daddy. Open!" I opened it and Aina got her biscuit.

There were raspberries growing beside the path. I picked a few and gave them to Aina. "Yum. More." I picked some more. Aina moved over to the raspberry bushes and tried to pick some herself but the berries just got squashed and the thorns pricked her hands when she grabbed the stems. "Aina, look, this is how you do it."

Eventually Aina managed to pick off a whole raspberry. She offered it proudly to me. "Daddy eat!"

\* \* \*

A young chimp is with its mother in the forest. Mum is cracking nuts with a rock. She places the nuts on a hard tree root in a little hollow where they cannot move around and hits them with the rock to break the shell. Then she removes the edible bits from among the pieces of shell and eats them. The young chimp is watching her and then grabs her pelt. Mum gives him a bit of the nut.

A yellow-beaked turaco flies past. The young chimp looks at it with interest but remains silent. His mother pays no attention to the bird.

Most of the nuts have now been cracked and the mother has eaten her fill. She sits beside a tree to rest. The young chimp searches through the bits of shell and finds a few flakes of the meat in the nut to eat. Then he finds a whole nut and tries to do what his mother did. He places the nut on the root and tries to hit it with the rock. With little success. The nut keeps moving and just flies away when he hits it. His mother watches but does nothing.

\* \* \*

Human beings help their children. We naturally help them to get food; we help them to learn how to do various things; we help them to acquire language, and with much else besides. Children are helpful themselves, even from a very early age.

Chimps are not in any way as helpful, not even towards their young. The mother will ensure that her baby has food and will defend it when required, but otherwise she does not appear to be bothered. She makes no attempt to try and teach her son to crack nuts other than by allowing him to watch while she does it.

This difference in helpfulness is probably one of the keys to why people, but not chimps, have evolved language. It may be useful to remind ourselves of what we learned in the passage about lying and in the section on the development of robot language: that cooperativeness and trust are required for language to develop.

## THE IMPORTANCE OF MIDWIVES

Humans help to keep each other informed in many ways, not just linguistically. And we take for granted that others will try to keep us informed: we interpret gestures and looks and so on from that perspective. In the raspberry wood Aina had no problem interpreting Daddy's glance at the box under the buggy as an intent on my part to tell her where the biscuits were.

Experiments on chimps have shown that they are not so ready to help, nor do they understand that human beings can be helpful. In experiments in which a human pointed out to a chimp where there were some sweets, the chimp was unable to understand what the human wanted. When the experiment involved a competitive situation rather than having to interpret a human pointing helpfully to something, the chimps managed much better. They had no difficulty interpreting looks and gestures on the part of a competitor and were able to use that information tactically in different situations.

Chimps are perfectly capable of cooperating with each other. But that cooperation is based on doing favours and getting favours in return, either in the short term – if I scratch your back, you'll scratch mine – or as part of long-term strategic partnerships, such as when two male chimps will cooperate to bring down the alpha male of the troop and take power together. Ordinary human helpfulness is all but foreign to them.

Chimps also find it remarkably difficult to trust one another. Humans will normally trust people they know unless they have particular reason to distrust a certain individual. The contrast becomes particularly evident when comparing how chimps and humans care for their children. A female chimp never lets go of her child until it is able to move around on its own. She watches over the baby twenty-four hours a day, seven days a week. The baby chimp's maternal grandmother or aunt might help out a bit, but the mother is by no means always willing to trust even her closest relatives with the care of her child. Allowing the father to help is not a real option because the love life of chimps is usually such that none of those concerned will know who is the father of whom.

Human beings, in contrast, accept help from all sides when it comes to babysitting. It is a common aspect of family life that many people become involved in helping to take care of a child. The father, of course, a grandmother, a grandfather, uncles, aunts, older siblings and even friends and acquaintances will often help look after the little ones. And the mother trusts them sufficiently to allow them to take care of what is most precious to her. We have no hesitation in entrusting even strangers with babysitting, not to mention leaving toddlers at nursery class.

The basic attitude of chimps to the world around them could very well be characterised in human terms as paranoia – were it not for the fact that chimps actually have good reason to distrust one another. It is not at all uncommon for young chimps to be killed by other members of their species, both males and females, despite all the mother's efforts. It is, however, extremely rare for human children to be intentionally killed by someone else. We may feel that child-killing happens a lot, but that is because it attracts a great deal of attention in the media on the rare occasions it does occur. It only takes one media storm a year to make ten million Swedes feel that it must happen often. In Sweden, one child in every 100,000 dies through violence before it has reached the age of one.[35] Among the chimps observed by researchers, that figure is more like one or more in every hundred. Infanticide is therefore at least a thousand times more common among chimps than among Swedish humans.

Murder is also relatively common among adult chimps. This usually involves conflicts between different groups. Chimps live

35  From Statistics Sweden's data on causes of death, http://www.statistikdatabasen. scb.se/sq/32928. I am using Swedish statistics purely as a matter of convenience. I have no reason to believe that there is any great discrepancy among different countries, those at least that are not at war or engaged in some other kind of conflict.

in troops that jealously defend their territories and God help the intruder who comes too close. One of the few things that chimps in a troop will work together on is guarding their territorial boundaries and making short work of any unknown males who have wandered across them. Females who want to change troop will sometimes be allowed to do so, but for all practical purposes the males are stuck with the troop they were born in.

There are of course other primates who do cooperate and trust one another more than chimps. Bonobos (pygmy chimps) are by no means as aggressive as common chimps, even if their reputation as the hippies of the animal kingdom is somewhat exaggerated. Even among bonobos, encounters across territorial boundaries occur with great caution and a good deal of mutual distrust.

A lot of primates live in family groups of various kinds with fairly peaceful relationships existing between the members. Within such groups it is usual for the father and older siblings to help with caring for the young, and the mother will trust them sufficiently to allow this. There are also primates, some species of baboon for example, that manage to live in troops without too much conflict and in which a mother will allow her female friends to hold her young for a little while. But she is not entirely comfortable doing so and makes sure to keep a watchful eye on the situation the whole time.

However, in most primates, relationships between different groups of the same species are characterised by distrust and enmity. It is rarely a good idea to put primates that do not know one another in the same cage in a zoo, and it is done with great caution when absolutely necessary. Frequently they will be allowed to get to know one another under supervision by first putting them in adjacent cages, so they can communicate through the bars.

Of course enmity towards strangers is not unknown among human beings either. But in day-to-day life we manage to tolerate strangers and that applies as well to the part of the human race who vote for xenophobic political parties. You can pack 300 people who do not know one another onto the same plane, and every single one of them will stay calmly in their seats throughout the flight. Not everyone will relish being squashed together and having to rub elbows with strangers in economy, but most of us will put up with it. Shutting three hundred primates who do not know one another in a plane would soon lead to bloodshed and complete chaos.[36]

\* \* \*

After many hours of difficult labour it will soon be over. The fair-haired crown of the child's head can already be glimpsed on its way out of its mother. Grandmother is sitting between Mum's legs ready to receive the child, while Mum is bearing down for that final stretch towards the goal. The head is out now, and the shoulders are visible. Granny takes careful hold of the child and helps to ease it out and then holds the little mite up for Mum to look at while he takes his first screaming breath. She lays him gently on Mum's breast and he wriggles around to find the nearest nipple and starts sucking. A new human has been born on a tiny croft in the rural heart of Småland in the midst of the Dacke war (a peasant uprising against the Swedish king in 1542).

Aunty, who has been holding Mum's hand, goes to find a cloth to wipe the baby dry with and a blanket to wrap him in. Grandmother cuts the umbilical cord and then deals with the afterbirth. The other grandmother, the father's mother, goes to find her son to tell him he has another son of his own.

\* \* \*

After a few hours of labour it will soon be over. The dark-haired crown of the child can already be glimpsed on its way out of its mother. Mum reaches down with her long hairy arms to catch the

36 The plane simile has been borrowed from Sarah Blaffer Hrdy, who uses it in the introduction to her book *Mothers and Others* (2009).

child and lifts the little mite to her breast herself once he is out. He wriggles around to find the nearest nipple and starts sucking while his mother bites off the umbilical cord and waits for the afterbirth. A new chimpanzee has been born, deep inside a stand of trees in the rain forest of the northern Congo.

* * *

Throughout history most people have been born more or less as in the first scene above, with the mother surrounded by helpers who support her and take care of practical matters. In today's Sweden, a professional midwife will usually take the place of the grand-mother, and Dad will be sitting beside Mum holding her hand, but traditionally it was the female relatives who assisted with the birth. In any case, extremely few women give birth entirely on their own. Chimps, in contrast, will withdraw as soon as they feel labour coming on, making sure to get away from the troop so that no-one will happen to find or hear them, and they normally give birth entirely without help. They have every reason to isolate themselves – researchers have directly observed another chimp in the troop grabbing hold of a newborn and killing it immediately after the delivery when the mother has failed to conceal herself well enough.

Childbirth is more than just another example of helpful humans and paranoid chimps. It may be one of the keys to why humans became so helpful and at the same time so successful. While female humans can manage childbirth on their own, the delivery is both extremely demanding and very risky. The process can sometimes end well, but both infantile and maternal mortal-ity are much higher for a woman giving birth alone. Infant mortality is, for that matter, high among chimps too, but there are very few female chimps who die in childbirth, despite the fact that they get no help at all.

When a child is due to come out of its mother the normal way, by vaginal delivery, it has to pass through a hole in the middle of her pelvis, the girdle of bone that sits in the centre of the body at the hips. In humans this is a very tight fit, exactly large enough for a baby's head, and the child has to wriggle out, twisting its head and body along the way. Things are very different for chimps who have plenty of space for the baby to pass through when it is being delivered. That difference arises from three factors in human evolution that conspire to make childbirth much more difficult.

The first has to do with the fact that our bodies are adapted to walk upright on two legs, and a crucial adaptation in this regard has been selected for in the pelvis, which has been set at a different angle from the way it is arranged in chimps and other primates and also made narrower. The narrower the hips, the more efficient bipedalism – and running in particular – are in purely mechanical terms, and this made it evolutionarily advantageous to have narrow hips once we had begun to walk upright. That is how our hips came to squeeze the space available for delivering babies, until the evolutionary gains from narrow hips were offset by complications in childbirth. The same process would nevertheless continue in men, with the result that they tend to have narrower hips than women. This is probably part of the explanation for why men run faster on average than women.

The second factor is connected to the first and has to do with the fact that our arms are shorter and weaker than those of other primates. We do not use our arms as much to climb with and so they have regressed somewhat. The arms we have are excellently suited to our needs in most situations, but in childbirth especially it would be useful if human mothers had those extra-long arms that chimps possess. Humans can reach between their legs with their hands, but only just, which makes it difficult for a woman to assist in bringing her own baby into the world, particularly when problems occur. This is not made any easier by the fact that human children are usually born facing backwards towards the mother's spine. If the mother tries to pull the child out in the only direction she can get any leverage in that position, she will bend the child's back in the wrong direction. A female chimp in labour can reach further between her legs and is more mobile and possesses greater strength in her arms, which makes it easier to be her own midwife when delivering her baby.

The third factor has to do with our large brains. As adults, our brains are three to four times larger than a chimp's and even a newborn human's head is much bigger than that of a baby chimp. As most women can testify, the head is the most difficult part to push out during childbirth.

Because human children are so difficult to deliver, having help can mean the difference between life and death – frequently for the child and, occasionally, for the mother as well. We have evolved bipedalism and large brains and they have clearly been of advantage in Darwinian terms. But they have also turned us into creatures that cannot even come into the world without the help of others, and this means that our helpfulness and our ability to trust others must have evolved hand in hand with our physical humanity. Our evolution towards thinking – and speaking – beings would have been arrested halfway had we not been able to get help in childbirth.

Is the midwife of childbirth also the midwife of language?

## LANGUAGE AND HELPFULNESS

Human beings are particularly fond of helping each other by providing information. This is obvious in children who have recently learned to talk: they gleefully use their newly acquired language ability to inform the people around them about everything they are noticing. "Look, bird!" – what parent could fail to recognise that? But even adults' language usage involves a great deal of informing other people. While this is frequently not information the recipient actually needs or has asked for, it will be supplied all the same. If you listen to a group of people having their tea break, it can sometimes feel as though they are competing as to who can supply the most information, usually about very mundane things. People are richly endowed with the need to communicate, a powerful urge to inform the world around them of what they are thinking.

Other apes lack that same impulse. Even apes that have been trained in language to the point where they would be capable in purely linguistic terms of expressing "Look, bird!" do not do so. They feel no need to tell the world around them that they have seen a bird. The other side of that coin is that the other apes do not ask questions either. They can ask for things, but they do not demand information – perhaps because they are not expecting helpful answers? The "why" stage I mentioned in the foreword to this book is entirely absent in the young of other species of ape.

That helpful communicativeness of human beings has a bearing on language when we remind ourselves once more about what was said about lies in the chapter on the boundaries of language. The communication systems used by most other animals have evolved in such a way as to make lying hard, and that means liars will incriminate themselves – because otherwise no-one would believe the message. But human language does not operate that way and yet we continue to listen to one another. At first sight language appears to be an evolutionary paradox, but this is a paradox that is resolved by our ability to cooperate and by our helpfulness. Or, to be more precise, the evolutionary puzzle at this point is about how we became so helpful and so trusting.

*Human language presupposes helpfulness. Language cannot have evolved, therefore, before we became helpful, which means the evolution of helpfulness is one of the keys to the origin of language.*

In the chapter on the linguistic abilities of other animals we observed how both apes and some other animal species have the capacity to learn a good deal that is linguistic in nature. They can learn words – connecting a concept to a label – and also learn to use words in appropriate situations. They can also combine words even though there tends to be little grammar involved and they can learn to understand quite a bit of a human language. While the language faculty apes evidently possess is not of the same calibre as that of human beings, it is quite extensive nonetheless and appears to be sufficient to serve a basic protolanguage. But that faculty is only expressed when the apes in question have been taught by human beings; they never learn anything like a language on their own in the wild.

There is apparently something lacking in the other apes that would allow them to spontaneously begin to use even a rudimentary form of language. But that something does not appear to be part of the language faculty itself. Something else is missing.

*Human helpfulness and trust are absent in chimps. And yet helpfulness is one of the prerequisites for language. This makes it even more likely that human helpfulness is one of the keys to language and, vice versa, that the absence of helpfulness is the underlying reason that chimps and other primates lack language.*


## HOW DID HELPFULNESS EVOLVE?

Working out how the qualities of helpfulness and cooperation can be produced through Darwinian evolution turns out to be quite tricky, and a great deal of intellectual effort has been devoted to this problem. The Swedish scientist Patrik Lindenfors, who specialises in biological and cultural evolution, has written an entire book about the origins of human cooperation with the title *For Whose Benefit?* The phrase echoes the Latin *cui bono?* – who stands to gain? – which is most frequently used in a criminal context but fits well here, too. Who benefits from a particular behaviour is, in fact, the key question when it comes to the evolution of cooperativeness.

Natural selection normally favours the animal that is good at surviving and good at reproducing itself. Normally, therefore, natural selection would favour the animal that helps itself and not the one that wastes its resources helping others in the struggle for existence. Most animals look out for themselves and stick to behaviours that benefit themselves in consequence. This is also why trust between most animals is extremely limited.

The only exception that is to any extent common in the animal kingdom is that parents help their offspring in various ways. But the offspring carry the parents' genes, and the parents are favouring their own reproduction and the continuation of their own genes by helping their young. Because other relatives also carry some of the same genes as I do, I can help spread my genes by helping those who are related to me. The concept of nepotism exists for good reason – favouring the offspring of your siblings (the Latin word for whom is *nepos*) pays off because they will be continuing your genes indirectly. This means that the kind of helpfulness that takes place within the family is not difficult to account for in Darwinian terms.

It is, however, only under very particular circumstances that helpfulness in any wider sense will evolve through natural selection. There is no obviously Darwinian advantage in helping individuals you are not related to or offering a helping hand to complete strangers even. This kind of more general helpfulness is therefore very rare in the animal kingdom and at first sight constitutes an evolutionary paradox.

Many researchers have attempted to invent models for how helpfulness – or altruistic behaviour in general – could evolve through natural selection. Some of these models are based on the same idea as nepotism: it is relatedness that forms the foundation for helpfulness, and this is obviously the case for many animal species. Ants and bees are well known examples of helpful animals: the workers devote all their efforts to helping the queen produce eggs and rear her young rather than to their own reproduction. This is explained by a peculiarity of the genetics of these insects which means that it is more advantageous in the Darwinian sense for the workers (who are usually daughters of the queen) to feed the children of the queen – their siblings – than offspring of their own. But that is not how human genetics operates.

Various other examples of helpfulness in animals can also be explained by relatedness. It is not at all unusual for brothers and sisters to help each other. There are normally two or three males and a larger number of females in a pride of lions for example. The males are often brothers who collaborate against other males in order to maintain their position.

What seems to be important in relation to help within the family and helpfulness more generally is both what benefit the help offers to the recipient and what cost it entails to the donor. Providing help appears to be more logical when the cost to the helper is low but the value to the recipient high. This means that helpfulness will evolve more readily when the helper enjoys an excess it can easily do without and when even a minor intervention is a matter of life or death to the recipient. Helpfulness will also become easier if the helper can expect to get back something for the help given in the currency of evolution. When relatives are helped, they "pay" for the help by distributing the helper's genes through their own offspring. Helping strangers, however, would require repayment in currency of some other kind.

Helpfulness within the group as a whole can sometimes be explained by inbreeding which results in all the animals in the group being related to one another to a greater or lesser extent. This means that it may pay to cooperate and help each other in exactly the same way that it pays more generally to help relatives. However, in most animal species there is a degree of exchange between groups – young animals will try to join another group when they are sexually mature – precisely because inbreeding is so harmful in the long term. This has the effect of suppressing more widespread relatedness within the population. Human beings function in the same way: in most communities, individuals look for partners outside the family; incest is taboo. Exactly where to draw the line for what counts as incest varies among cultures –

relationships between cousins are legal in Sweden, for example, but illegal in quite a few other countries – but the fact that some kind of line *does* exist is as close as you can come to finding a universal characteristic in human cultures. Primates, too, normally avoid incest in one way or another, usually by swapping troops. Inbreeding as an explanation for human helpfulness would therefore seem unlikely even if isolated groups of humans occasionally become rather inbred for want of any better alternative.

The next kind of explanation involves what is known as group selection – natural selection among groups, rather than between individuals. The idea here is that a group made up of helpful individuals will be much more successful than a group of egoists. The helpful group will therefore triumph in any competition, and be able to expand at the cost of the selfish group. That might sound plausible initially, but the problem is that the helpful group is vulnerable from within. If an egoist is born in the helpful group, then that individual will gain from the strength of the group but not pay the cost owed in terms of helpfulness. An egoist in a helpful group will therefore do even better than an altruist in the same group. This would lead to helpful groups becoming unstable: it would pay for individuals in the group to cheat the system and receive help without having to help others themselves.

In order to make helpfulness more robust in evolutionary terms, something would be required that stops cheats from undermining cooperation. There are two solutions that are frequently put forward, and that may work either on their own or in tandem. One has to do with reciprocity: limiting your helpfulness to those who can help you in return. This is called reciprocal altruism and can be found in a few different species, even if it is relatively rare in nature. Vampire bats help each other in this way. These bats deserve their name; they live off the blood they suck from larger animals and after a successful hunt a bat may return to the colony with an excess of blood that will have spoiled by the following night. The bats will frequently help one another as a result: the bat who has done better on the night in question will give a portion of the excess to another bat whose hunt went less well, and on another night, when fortunes change, the help will be repaid. This is how the bats do better than they would in the absence of helpfulness, and they solve the problem posed by cheats inasmuch as only the bat who has been generous with its excess can count on help from others when its own belly is empty. This type of reciprocity can either be direct, so that it is the same individuals who exchange blood on different nights, or it can be networked with many individuals belonging to the same group all helping the other members when necessary.

The second solution involves the group acting more directly against cheats by punishing them in one way or another. This is a normal and common feature of all human societies; the person who violates the norms of the group and fails to do his duty by it can expect consequences ranging from a scolding to exclusion, and *in extremis* to capital punishment. Rule-based punishment is, however, very unusual among other animals.

Human societies and cultures can vary enormously, but helpfulness and trust, within the group at least, are all but universal. All cultures also keep track of relatedness and we trust and help relatives more than others. We also distinguish between *Us* and *Them* and are more helpful within the group to which we belong, primarily aiding those we consider to be *Us*. Reciprocity and punishment are also important in most cultures; the individual who is helpful finds it easier to get help when the need arises, and the person who fails to return helpfulness risks facing the consequences.

Another prominent feature of human cultures is social control. We monitor one another, we observe who is doing what and with whom and we listen to gossip about who is doing what with whom. We collect social information about other members of our group on a systematic basis, and we are very aware of who is rumoured to be a good and helpful person and who is not. An individual's foremost asset in a social situation is her good name.

In conclusion: for helpfulness to evolve, a situation is required in which helpers gain an evolutionary advantage from their helpfulness great enough to outweigh the cost of that help. The advantage may be in the form of relatives surviving and indirectly reproducing the helper's genes, or as the benefit the helper derives from the whole group becoming so much more successful, or from the helper receiving help in turn, or from the person who refuses to help being punished. Or from a combination of all these factors.

We can now start piecing together the bits of the puzzle of the evolution of human helpfulness and begin to make out a possible pattern. These pieces will serve as the basis for the evolution of language first of all, and then interact with it.

Childbirth and childcare may be the most important part of the puzzle. The childcare argument is largely inspired by the American anthropologist Sarah Blaffer Hrdy, already mentioned in the context of the aeroplane simile at the beginning of this chapter. Crucial to her thesis is the idea that cooperative childcare played a vital role in human evolution.

Childcare provides a context in which cooperation and helpfulness make a real difference, in which a helping hand at the right moment may be of crucial importance to the mother and child without any great cost to the helper. Those helping to take care of the children are usually relatives, which makes repayment of the help straightforward – the survival of the child is repayment in itself. A grandmother spending a few hours of her time to assist at the delivery may mean life or death to her grandchild, which makes for a very high hourly wage for her labour in evolutionary terms. Assisting at deliveries and providing childcare set a very low bar for getting helpfulness started.

In order for that to work, however, a different family and group structure is required from that of chimps and most of the other primates. Female chimps usually move to a new troop when they reach sexual maturity, and their mothers and other relatives are not available as a result when they need help with childcare. Male chimps stay with their birth troop and are often helped by their mothers in various ways. But expecting the paternal grandmother to help with the care of her grandchildren is not a real option for the simple reason that chimps have no idea who is the father of which child. Not because male chimps do not understand the link between mating and paternity – they do – but the females exploit that understanding to try and protect their young from infanticide. A female chimp will make sure to mate with many different males in the troop in order to ensure that as many males as possible will believe that they might be the father to her child – because a male will not readily kill an infant he might be the father of. So having many possible fathers becomes a form of life insurance for the child. But that tactic will not protect the child from the other females in the troop, nor against the males that the mother had no opportunity to mate with or deliberately chose not to, which means the mother has good reason to be paranoid. And the fact that everyone mates with everyone else is not a sound foundation for creating secure and helpful family constellations.

Even though gorillas and orang-utans have very different family systems, their relationships do not offer fertile ground for helpfulness of the human variety. The gibbons live in family groups that greatly resemble human nuclear families – including adultery, divorce, and stepbrothers and sisters – and gibbons are helpful within the family. But all the families defend their territory against all the other families in the neighbourhood, which prevents the development of any wider degree of social cohesion. Pygmy marmosets are also of interest in this context: they live in extended families and, like humans, help each other within the group with childcare and other matters. They also employ a complex system of sounds that the young learn gradually as they grow up. So why have their sounds not become a language?

What is special about the social structures of human beings is that we combine the nuclear families of the gibbons with the large and loosely interconnected troops of the chimps, or indeed the baboons. This is a very rare combination among mammals even if it is relatively common among birds – jackdaws and rooks, for example. This combination initially made helpfulness within the family, with childcare and so on, possible for humans because a woman actually had her family around her – a father at least, and either the maternal or paternal grandmother depending on who moved into whose home when they set up house. But the human group structure also made possible the evolution of helpfulness in a broader context that extended beyond close relatives. Reciprocity was presumably a crucial factor to begin with: through networks of mutual help based on the families within the group that was then extended to include increasingly distant relatives and eventually even strangers.

But if a climate of trust and helpfulness is to permeate the whole group, a considerable degree of social control against cheats and swindlers is also required. This is a characteristic aspect of human communities but not those of chimps or baboons, nor the flocks of birds that would otherwise appear to provide such promising family structures. A measure of social control can be found in baboon troops in relation to aggression and conflict, but not in relation to freeloaders. There are very few rules in chimpanzee troops, as far as we have been able to observe, and a chimp can behave almost any way it likes without the group acting collectively against it. Occasionally the females in a troop have been observed banding together to stop an excessively aggressive male, but these instances are the exception. Normally a chimp can get away with murder without facing any real consequences.

Can social control at the level required for helpfulness develop without a broad exchange of social information? Can social information be exchanged at the level required without a language?

*Once the ground had been laid so we could get over the first threshold to cooperation, perhaps with the help of grandmothers and midwives, the evolution of cooperation and the evolution of language would have buttressed each other in a positive spiral as language made social control easier and social control favoured the development of the trust that is the prerequisite for any further evolution of language.*

We have now explained how language became *possible* for human beings but remained impossible for chimps. But what still has to be explained is how that possibility was turned into reality by our ancestors but not those of other cooperative species of animals – why do rooks and pygmy marmosets not have a language? Before that, however, we will take a look at the time frame that fossils can provide us with for these developments.

## WHEN DID WE BECOME HELPFUL?

Helpfulness, like language, leaves no fossils behind, and determining when our ancestors began helping one another and felt trusting enough to accept help is far from easy. When it comes to help with childbirth we are at an advantage inasmuch as both the pelvis and children's heads get preserved as fossils from time to time, and this allows us to deduce how difficult labour must have been for a species and whether they would have needed help with the delivery.

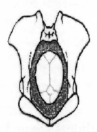  

A comparison between the infant and the pelvis: in chimps (left), *Australopithecus* (centre) and modern humans (right). The images are from a "midwife's perspective" of a delivery, with the infant's head in the centre of the birth canal.

Changes to the pelvis arrived at a fairly early stage in human evolution. *Australopithecus* was already walking upright much the way we do now three to four million years ago and had a pelvis that was as narrow as a modern human's. On the other hand *Australopithecus'* brain was no larger than a chimp's and giving birth would therefore have presented little problem because of the small size of the infant's head. Deliveries probably did not become difficult enough to require help during labour until the advent of *Homo erectus* about 1.8 million years ago. The pelvis in *erectus* was virtually identical to ours and their brains had begun to approach ours in size. They probably had a growth pattern that resembled our own and ought to have had similar problems with giving birth.

This business of growth patterns is particularly interesting because the human version is rather odd. It takes many years for us to become adult, which is not the norm at all for mammals. Horses, for instance, reach sexual maturity by the age of two if not earlier. In contrast it takes twelve to fifteen years for a human to reach puberty and we do not become fully adult until our twenties, even allowing for a considerable degree of individual variation.

The other apes also grow slowly although not quite as slowly as humans. It can take them up to ten years to reach adulthood. But in addition to its slow pace there are another few peculiarities to the human growth pattern that are completely absent in apes.

First, newborn humans are completely helpless and it takes many months before they can even move on their own. Infant apes are much more precocious from birth. This is to do with the fact that the brain in a newborn human does not finish growing in the womb. The norm in the other apes is for the brain to grow very rapidly in the womb and to be in a more or less usable state when the child is born, after which the brain will grow much more slowly during childhood. In humans the rapid growth of the brain continues for a further few years after birth.

Second, humans grow remarkably slowly for a number of

years. The brain reaches adult size by the age of six or so, while the body is only half-grown at that point. Then, as teenagers, we start to sprint in height and reach full adult size in just a couple of years.

No other mammal has a growth pattern anything like ours. Helpless infants are fairly common – think of kittens or baby mice – but they only occur in animals that give birth to many offspring in a single litter and the young then grow very quickly. In the case of mammals that give birth to only one or two young at a time – think of cattle or sheep – the young are usually perfectly capable of standing and walking from day one.

For there to be a pause in growth and a delay to the onset of adulthood of several years is also extremely unusual and would appear to be counterproductive in evolutionary terms. At first sight, natural selection ought to favour the individual that grows fastest and starts reproducing as soon as possible. That is why most animals grow as quickly as they can with the resources they have available; this does not apply to the apes, however, and even less so to human beings. It is as if our growth were being deliberately retarded. The likely explanation is that the brain has to be given time to learn all it needs before maturity, language in particular, and all the social skills required to function as an adult and autonomous individual in society, as well as the practical know-how necessary to be able to provide for oneself.

Anthropologists have conducted several systematic studies of how much food hunter-gatherers are capable of hunting and gathering and how that varies with age and gender. One clear trend is for hunters, especially, to reach their peak relatively late in life, around thirty-five to forty years of age, and then remain highly productive for another decade or two before age takes its toll. But on average a young and inexperienced hunter in his twenties can barely procure enough food to feed himself. The productivity of gatherers increases with age as well, although not as dramatically.

One explanation for our long childhoods probably lies in these productivity curves. The human way of life, be it that of hunter-gatherers or of a modern high-tech society, is based on sophisticated knowledge and skills that take a long time – decades – to acquire but provide a very high return once they have been acquired. A slow life-cycle thus pays for itself, and it pays to keep the body small (and therefore cheap to run) until an individual has learned enough to provide for a larger body. Language is a crucial part of the human way of life and is essential for other forms of learning. That is the reason for the pause in growth in childhood – the child spends most of that interval learning its mother tongue.

But our long childhood is still a Darwinian problem, particularly when you bear in mind how the other great apes care for their young. A chimp or an orang-utan has one child at a time, after which the mother's sole occupation is to take care of it until it is big enough to look after itself. During that entire period she will not go into heat nor have any more children. This means that there are usually at least five years between births for chimps and even longer for orang-utans. If humans behaved the same way there would have to be 15–20 years between children, and a woman could only have two children at most while she remained fertile. That would not be sustainable and it is not what humans actually do. But how can we have children at so much shorter intervals than chimps, despite the fact that our children need more care for a longer time than young chimps do?

Another peculiarity of the human life cycle may be of help here – the fact that women generally survive for many years after they reach menopause and can no longer conceive. Survival after an animal has stopped reproducing is pointless in Darwinian terms, which is why most species remain fertile throughout their lives in their natural state. As it turns out, some other mammals will also enter menopause in captivity: female chimps at roughly the same age as human women, but in the wild few mammals survive for any considerable time after menopause. Fertility for most mammals appears to be adapted to the length of their lives in their natural state, which is logical from an evolutionary perspective.

But women live much longer than that; even without modern medicine many women used to live for another twenty to thirty years beyond their fertility. This peculiarity needs to be explained.

One popular theory is called the "grandmother hypothesis". It attempts to link the issue of menopause to the fact that humans have children considerably more frequently than our nearest animal relatives. How closely pregnancies follow one another varies a good deal, but in societies without access to contraception, two to three years is normal between children, and even more frequently is entirely possible because women become fertile again fairly soon after childbirth. Continuing to breastfeed can lower fertility somewhat and in many societies children continue to be breastfed until they are two years old or thereabouts, but numerous parents can testify that breastfeeding is not a reliable form of contraception. The result in any case is that people "in the wild" can have children much more often than chimps, even twice as often if they want.

Being able to have children twice as frequently and therefore having twice as many children in the course of a lifetime is an enormous evolutionary advantage and in all likelihood a key ingredient in the success of humans as a species compared with the other primates. And this is where our ability to cooperate proves crucial. The fact that a female chimp has to take sole responsibility for each of her young is what limits her fertility. Having several young at the same time in those circumstances would just not be possible. Imagine you are out in the jungle with a newborn on your back and a two-year-old and a four-year-old scampering about. You are entirely on your own and you have to keep an eye on all the kids and make sure nothing happens to them while also gathering food and picking fruit high up in the trees so you have enough to feed both yourself and all those children. Living like that would be completely unsustainable, which is why chimps wait for five years between pregnancies.

It would also prove completely unsustainable for humans if the mother were as isolated as her chimpanzee counterpart. For humans, though, it is perfectly normal to have several small children at the same time. What makes it possible for women to have children so closely one after the other is that the mother does not have to do everything on her own. In an ordinary human community there are always several other people available to help not just with assisting at the delivery, but until the child is able to fend for itself. It is the fact that helpfulness permeates a human community which allows women to have children at such short intervals, and to have so many children in total.

In a traditional society it is usually the maternal grandmother who represents the greatest practical source of help to her daughter's children. The father may frequently be responsible for most of the providing, but less often for the practicalities of childcare. Our traditional gender roles, with men as the providers and women taking responsibility for childcare are, of course, not a universal pattern in all societies, but it is the most common one by a long way.

And it is the role of the maternal grandmother that comes into focus when explaining the menopause question. Because granny will only be available for her daughter's children if she is still alive and with her health intact and does not have small children of her own to look after. This is the core of the grandmother hypothesis: that the help a grandmother can give her grandchildren is so valuable that – beyond a certain age – it is more advantageous in evolutionary terms to help her daughters bring up her grandchildren than to bring more children of her own into the world. This would be the reason behind the many years of life women enjoy beyond their own fertility, which also ends at just the right time to help with the grandchildren.

*The fact that the maternal (or paternal) grandmother is both avail-able and helpful means that women can have children much more often – or, looked at from another angle, that humans can afford to allow children to remain children for many years and to invest as much as we do in their learning – without our fertility suffering. Our long childhoods are a fundamental prerequisite for both human intelligence and human language.*

And this brings us back to the question of when we began to cooperate. It must have been at the same time as the changes occurred in our growth pattern and our fertility. It is difficult to get a read on our growth pattern from fossils. Some rough con-clusions may be drawn nonetheless about how that pattern has changed during our evolutionary history. There is nothing about *Australopithecus* to suggest that they grew any differently from the way other apes do nor is there anything to suggest that they were noticeably more fertile – or more helpful – than chimps.

We have found numerous fossils of Neandertal children, and these indicate by and large that they grew along much the same lines as we do. The details differ a little but on the whole Neander-tals had a human childhood. There is also a good deal of evidence to suggest that Neandertals were helpful within their social unit. Many of the Neandertals that we have discovered had old healed wounds on their skeletons; they had broken limbs more than once and had clearly led hard lives. Some were almost invalids but had still managed to survive for many years with their wounds. The Neandertals evidently helped one another when someone had broken a leg and could no longer hunt, and they also helped those who were permanently incapable of providing for them-selves. The Neandertals were human beings, at least in terms of their childhoods and their helpfulness.

Things get particularly interesting when we turn to *Homo erec-tus* because here the answer is much less clear-cut. *Homo erectus* is the first species with the same body structure as modern humans, tall with long straight legs and relatively short arms. We have

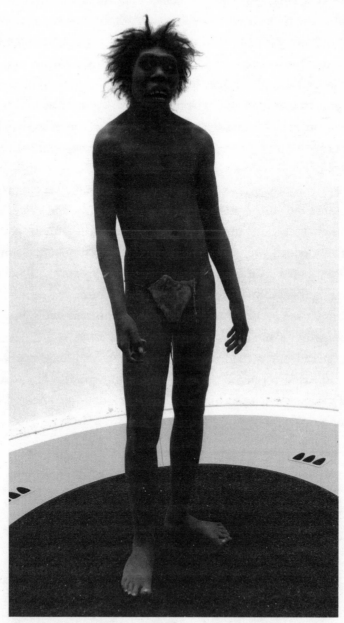

Reconstruction of a young Homo erectus based on the
skeleton known as the Turkana boy.

also discovered an early fossil of *Homo erectus*[37] which appears to be that of a lanky and gangly teenage boy with a body structure typical of the pubescent males that can be found in any secondary school, although never among the other apes. This suggests that *erectus* had evolved something similar to the growth spurt that humans go through in their teenage years. The pattern of use on this young man's teeth could be interpreted, however, as indicating he was younger than modern pubescent males usually are when their growth spurt hits – he may have been only eight or nine years old.

*Homo erectus* was also the first human species to become really successful and whose population expanded around the globe. This could be taken to mean that they had evolved the human pattern of fertility which produces many children in close succession or that they had become that much better at procuring food and defending themselves against predators, or both.

In any case it seems probable that the human willingness to work together came into being with *Homo erectus*.

Cooperativeness made language possible and language in its turn increased cooperation in an ascending spiral. This positive spiral probably began to form at this time, just over one and half million years or so ago.

37 Some scientists consider these early *erectus*-like fossils to belong to a species of their own: *Homo ergaster*. The name *Homo georgicus* is also used for other early *erectus*-fossils. I am not convinced that separate species names are justified.

# PART THREE

# ON THE ORIGIN OF
# LANGUAGE

# The First Speaker

A large troop of more than three hundred red baboons are roaming across the plain in western Mali while the sun casts long shadows ahead of them. They are on their way back to the strip of forest around the river Bafing, where they usually spend the night. When they reach the river they are tired and thirsty and drink from its waters before doing anything else. The larger males take it in turns to keep watch while the others drink – there are plenty of leopards in the area that like to hunt along the banks.

Once everyone has slaked their thirst the troop takes it easy in the dusk. Two young males chase each other and bark "eh-eh-eh-eh", a third male confronts them with an "eh-hoo eh-hoo" sound. A female is mating with a large male in a thicket; she is making an "ooh-ooh-ooh" noise. Some other females passing by grunt "uh-uh-uh-uh".

\* \* \*

In transcribing the sounds these red baboons were making I have attempted to capture how remarkably similar they are to human vowels in acoustic terms. The baboons make use of some four or five different vowels in the sounds they produce, which are as many as are used by numerous human languages. While English and Swedish use considerably more than that, there are languages that manage with only three. And yet the presumed inability of primates and prehumans to produce all the human vowels has for many years been a predominant theme in the debate on who the first speaker was.

I can think of two different reasons why this idea has taken root so strongly and for as long as it has. One is the total failure of all those experiments in which attempts have been made to teach apes to imitate human speech. Even when the apes in question have evidently understood what is expected of them and equally evidently have done their best to produce something resembling speech, their best has been remarkably bad. The consonants were especially conspicuous by their absence from the sounds the apes produced. This led to the far too hasty conclusion that apes are physically incapable of producing human speech sounds. The second reason is that there are crucial differences in the anatomy of the vocal tract between humans and other apes. Both apes and humans, like most other mammals, make sounds by blowing air from the lungs past the larynx or voice box and up that part of the throat known as the pharynx and on through the mouth. The vocal cords are located in the larynx, and it is the vibrations they make that are the chief source of sound production. Those vibrations are transmitted to the air passing over the vocal cords to become sound waves. The sound waves are shaped on their ascent through the pharynx and the mouth to form the speech sounds that we use.

The larynx is that lump on the front of the human throat. It is larger and more prominent in men than in women and is sometimes known as the Adam's apple. The vocal cords are small folds of skin that are located inside the larynx, one on each side of the central airway. We have muscles around the larynx that can both move the cords closer together or further apart and pull them taut or relax them. If they are tightened enough and kept just the right distance apart they begin to vibrate when the correct amount of air is exhaled. We do not usually do this consciously; it just happens when we need the vocal cords to work in order for us to be able to say something. But we can turn the vocal cords on and off deliberately if we want to. Whispering is talking with the vocal cords turned off. Try saying "aaaah", first normally and then in a

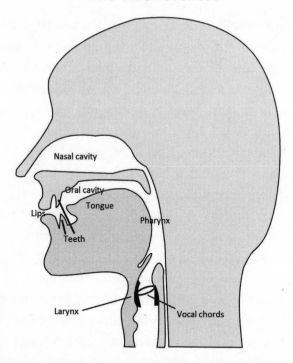

The human vocal apparatus

whisper. You can feel the difference if you put your finger on your Adam's apple: it vibrates when you are not whispering.

This is to some extent reminiscent of the way wind instruments work – clarinets, saxophones, bassoons and so on. To play them you also blow air over something that is capable of vibrating. In these instruments it is one or two "reeds" that do the vibrating, thin strips made of straw from certain types of grass. The notes are then formed by the tube that makes up the main part of the instrument, and you can control what kind of notes are produced by manipulating the length and shape of the tube.

Human beings are basically doing the same thing when we produce different speech sounds. Our pharynx and oral cavity together form a tube bent at a right angle in the middle. We can alter the shape of the tube by moving the tongue and lower jaw around. Try saying "aaah" once more and think about what you are doing with your tongue as you say it. The sound becomes an "ah" by pressing the tongue down and opening the mouth so you can breathe through the tube without any obstruction. To say "oooh" you pull your tongue back and up, while forward and up becomes an "ee" sound. You can try this out with other vowels while attempting to get a feel for what you are doing with your tongue (and sometimes your lips) in order to shape the tube so the sound that is produced is "eh", "uh" or "oh" and so on. On a clarinet or a saxophone what you would do instead is manipulate the shape of the tube by opening or closing holes along it. This is the same basic concept as applies in the human vocal tract, although having holes along the tube is a good deal simpler in technical terms than a tongue moving inside a saxophone.

The shape of the tube is one of the keys to how various wind instruments sound and what timbre is produced. Similarly the shape of the tube in the human vocal apparatus is crucial to the way we sound, what the timbre of our voices is like. The ways in which we can manipulate that shape will determine the nature of the different sounds we are able to produce. There is a difference on this point between human beings and most other mammals that was long thought to be definitive. The tube we shape sounds with is made up of the pharynx and the oral cavity. In most mammals, the other apes in particular, the oral cavity is considerably longer than the pharynx. Humans do not have the protruding muzzle that most mammals are endowed with, and therefore possess a shorter oral cavity, while our larynx is located rather far down our throats, which allows the pharynx to be long. As a result the pharynx and oral cavity are roughly equivalent in length in human beings, a feature that distinguishes us from our relatives.

The human proportions of the vocal apparatus have been assumed to be the best for producing speech. This assumption is not entirely unfounded: two tube parts of equal length that can be manipulated independently of one another make for a very versatile vocal instrument. What the baboons at the beginning of this section were demonstrating, however, is that a long muzzle is not a barrier to producing a range of vowels that are entirely adequate for language. It is true that that they would find it difficult to produce all the eighteen different vowels of Swedish, but that is a problem they also share with large parts of the human race. Many languages only have a handful of vowels, which baboons could manage with flying colours.

This is something that would, in fact, have occurred to experts on the evolution of language long ago if only they had spent more time talking to experts on child development. Human infants are actually born with the larynx situated much higher up than in adults so that suckling is painless – if the larynx was where it is in adults they could not be breastfed and breathe at the same time without choking on the milk. It then takes a couple of years for the larynx to descend and for the child's vocal apparatus to take on adult proportions. Although children start talking long before that! When the child starts babbling "da-da-da" and "goo-goo-goo" using perfectly recognisable speech sounds, it is making use of a vocal apparatus with near enough the same proportions as a chimp, but it is one that works just fine as every parent knows.

*The design of the vocal apparatus in our most ancient ancestors would not therefore have been a barrier to speaking a protolanguage using a modest number of speech sounds.*

The human vocal apparatus has, however, been refined to some extent compared with the other primates. Although baboons can produce quite enough vowels for a working language, their anatomy imposes certain restrictions nonetheless. In the course of evolution our vocal apparatus has been changed in several respects and has become better adapted to producing a wide range of speech sounds – the price we pay is that we have become less good at chewing and swallowing. In order to produce the optimal vocal tract our speech organs have been moved a little down the throat, which makes it easier to choke when swallowing. Food getting stuck in the throat is not an uncommon cause of death in human beings, which means that we have ended up paying rather a high evolutionary cost simply to be able to speak better.

Simultaneously the muzzles our ancestors possessed were evolving so that our lower faces would no longer project as they do in other mammals. This serves to shorten the oral cavity and may also form part of the optimisation of the vocal apparatus, but that is less certain. One effect of the shortening is that the root of the tongue has been pushed back so it is now situated in humans right at the bend in the vocal tube between the pharynx and the oral cavity. As a result the tongue has a greater degree of freedom of movement than in other primates, which is particularly impor-tant when it comes to the production of consonants. This process of optimisation for speech may have been the driving force behind the shortening of the muzzle. The price we pay is that there is less room for the teeth. Our teeth are also smaller than those of other primates but the wisdom teeth are still squeezed for space and can become a problem for many people.

*The restructuring of the vocal apparatus was costly in evolutionary terms and driven by what were actually rather marginal improvements in our speech abilities. This tells us a good deal about the evolutionary value of speech, and also confirms that natural selection played an important role in the evolution of language.*

So we can produce a greater range of different sounds than other primates. It is mainly the vowels, which are articulated with the tongue raised towards the roof of the mouth, that apes find difficult – the "ee" sound is the vowel that stretches the vocal apparatus the most, and therefore was probably the vowel that was last to develop in the course of human evolution. It is also unusual to hear "dee-dee-dee" when babies babble – "da-da-da" or "goo-goo-goo" are much more common, which makes sense because babies still have an ape-shaped vocal apparatus during the babbling stage.

There are other changes to our physiognomy that may be linked to our speech faculty. One area to have been affected is respiration.

The sounds primates make are often adapted to the rhythm of their breathing. The "wah-hoo" sound that chimps make is one example, with every "wah-hoo" being a complete breath (in and out). This is quite unlike what humans do when talking; we adapt our breathing to the rhythm of speech instead. Normally we can squeeze many words and dozens of speech sounds into a single exhalation while speaking. Then we inhale quickly and continue with another lengthy harangue in the course of the next outbreath. Producing speech this way requires very detailed control of the airflow from the lungs in order to make it vary in the course of a single breath in accordance with the sound pattern of the language. For this reason, humans have more neural pathways between the brain and the respiratory muscles than apes do; these allow us to control respiration with greater precision. Otherwise we would never be able to speak as fast as we do.

It is the consonants in the main that require detailed control and timing of both respiration and the parts of the mouth – tongue, lips, jaws and so on. The difference between a "p" and a "b" is a matter of a few hundredths of a second here or there in the timing of the lips opening and the vocal cords switching on. A consonant such as "p", by the way, which is made with the lips, may have been a fairly early component of speech because apes have enough control of their lips to produce it and various other sounds. Consonants that require very precise movements of the tongue, such as "r", may have developed later – they often prove difficult for human children and the tongues of apes are positioned slightly differently from ours.

# Fossil Speakers

Changes to the vocal tract were not essential in order to make speech possible, but they are in all likelihood adaptations for becoming better speakers. However, acquiring an improved vocal apparatus would only become a Darwinian advantage once we possessed a spoken language. Language must predate the changes to our organs of speech.

If we can find traces in our fossil ancestors of evolutionary changes in this area, that might be able to tell us how old language must be at the very least. Language could very well be older than the human vocal apparatus as it appears today, and it certainly cannot be younger.

The vocal apparatus is, however, made up almost entirely of soft tissue, which is not preserved in fossils. The only clearly visible evidence from skeletons relates to when our muzzle disappeared and the face was flattened, and this occurred very late in our evolutionary history. While *Homo erectus* had slightly shorter jaws than both *Australopithecus* and modern chimpanzees, they still jutted out a couple of centimetres in front of the rest of the face. Neandertals retained that form of prognathism. It was only with *Homo sapiens*, our own species, that it vanished for ever about 200,000 years ago and the human face became relatively flat.

As regards the rest, we have to focus on indirect evidence from the surrounding parts of the skeleton. Among the attachment points for both the muscles of the tongue and the larynx is the small bone known as the hyoid. This is an odd bone that is not connected to the rest of the body but is free floating under our jaws in the area between the throat and the lower jaw. In apes the hyoid bone does not look at all similar to ours, which may have to do with the fact that the larynx is positioned differently in our throats and we use it in different ways. Fossil hyoid bones should therefore be able to tell us something about the evolution of the vocal apparatus.

In *Australopithecus* the hyoid looks much the same as it does in any other ape. Neandertals, on the other hand, possessed an essentially human hyoid and so did the ancestors of the Neandertals who lived in Spain half a million years ago. The hyoid in *Homo erectus* falls somewhere in between: its shape is basically human, but the muscle attachments are different. It is therefore likely that *erectus* used his vocal apparatus for more than apes are able to accomplish with theirs, but for less than we do. It would appear that the adaptations relating to the hyoid bone began with *erectus* and were completed by the time of our common ancestor with the Neandertals.

The nerves that control breathing are obviously not preserved in fossil form. But there are holes here and there in the skeleton where nerves need to pass through a bone. The more nerve fibres that need to pass through a hole, the larger the hole needs to be. These holes can still be seen in fossils that have been well preserved. The respiratory nerves travel from the brain along the inside of the spinal cord and then move out of the spinal column through a hole in a particular vertebra. That hole is a great deal larger in humans than in chimps.

Once again we find the same pattern as with the hyoid bone. The Neandertals had nerve holes with the same dimensions as humans, while the holes in early *Homo erectus* are smaller. More sophisticated breath control ought therefore to have evolved as recently as in the common ancestor we share with the Neandertals, or perhaps at some earlier point during the long period that *Homo erectus* roamed the earth.

One odd detail relating to our speech organs is that many

primates, including our closest relatives, have a pair of substantial air sacs low in their throats. The air sacs are connected to the windpipe, and a primate can inflate its air sacs and then release the air. These air sacs appear to serve as extra amplification for the various sounds that primates are able to make. Humans lack these sacs, and it may seem rather odd that they should have disappeared in the course of evolution in a species that uses its voice as much as we do. But computer studies have shown that while the air sacs may amplify the voice, they also blur the sounds of speech. Human speech requires us to be able to rapidly utter long sequences of distinct sounds but with air sacs we would have had to articulate them more slowly and more clearly. This is why we no longer have them.

The air sacs also leave impressions on the hyoid bone we have just referred to. From the available fossil evidence, these impressions lead us to conclude that while *Australopithecus* probably still had laryngeal air sacs, *Homo erectus* did not.

## FOSSIL LISTENERS

The hearing of most mammals is quite good enough to perceive human speech. The extent to which they understand what we say is another matter, but most of us have experience of speaking to animals and being heard. It is perfectly obvious that dogs, for example, are quite capable of hearing the words we use to give them orders. This applies not only to hearing itself but also to the ability to analyse the speech sounds in what is said in order to understand a particular word even when spoken by an unfamiliar speaker. Sound analysis at the level required for language is actually an ability that is fairly widespread among various animals, from chinchillas to songbirds. This tells us our capacity to analyse sounds did not evolve for linguistic reasons and that the sound patterns of language were adapted instead to the hearing and ability to analyse sounds that we already possessed.

Apes have no difficulty either with hearing or sound analysis. However, the ears of humans and chimps are not completely identical; the shapes of the tiny hearing bones in the middle ear are different. This matters as far as hearing is concerned – for low tones it makes no difference but humans are remarkably better than chimps at hearing sounds with frequencies between 3 and 5 kilohertz. These are quite high tones that are not used very much in everyday situations but which matter for language to some degree. What distinguishes the fricative or "hissing" speech sounds, such as "ss" and "sh", is mostly voiced at those frequencies.

It may be purely a matter of chance that our ability to perceive speech sounds improved at the same time as we started using them, but maybe not. Whatever the case, it is possible to examine hearing in ancient fossils. When the hearing bones have been preserved, we can calculate from their shape the sensitivity of the ear to various tones. Neandertals, and even their ancestors from half a million years ago, had hearing bones that, while not completely identical to ours, nevertheless gave them hearing as good as ours. The hearing bones in *Australopithecus* come in a slightly hybrid form; some of them look like those of chimps and some those of humans. It is unclear how good their hearing was. Unfortunately we have not found any hearing bones from *Homo erectus* – these are really tiny bones that are easily destroyed or lost from the skeleton, and it is rare to find them in fossil form.

## FOSSIL CONCLUSIONS

All this information relates to tiny details on the skeleton that could possibly be interpreted as evolutionary adaptations to a spoken language. Not one of these details is incontrovertible proof of prehistoric language, but it is interesting nonetheless that the pattern is so uniform. *Australopithecus* is consistently rather ape-like in these as in so many other respects. It is also consistently the case that the vocal apparatus in Neandertals and their closest ancestors is almost identical to that of humans. This consistency gives us good reason to believe that Neandertals, but not *Australopithecus*, could speak.

*The vocal apparatus was gradually humanised during our evolution – primarily during the period that* Homo erectus *existed – and this process was essentially complete half a million years ago. Spoken language must be at least that old. On the other hand, there is no evidence of speech adaptations in* Australopithecus. *While this does not prove that they were language-less, it seems most probable nevertheless that spoken language first arose within the genus* Homo, *two and half million years ago at the earliest.*

That apart, though, we have no evidence to support any really robust conclusions about when language arose. And we are referring to a very broad interval indeed: there are almost two million years between *Australopithecus* and the Neandertals, and much could have happened in that time.

## DID THE FIRST SPEAKER REALLY SPEAK?

In this chapter we have been assuming thus far that the first speaker was also the first person to use language. But it is far from self-evident that language began as something that was spoken out loud. There are at least two other theories, both of which have prominent scientists among their advocates. One theory holds that the first language would have been a purely cognitive one that was used only inside the brain. The other theory holds that the first language was a sign language roughly like the languages deaf people use today.

* * *

## The First Thinker

According to the first theory, we used language as a tool to think with before it occurred to us that language could be used for communicating with others. The foremost advocate of the idea that language arose as a cognitive tool is Noam Chomsky. The theory is connected to Chomsky's ideas about the way language operates in the brain using a built-in form of grammar. In Chomsky's view it is the brain's internal grammar that is the core of language, while the possibility of externalising it – expressing it to the surrounding world – is just a later addition.

It is, of course, true that a large part of our language use today is in the form of the internal monologue flowing incessantly through our minds. Chomsky maintains that this makes up the greater part by far, and that may be true both for him and for me. But I am not as convinced that this is the case for all human beings – I am less talkative by nature than most people and spend a lot of time lost in thought. But what I use language most for today cannot prove much about the original purpose of language – I use my fingers mostly for tapping away at a keyboard, which can hardly have been what originally determined the way our fingers evolved.

According to Chomsky it was a small mutation in one of the genes that govern the development of the brain that led to a certain human suddenly being born with a working grammar module inside his head. That individual, whom Chomsky calls Prometheus, would have been capable of thinking much better than his fellows as a result, and this would have lent him and his descendants so great an evolutionary advantage that the mutation in question would soon have become dominant throughout the entire population. It was only at a much later point, when everyone possessed that grammar gene, that it finally occurred to someone that language could also be used for communicating with others.

The arguments that Chomsky presents in favour of the cognitive tool theory of language are as follows:

- What Chomsky refers to as the "asymmetry of the interfaces": the notion that the interface between language and our cognitive world is more optimally designed than that between language and the external world.
- Language is poorly adapted for communication.
- The various ways of externalising language – speech, signing and so on – all work equally well (or just as poorly)
- The words in a language have no clear connection to objects in the external world.
- Language arose suddenly and relatively recently in the history of the human race.

However, none of these arguments ultimately prove tenable.

- As an argument, the asymmetry of the interfaces is based entirely on Chomsky's assumption that the human language faculty as a whole is in some sense perfect. The interface between language and the external world is evidently not perfect, so that perfection must lie elsewhere, conveniently in the interface to the cognitive world. But if you do not rely on perfection, the argument no longer holds. Evolution rarely produces perfect results; the normal outcome is something that works well enough instead and cannot be improved in small and simple steps. Language per se fits in well with that description.
- The proposition that language is poorly adapted for communication is closely related to the idea of the asymmetry of the interfaces. This notion, too, loses its force if one does not assume that language is perfect. And it could also be countered that language is not that poorly adapted to the kind of personal puzzle communication that has dominated the historical development of language.

- While it may be an interesting feature of the human language faculty that both speech and signing work equally well, what this would actually suggest is that signing played a role in the evolution of language: an idea we will be considering in this book.

- The connection between words and the external world may be indirect and sometimes very loose, but I consider this to be a natural consequence of our possessing such a flexible and wide-ranging language that we are not restricted to using words solely to discuss concrete objects in the world around us, nor solely in the here and now. A language with more straightforward connections to objects would not be able to do all the things that human language can. And in any case the problem of relating words to the external world would still pertain to a purely cognitive language. In order to use language to think thoughts about something external you would need to be able to connect those thoughts to external objects.

- The notion that language arose suddenly is a myth that is based on an older and more Eurocentric understanding of the archaeological evidence for the origins of human culture. We will be returning to that myth in the chapter "Cultural Man".

If the cognitive language came first it is also odd that the monologue inside our heads sounds exactly like an internal copy of externalised speech with all its limitations. An internal language that was a cognitive language from the beginning ought not to sound like that – it ought not to sound at all.

Furthermore it is the requirements of externalised speech that are deeply woven into the internal structures of language. Spoken language is by its nature linear, a long straight sequence of words and sounds. The natural and logical internal structure of language is in contrast hierarchical and like a tree, but externalised speech forces us to squeeze that tree into a single long sequence of sounds without any branches. The purpose of much of the machinery of grammar, which is deeply embedded in the very heart of language, is to provide the utterances of the speaker with structural markers that help the listener reconstruct the structure of the tree; all of which would be entirely unnecessary in the case of a purely cognitive language.

Additionally, and as we have already observed, it would be extremely unlikely in biological terms for a single mutation to have given rise to anything as complex and all-embracing as the human language faculty.

But the thorniest problem associated with the idea of a cognitive language would surely be that there is no realistic way that a child could learn a language of that kind. All due respect to the poverty of the stimulus, but children still need a foundation for learning a language and if they fail to be exposed to linguistic material from the external world they will not develop language – remember Genie, the girl who grew up in confinement with no exposure to language. And if parents were using a purely cognitive language inside their heads, no aspect of language could be transmitted to their children and all children would end up like Genie.

In sum, the notion that language could have arisen without any connection to the outside world is a far-fetched one that lacks any foundation whatsoever outside Chomsky's own theoretical framework.

### The First Signer

The idea that the first language would have been a sign language is one that has been in circulation since at least the eighteenth century. As mentioned in the historical survey in the introduction to this book, the French philosopher Condillac was among its first proponents.

Condillac's scenario of 1746 was that, while our ancestors made various movements entirely without any communicative purpose, these actions nevertheless carried information about their aims and thoughts. One example of a gesture of this kind is when someone reaches up for a fruit hanging from a tree and fails to pluck it. This is a natural movement entirely without communicative intent, but it nevertheless signals to the surrounding world that the person in question wants that fruit. Someone else located higher up that tree and within reach of the fruit might then be kind enough to grab it and drop it to the person who reached for it. If this process is repeated several times the people involved might learn to deliberately reach up to signal what they want and to get someone to come to their aid. After a while a minor gesture of the hand along these lines might be enough to be given that help. The motion of stretching up would then become a ritualised and conventionalised gesture, dissociated from its original function as a serious attempt to reach something. And gestures of this kind might then have developed into a sign language.

Many parents will also have noticed their children developing communicative gestures based on functional movements even before they have learned to talk properly. The little one-year-old reaching his arms up to Daddy to be lifted is a common example. Among adults at a dinner table it is also rather common for someone to reach for the salt only for another person seeing the gesture to pass them the condiment. This works perfectly well as communication, particularly when combined with a bit of eye contact.

And if you are travelling in a foreign country and need to communicate with someone who does not speak any language you know, what do you do? Most of us will employ gestures of various kinds. We can point, use our hands to demonstrate, or even perform a little mime to get our message across. This often works well enough for some communication to take place although the limitations of the technique will readily be apparent as soon as the message becomes more complicated.

It is also worth noting that we rarely speak without also using our hands. Most of us gesticulate more or less constantly while talking. We use our hands in roughly the same way that we use intonation and vocal pitch, to emphasise different elements of what we are saying. Gesticulation occurs more or less automatically; we will often continue gesticulating even when the person we are talking to cannot see us – next time you have the opportunity, watch someone speaking on the phone and pay attention to what their hand, the one that is not holding the phone, is doing. If that hand is free, it will be moving. People who have been blind since birth will also use gestures as they talk. All of this tells us that speech and gestures have become profoundly integrated into our language faculty.

The sign languages of today are, of course, quite different from the various gestures employed by children, tourists and people speaking. The different sign languages in use are just as structured and formalised as spoken languages and differ from each other just as spoken languages do. They are as far removed from the gestures of children and the pantomime of tourists as spoken language is from the child's imitative "woof-woof" sound. But the fact that pure sign languages work perfectly well for human beings today demonstrates that our language faculty is not restricted to spoken language, which lends further support to the idea that gestures and signing may have played a role in the evolutionary history of language. If language had been purely speech-based from the beginning, it would become more difficult to explain why our language faculty can be used just as readily for signed as for spoken language.

*There are therefore good reasons to believe that gestures and signs played a role in the history of language. The question is, what kind of role?*

If the original language were a purely signed language without sound, that would get round the problem of the lack of vocal control on the part of the apes. In terms of their motor skills alone any of the apes is sufficiently dextrous to be able to handle a sign language without difficulty. The fact that our ancestors had started to walk upright on two legs at an early stage, long before language was born, would have further facilitated the use of a possible sign language, because their hands would have been free most of the time.

A fundamental difficulty for all scenarios involving an original signed language is, however, how to explain why virtually all hearing people use a spoken language today. Spoken language is not in any obvious way superior to sign language; instead, as every deaf person can testify, signed languages work just as well. Speech and signing both have their advantages and disadvantages – speech, for example, works better when it is dark or vision is obscured, while signing works better when there is a lot of noise – but neither is superior overall to the other. So if our ancestors possessed a functioning sign language, why did they switch to speech?

There are a few marginal advantages that spoken language enjoys over the signed variety:

- Speech can be used to call attention to someone who is not looking whereas sign language presupposes that the other person is already looking at the person signing. The flipside is that speech is harder to use discreetly when you do *not* wish to attract attention.
- The hands of the person speaking are free and can work or carry things while communicating.

But neither of these advantages seems so clearly decisive as to justify something as drastic as changing an entire linguistic system.

A more likely scenario is that our early ancestors did exactly what other apes do: communicate pragmatically using all the means at their disposal. Apes employ various sounds but they also use gestures to communicate with each other and can make use of sticks and other things to attract the attention of someone

else. Apes that have a great deal to do with humans have no difficulty getting their message across to us with gestures either.
Santino the chimp, whose well-planned stone-throwing we are
already acquainted with, clearly had strong views on the level of
service when I was watching the chimps at Furuvik zoo being
fed recently. At first he clapped his hands to attract the attention
of the keeper and then extended his hand in a way that looked
more like an order than a begging gesture.

An initial language may very well have consisted of a combination of gestures and sounds that eventually evolved into a
protolanguage that contained elements of both speech and signs.
Languages come in a more refined form nowadays, either pure
speech or pure signing. Mixed languages basically never occur –
the gestures that often accompany spoken language are fundamentally different from those of sign language. Bilingualism is,
of course, not that rare and it would be no odder to know how to
speak Swedish and a sign language – or for that matter two different sign languages – than to be able to speak both Swedish and
English. While bilingual people are clearly capable of alternating
between their languages – switching between speech and signing
if that is the case – or even combining different languages in the
same sentence, they are perfectly aware that they are dealing with
two separate systems.

But this situation need not always have been so clear-cut.
When language began it is by no means certain that speech and
signing would have been such distinct entities as they clearly are
today. Before language became as advanced and as systematic as
it currently is, it may have made use of every possible kind of
communicative tool.

As has already been observed, people will readily use gestures
when they lack a common language but are keen to communicate
nonetheless. In which case the gestures employed are mainly
those that are in some sense obvious to the extent that they bear
some resemblance to what is meant and should therefore be

easy to interpret for someone from an entirely different culture. If you want to communicate something about a bird you flap your arms, if you want to say something about eating instead you pretend to put food in your mouth. Representational gestures like these can be understood by almost anyone. It is not only gestures that can be deployed: if you want to communicate something about a cat you are more likely to imitate a "miaow" sound than try to move stealthily the way a cat does, and if driving a car is the topic you might combine sounds and gestures and imitate holding a wheel while saying "brrm brrm".

If we look back in time and imagine the lives of a group of hunter-gatherers, it could well have been vital to be able to communicate about the natural world in some detail. It may have been important every now and then to be able to distinguish between different species of birds, for example. Communicating the difference between a blue tit and a great tit using only gestures would be a real challenge, however – but no problem at all if you could imitate their song. Imitation of this kind could have played a key role at the dawn of language, before our ancestors had started to reach agreement on what different signs and words would mean. In that case all they would have available were "words" that could be understood without any pre-existing knowledge and that would have involved self-explanatory gestures and sounds. These will actually take you a long way; it is possible to get across a complete narrative by performing a mime that depicts the whole story.

*This is what the roots of language may have been like, in which case there is no longer any point in wondering whether the first language was a spoken or a signed one because it would have contained a mishmash of sounds and gestures. This chimes well with our previous conclusion that it was the original form of language that prompted the evolution of a highly flexible language faculty.*

In a setup like this our ancestors would have derived great benefit from an ability to imitate different sounds, which, as we have learned, is a skill apes are bad at.

*It may have been the need to both communicate about and imitate birds and other creatures, rather than language in the strict sense, that first prompted the evolution of our ability to imitate sounds.*

## THE ORIGINS OF THE SOUNDS OF SPEECH

Our vocal apparatus has evolved so that we can imitate both one another and birdsong, as well as almost any sound at all. And yet in language we do not make use of any old sound: for speech we employ only a limited range of distinct sounds.

One very clear pattern to emerge from a study of the sounds of speech is that the various sounds employed within the same language are clearly distinct from each other; they need to be easily distinguishable. It has to be easy for a listener to determine which sound a speaker meant to utter, even if the speaker is unfamiliar and even when there is a lot of background noise in the environment. Sliding scales and hybrids of different sounds are therefore not normally used because they would cause problems of interpretation. Spoken language is a digital system, not an analogue one, despite the fact that it is produced by what is a fundamentally analogue vocal apparatus.

This can be seen most clearly when we take a look at the vowels. As previously mentioned in this chapter, the vowels are formed by placing the tongue in different positions inside the oral cavity and then allowing air to pass while the vocal cords are switched on. The tongue can move fairly freely both backwards and forwards and up and down. This allows us to create whichever vowel sound we want that is within the range of the tongue, and there are no distinct boundaries in the oral cavity between the vowels so that if we want we can easily come out with something that gradually shifts from "ah" to "eh" to "ee" just by raising our tongue in stages. I noticed when I tried this out myself that the sounds of speech are so ingrained that my tongue "wants" to jump from the "ah" position to the "eh" position, but with a bit of self-control it is possible to get it to move slowly between the intervening stages so that the sound changes gradually.

Those intervening stages are not used in language, however. Those of us who speak Swedish have agreed that only certain tongue positions are valid for producing the vowels of our language. In other languages, such as English, different conventions have been agreed that involve different sets of vowel sounds. Children learn the vowels they come in contact with as infants, acquiring the skills to distinguish between them and to make the correct movement of the tongue required to produce them. Simultaneously children learn *not* to distinguish between variants of a sound that are one and the same speech sound in their mother tongue and not to allow their tongues to adopt positions that will create speech sounds that are invalid in the same language. This is why it is so difficult to learn to pronounce a new language correctly as an adult: the hearing has become attuned to ignore sound differences that do not mean anything in the hearer's mother tongue while the tongue has been trained not to produce deviant vowels. Overcoming those restrictions as a grown-up can be close to impossible and rarely turns out well.

The different vowel systems are not an arbitrary matter either; there are definite patterns and connections between them. So how did such systems of distinct vowels arise at the dawn of language? This has long been a topic of discussion among researchers with much speculation about innate systems of vowels and other ideas. But for all essential purposes the debate came to an end in 1999 when the Dutch linguist Bart de Boer presented a simple and elegant solution to this problem in his doctoral dissertation.[38]

That solution is based on the notion of self-organisation among

38 De Boer, Bart, "Evolution and selforganization in vowel systems" Evolution of Communication 3:79–102. http://ai.vub.ac.be/~bart/papers/deBoerEvoComm99. pdf (abbreviated version of doctoral thesis published in journal) (1999)

a group of speakers and makes certain basic assumptions about how speakers behave. If each speaker wants to be understood and each listener wants to understand, and both parties adapt their vowel sounds accordingly when misunderstandings occur, a structured system of vowels will spontaneously arise. Bart de Boer ran a huge number of computer simulations using virtual beings who attempted to communicate in this way. The vowel systems that came into being in the simulations had essentially the same structure and shared the same features as the vowel systems of real languages. A more sophisticated explanation would clearly be superfluous, as all that is actually required is a group of speakers all of whom want to understand each other and all of whom adapt their speech and the way they interpret sounds to facilitate that understanding.

Consonants are a more complicated matter because they involve more freedom of articulation: they can be created in other ways than by just moving the tongue this way or that. The airflow in the oral cavity is obstructed either wholly or partially in order to utter this kind of speech sound. This can be done at a number of different locations from the vocal cords to the lips. Most consonants are shaped with the tongue pressing against the roof of the mouth at one spot or another, although other parts of the vocal apparatus may also be used. Even though we can actually allow the occlusion points and the leakage of air to gradually alter, we do not do so but stick instead to a handful of fixed points and allow things like airflow to leak in binary fashion, either on or off, in a variety of different ways.

Although they are more complex, the system of consonants displays much the same pattern as the vowel system, and there have been the same kind of discussions about its origin. Following the work of Bart de Boer, however, most researchers have been convinced that the consonant system can be self-regulating in the same way the vowel system is. In 2009, De Boer, together with his colleague Willem Zuidema, was able to show that the entire combinatorial system of sounds could be explained on the basis of the same self-organising principles.

*On the whole therefore there is no compelling reason to dig more deeply into the origin of the sounds of speech when exploring the origins of language. Given creatures that can freely control their vocal organs and who want to communicate and make themselves under-stood to their fellows, a system of speech sounds will soon establish itself autonomously.*

# The First Topic of Conversation

What did we evolve language to be able to talk about? In order even to begin to answer that question we need to recall Tinbergen's four "why?" questions (see pp. 117–18) and above all the question that related to evolutionary advantages:

- Adaptation – what advantage in evolutionary terms do we gain from language; in what way does language make us better able to survive and reproduce?

In all likelihood we evolved language in order to be able to talk to each other and in order to be able to communicate better than we could before we had language. In what way, however, did our ability to communicate make us better at surviving and reproducing?

It may appear obvious that good communication offers an evolutionary advantage and that being able to talk benefits us in Darwinian terms – but if communication is so obviously and self-evidently advantageous, we end up with the opposite problem: why did language *not* evolve in all the other primates as well? If language is that good, why are we the sole species of animal to possess it?

So we need to discover something more specific: what it was that made language advantageous to our ancestors, in particular, but not to the ancestors of chimps or baboons or nightingales or squid. This might have involved traits that were possessed by our ancestors, but not those of the chimps and other animals, and that facilitated the creation of language. It could also have involved environmental factors or behaviours that affected our ancestors, but not the chimps, and for which language could have offered an advantage.

In this book I have devoted an entire chapter to the cooperative human being because cooperation is high up the list of possible human attributes that favoured the evolution of language. Language would never have come into being if we had been as paranoid and unhelpful as the chimpanzees.

However, the fact that midwives made cooperation possible and that cooperation made language possible is simply not enough. There also needs to be an obvious evolutionary advantage to language if that possibility is to become reality. Was there some essential aspect of our ancestors' ecology or behavioural repertoire that particularly favoured the creation of language in us rather than in other animals that cooperate? We can leave aside the paranoid chimps (even though "the chimp test" – see p. 78 – remains the accepted term for the issue) but there are many species of animal, primates as well, that are more helpful than chimps. Why have none of them evolved a language? When we refer to "the chimp test" below we will not actually be thinking of chimps but of all animals that collaborate socially.

There is a wide range of different theories about what the first conversation would actually have been about. The problem is not of finding a context in which language provides advantages – on the contrary, as we currently use language, it is advantageous in almost every situation. What is difficult is finding which one of all the possible areas of application for language provides the key to its origin: the original topic of conversation that made language take off in evolutionary terms. We will be examining some ideas about this in what follows.

## THE BATTLE OF THE SINGERS

The group have gathered at their campsite for the night, high in the branches of a baobab tree on the savannah, not far from the spot where Nairobi will be expanding two million years from now. They climb up the thick trunk in practised fashion and find comfortable perches among the broad branches. The temperature drops rapidly once the sun has set but their dark fur keeps them warm.

Just before it gets completely dark a youngster strikes up a song. There are no words to the song, and yet it consists of a complex arrangement of sounds with a distinct rhythm. He peers at a girl of the same age while singing but she looks away. Another youngster gets up and begins singing as well. He joins in the first song to start with but is soon embellishing it with a theme and variations of his own and it rapidly becomes apparent that he is a skilled singer, with a better sense of pitch along with several patterns of sound in his repertoire. The girl is now listening avidly. The first youngster tries to counter with variations of his own but cannot keep pace with all the trills and soon gives up and sits down.

* * *

The idea that song and music may have played a role in the evolution of language has been put forward in various forms by a number of scientists over the years, with Darwin very much the pioneer. Singing and music exist in one form or another in all human cultures and often have a ritual or socially cohesive function. Singing also occurs among a few other primate species, although not our closest relatives. The singers closest to us are the gibbons who, like songbirds, sing to mark their territory and to attract the opposite sex. Established gibbon couples sing duets on a daily basis to proclaim their shared territory and also, perhaps, to affirm their relationship. Instrumental music, however, is very rare in the animal kingdom although apes have been observed drumming.

Darwin thought that there must have been a stage in the evolution of the human being when we sang in the same way gibbons do and that it was this that prompted the evolution of the human vocal apparatus. What he envisaged first and foremost were mating songs with singing youths competing to gain the favour of the local ladies much as in the story above, the same way birds do, and young male gibbons for that matter.

Some contemporary researchers have taken this notion a stage further and added lullabies to the mix along with other sounds that we use to calm babies. Common both to Darwin's scenario and those of his successors is the idea that we became singers before we became speakers and that the voice evolved to produce lovely sounds without those sounds necessarily meaning anything. A singing phase of this kind would need to have occurred at an early stage in our evolution. Various researchers have come up with different timelines but if I wanted to include singing in mine it would have to be heading for two million years ago.

There were no semantics in these songs so language in the real sense would have to have evolved in a subsequent and separate stage. There are also some researchers who are inclined to see a role for singing in that stage too: with a meaningful protolanguage evolving that still retained the form of singing, a language that was sung and in which melody was important. The best-known proponent of this idea would probably be Steven Mithen.[39]

Music and singing are, of course, important aspects of human life, so important that we have what would appear to be evolutionary adaptations to music-making – we possess a very different sense of rhythm to that of our relatives. And the idea that singing might have helped prompt the evolution of our vocal organs is

39 Mithen, Steven, *The Singing Neanderthals* (2005).

not an implausible notion, even though direct evidence to support it is lacking.

But while there is some degree of overlap, music and language are managed for the most part in separate areas of the brain. There are plenty of examples of patients who have had their language faculty destroyed by brain damage but who can still sing songs or play music – and vice versa. Musical ability is also much less evenly distributed in the population than linguistic ability – virtually every human being possesses a functioning language faculty and is able to learn language spontaneously as a child, but even when we have been provided with proper training not many of us can do more than sing a few simple songs.

Some kinds of music possess very sophisticated hierarchical structures – think of Bach – and these structures share a great many features with the grammar of language and probably use part of the same brain machinery. But few of us are able to relate to that kind of music properly; it is not spontaneously available to us in the same way that grammar is. Nor is that kind of music universal to humanity; it only occurs in certain cultures, including our European culture. It makes better sense therefore to conceive of that kind of music as a development based on our faculty for grammar, rather than of grammar as evolving from music.

Another aspect to consider of the idea that the habilines sang like canaries is that among canaries and most other songbirds it is only the males that sing. But the human language faculty is equally distributed between the sexes. Gibbons of both genders sing, it is true, but males and females do not sing to an equal extent nor in the same way. Additionally, both birdsong and gibbonsong are very largely to do with the marking of territory by individual males or couples, and there is nothing to suggest that the habilines defended individual territories in that manner.

The singing of songbirds has never evolved into anything like a language, nor has that of the gibbons. Their songs work just fine as they are, employing abstract melodies that carry no real message. This is a weakness in the theories that postulate a singing phase in the origins of language. It is difficult to find a convincing explanation of how and why song would have evolved into a language that conveyed meaning. And even if that explanation could be found, one would also need to explain why gibbons and nightingales do *not* possess language.

## THE CARRION HUNTERS

It is early in the spring and there is still snow in the dips in the ground that the sun fails to reach. In a million years' time, one of Beijing's suburbs will be growing steadily here but now it is just endless grass plains with mountains visible on the horizon in air that is still crystal clear.

A couple of large animal hides have been erected as a windbreak and twenty or so people – men, women and children – are sitting in front of them. They have low brows and no chin beneath their prognathous jaws but otherwise they look much like us. They are wrapped in animal furs as protection from the biting wind. They are all hungry and thin after the long hard winter but there is still not much that is edible in the land around them. At this point all the prey in the area around the cave where they spent the winter has already been hunted and they are hoping to have better luck out on the plains.

A young teenage girl comes running over. All the young people in the group have been sent off in different directions to search for food, and she is the first of them to return.

She stands in front of the group and starts her report with a wordless cry to attract everyone's attention. Then she raises one index finger and holds the same hand in front of her nose. So what she has found is a woolly rhinoceros. She drops that hand heavily towards the ground and then puts that arm on the ground. The rhino is already dead. Then she utters a muffled laughing sound and repeats it three times. Three cave hyenas have already found the carcass, or perhaps it was the hyenas who actually administered the *coup de grâce*. She points first in the direction she came from and then to the sun. Her hand traces the arc the sun will make against the sky as far as the sun will move in half an hour. So the rhino is half an hour's walk from the camp.

In order to drive off three hyenas in safety at least five adults will be needed. But a rhino will provide hundreds of kilos of meat, even though it too is bound to be on the thin side after the winter, and the hyenas may already have managed to chew through the thick hide and eaten some of it. The leader of the group looks a question at the girl and says the word that means "meat". The girl responds keenly "meat-meat-meat", so there is still a lot of meat left on the rhino. Definitely worth the effort.

The leader looks around the group and calls out five names. The five in question look back at her as they make hand gestures of affirmation and then go to fetch their hand axes and wooden spears. Afterwards the teenage girl leads them back towards the rhinoceros.

* * *

Language is, after all, what we use to inform one another about things. Using it to inform one another about important practical matters such as food and then to plan how to obtain that food is a popular explanation of the origin of language that comes in many different variants. The driving force behind language in that case would be purely functional and its Darwinian value expressed in so far as those who were better at talking would become better at procuring food.

The scenario above – with the scout recruiting help to deal with a large amount of carrion – is based on a book by Derek Bickerton, one of the pioneers in research into the origin of language, in which he identifies this kind of large carcass as an unexploited niche.[40] Many carrion-eaters find it difficult to get through the hide of an elephant or rhinoceros, and the carcass can remain in place for days encircled by vultures that are waiting for a larger predator to tear it open. People with hand axes and a basic language would have been able to exploit this opportunity by sending scouts out in every direction who could then return to fetch the right number of helpers to drive off the waiting carrion eaters and take possession of the carcass.

This would require a certain degree of communication but not an advanced form of language – what I have described above would suffice. But several points should be noted which mean that the language of these people, simple though it may have been, would still have been beyond the reach of most other animals. The most important point is that throughout the episode they are dealing with matters that are not present in the here and now. At issue is a carcass that is out of sight of the group by a long way and that was seen by one of their number half an hour ago but remains unseen by any of the others; it also involves a future scenario about what will happen when they reach the carcass. Mental time travel plays a crucial role here.

The discussion also employs simple techniques for indicating number, direction and time. These abilities are not widespread in the animal world either. While there are animals that have some awareness of such matters, extremely few of them can communicate the concepts involved. The only animals that can manage something along these lines are the bees we met earlier in this book that have the ability to waggle dance a road map to a flower bed. But the communication system of bees is both very specific and very restricted and lacks the flexibility that is taken for granted in the way human beings communicate. The scout could have reported on basically any kind of animal carcass and any kind of carrion eater while also providing significantly more varied

40 Bickerton, Derek, *Adam's Tongue* (2009).

information than bees can manage. That is why the bees are stuck at the dancing stage in evolutionary terms while we have moved on to the point where we can write books.

The particular niche that Bickerton describes only works for those humans who have already developed sharp stone tools; otherwise they would not be able to drive hyenas away or cut through the hide of a rhino. Other cooperative animal species lack those prerequisites and, what is more, most of them do not live in the right kind of environment. For this reason the scenario passes the chimp test: it contains a plausible explanation of why other animals have not evolved language. This episode should be also be dated a bit later down the timeline than the battle of the singers because it would require at least the technical level achieved by *Homo erectus* one and half million years ago.

* * *

I opted in this scenario to have both the scout and the leader be women. That is rarely the way things are arranged among *Homo sapiens* in their natural state; these roles in the vast majority of cultures – including that of Sweden – are traditionally male. I also deliberately avoided specifying the gender of the five people sent along to the carcass – did it actually occur to you that it was five women who were despatched to confront a pack of hyenas? Probably not – but it would be wrong to simply assume that our traditional gender roles applied in the same way among *Homo erectus*.

# THE LANGUAGE OF POWER
# AND THE POWER OF
# LANGUAGE

The alpha male has ruled his troop for more than five years – a long time in the chimpanzee world. He still has his strength, however, even though grey hairs have begun to appear in his otherwise pitch-black fur. None of the others is a proper match for him, not yet. That was all too apparent only yesterday when number two in the ranking failed to cower quickly enough and grunt submission when he came upon the alpha unexpectedly at a bend in the path. The troop second got away with only a few bruises and some superficial scratches, but the match was far from even.

Number three approaches number two as he is sitting in the shade under a tree, feeling sorry for himself. Three is cautious in his approach, uttering quiet little grunts and wearing a smile meant to disarm. Two grunts in response, and Three sidles up to him and starts grooming the other chimp's fur, removing lice and ticks and other vermin.

The next day Three finds another opportunity to approach Two. This time the grooming is mutual, and they take it in turns to remove the vermin from each other's fur.

Two and Three have soon become the best of friends and spend more and more time together. One day they are sitting together watching the alpha male who is some way off. Three looks at the alpha and makes a very cautious barking noise so quietly that only Two sitting beside him can hear it. Two looks at Three, then at the alpha, has a think for a while and then barks just as quietly and cautiously. The alpha moves closer and they pick up their grooming again, pretending nothing is going on.

More days pass. Two and Three continue to spend time together, communicating with each other, while grooming, about their feelings and intentions using the limited repertoire of gestures and sounds they have available. They are able to understand each other well enough though, and they both know what they will do when the moment presents itself.

The alpha male is walking along a path. Although the rest of the troop are within hearing range, none are close by. Two and Three have been watching the alpha, and they move together to intercept him. Two takes up position where the alpha will soon pass, while Three stands behind a nearby bush. This time Two shows not the slightest sign of submission, and the alpha attacks him in a rage. But then Three joins in the fight on the side of Two and the alpha has no chance against both of them combined. Before long he is slinking away covered in blood and grunting submission, while Two utters a rhythmic panting hoot to proclaim his victory. He is now the alpha male.

Shortly afterwards one of the older females comes into season – and male chimps, unlike most human males, regard older females as more attractive than younger ones. The old alpha used to monopolise her each time she was in heat, and no other male would dare so much as even touch her. The new alpha – the former number two – would have liked to do the same. But the former Three, now number two in the troop, approaches her quite blatantly while looking meaningfully at the alpha who is quick to suppress his rising anger. He is being forcefully reminded of what his power rests on and whom he has to thank. The female goes off with the new second and all the alpha male can do is look on.

\* \* \*

Chimps are quite capable of this much scheming. They can communicate well enough to agree to stage a coup. Humans have not been able to observe how the conspirators communicate details of the plot with their fellows, but we have witnessed the outcome: an overthrown alpha male replaced by a new one who is clearly dependent on his co-conspirator to maintain power. That is evidently how they do it. Chimp politics are distressingly similar to the human version.[41]

Politics is a rewarding game, both for humans and chimps, because status is worth the effort and status is achieved among both species through politics rather than through brute strength alone. Whoever has high status within the group will enjoy more reproductive success while the low-status group member may have none at all. Males with high status are allowed to mate with more females and sire more young. Females with high status have better access to food and protection and therefore produce more young that survive. This applies both to chimps and humans in their natural state. Polygamy is accepted in many human cultures and it is virtually always the men with high status who have several wives. But even in human societies that are officially monogamous, like those of the West, it is very common for men with high status to enjoy extra reproductive opportunities on the side. The practical outcome is the same – in both humans and chimps there is a clear connection between the status of the males and their reproductive success, with alpha males siring considerably more offspring than males with low status.[42] Alpha females may not give birth to more young than other females but more of their offspring survive when times are tough. Status is therefore hard currency in Darwinian terms.

And yet it is obvious from the chimp politics above that if status can be gained through politics then communication plays a vital role in acquiring status. The notion that language evolved as a tool for gaining status has become a popular idea as a result and one that is presented in many different variants.

In the political scenario, language evolved as a tool in the

41 *Chimpanzee Politics* is also the title of a book by the Dutch primatologist Frans de Waal. It provided the inspiration for this scenario.

42 The difference is obvious even in modern-day Sweden; see e.g. Henrik Höjer's article "Färre män blir pappor" (Fewer men are becoming fathers) in Forskning & Framsteg 8/2018 – many low-status males in Sweden have no children at all.

pursuit of status; it is used to gain friends and influence and thereby to acquire power and status and their attendant evolutionary advantages. But gender equality poses a snag in this regard as well – among both chimps and *Homo sapiens* the pursuit of status takes very different forms for men and women, and is conducted using dissimilar means and requires varying degrees of effort. It is therefore doubtful whether the political scenario really could result in the kind of gender-equal language faculty we possess today, even though we should not, as has been said before, take for granted that gender roles have remained the same throughout the ages.

This scenario also encounters real problems in meeting the chimp test: this is already obvious inasmuch as it could be illustrated using chimps. If language evolved for political ends, there is no satisfactory answer to the question why chimps or many other social animals do not have language – they would clearly benefit from it. Nor can this scenario be dated because it would have been possible at more or less any point in our evolutionary history.

* * *

An ordinary coffee break one ordinary day in an ordinary office in an ordinary town. Colleagues drop in to the staff room one by one and gather around the coffee machine, waiting for it to see fit to dispense its usual poison. Conversations quickly start up; a lot of the staff are keen to talk, many of them are looking for listeners while just as many are keen to talk about anything at all. More of them want to talk rather than listen, and the noise level rises quickly in volume.

Once they have all got their cups filled with the bitter brew, they sit at the various small tables in the room. Competition for speaking space continues around each table. Someone starts talking about the hassle they were just having with the photocopier but then another person interrupts almost immediately, trying to outdo the first person with a story about how she'd had to clean out 37 different scraps of paper from the bowels of the machine the week before when she'd been unlucky enough to arrive at the copier just after the boss had used it. A third person butts in with his own story about what an idiot the boss is when it comes to anything technical – someone ought to write: "This way up" on the front of his keyboard. The next individual tries to come up with practical tips for using short cuts on the keyboard but no-one is listening; they just keep telling stories about the boss instead, each one more awful than the last.

* * *

This is fairly typical of human interaction. Telling each other a variety of different stories accounts for a very great deal of what we use language for. This is not so much a matter of exchanging practical information – the guy with the keyboard routines couldn't find many takers – but of sharing good stories. It could be something that happened to you, embellished to a greater or lesser extent, or that you witnessed, or you could just be passing on a good story you read about on Facebook. On social media they refer to "clickbait" – links with a seductive header and opening statement that prompt you to click further – in our workplace canteens we are continually offering clickbait in the stories we tell and doing it skilfully as well without even having to think about it. We bait the hook with something juicy to attract an audience for our stories.

We compete for listeners when we talk. Competition for the role of speaker is intense at almost every human gathering, but there is rarely any competition to be the listener. If language is considered to be a tool for transmitting information it ought to be the reverse. Information is valuable: access to the right information at the right time can mean the difference between life and death. If human conversation was about providing information we ought not to be competing for the right to speak, we ought to be competing for the right to listen. The person speaking is in fact donating valuable information while the person listening is being given valuable information for free. And yet we compete for the right to speak. This tells us that conversation is probably not primarily about providing information.

The French scientist Jean-Louis Dessalles, who had made a study of human conversations, observed this paradox at work and used it as the basis for his theory about the origins of language. Just as in the political scenario, his focus is on language as a tool for acquiring status, although he considers the route from language to status to be a more direct one. High status means being listened to. High status in the canteen is gained by being able to tell stories that are interesting and relevant enough that other people want to listen.

In this everyday interpersonal context it is the person who is a better storyteller who will gain higher status along with the attendant evolutionary benefits. According to Dessalles' theory, this is what drives the evolution of language. The observations that underpin his theory chime rather well with many people's everyday lives: an extraordinary amount of language use consists of storytelling in various forms, and there is far more competition for the right to speak than the right to listen.

The structure of language also provides support for the idea that storytelling may have played a role in the evolution of language. There is a great deal about grammar that is perfectly adapted for storytelling, particularly the entire grammatical machinery to be found in most languages for relating different points in time and the flow of events to each other:

> I should have been at work today but I stayed home ill because I got a cold from being infected by my kids who brought a virus back from nursery school while I was at work the day before yesterday, but I'm hoping to be back at

work tomorrow and for the children to go back to nursery school as soon as possible but not until they haven't got a temperature anymore.

In that sentence there are ten different clauses, each with a main verb of its own. The grammar puts a time stamp on each clause, and all ten clauses can be sorted according to the order in which the events they describe happened and according to how probable the future events are. If language had evolved purely for communicating information – would we really have needed such an intricate system of time markers in relation to different reference points? No, this machinery is better suited to narrative contexts when it is important for the story to relate events to each other in time. Being able to talk about both the past and the future is appropriate in many situations, but being able to relate different times in the past to each other is rarely necessary – apart from in stories.

Storytelling ought to have played some role in the evolution of language, but it is difficult to find evidence that this role really was as direct as Dessalles would have it. It is also difficult to date when storytelling might have become important. Storytelling could have started at the mime stage before we actually had a real language and, in that case, would date to as far back as a million years ago, or storytelling might have been a factor in the transition from a basic protolanguage to a fully grammatical one, in which case we would be looking at something more recent, maybe only half a million years ago.

## SILENCE IN CLASS?

We're back with the rhinoceros scouts we met before. Taking possession of the rhino carcass went exactly as planned: the hyenas had had enough experience of humans and their sharp stones to quickly give way. There was far more meat left than the five hunters could carry, so four of them started cutting off the best bits while the fifth went to fetch the rest of the group. They quickly took down their windbreak and moved their entire camp over to the rhinoceros where they put the windbreak up again within sight of the carcass. Not right next to it, however, and they were careful to take the wind direction into account before choosing the spot. Rhinoceroses do not smell sweet even when they are alive, and this one would have passed its sell-by date long before they could make the most of it.

Everyone in the group has now eaten their fill. Strips of rhino meat have been hung out to dry wherever they can on the few straggly bushes growing nearby. The smaller children are running around with sticks, chasing off the flies, crows, rats and other interested parties. The adults are sitting in small groups and talking while both keeping an eye on the kids and busying themselves with their tools. They have got time for that kind of thing now that there's no need to think about food for a bit.

Just beyond the windbreak, an older man is squatting on the ground surrounded by four of the slightly bigger children who are looking at him expectantly. The man holds up a stone axe in one hand, while in the other he has a round chunk of rock. He is telling the children that this rock will become a stone axe just like the other one. Using words and gestures he explains how they should look at the rock so they can visualise the stone axe that the rock will turn into. Then he goes through the different elements of the process, step by step; slowly the man strikes flake after stone flake from the rock while telling them why he selected that particular flake and slowly, ever so slowly, a stone axe emerges.

Then the two eldest children are allowed to experiment with a lump of rock of their own. It doesn't turn out particularly well even after the explanations the old man provided – it is a difficult skill they have to learn. But they end up with something sharp enough at least to help turn the rhino meat into strips; there are still several loads big enough for a man to carry left for them to tackle.

They proudly take their new axes over to the carcass and get to work on their own chunk of meat.

\* \* \*

Teaching is a typically human activity. Children spend a large part of their childhood learning everything they will need to know as adults, and the adults around the children spend a lot of time demonstrating and explaining things to them. That's the way it works nowadays with our compulsory education and professional educators, and that is how it worked in traditional societies as well, even though the timetable and the methods of teaching would have been different among hunter-gatherers.

There are other animals that teach, but it is very uncommon. Some predators teach their young to hunt in a very systematic way too. Meerkats, for instance, teach their young to hunt scorpions by providing them with carefully prepared specimens to practise on. Many felines do the same – even ordinary domestic cats teach their kittens how to hunt. But there is still something missing from the pedagogic efforts of meerkats and felines. The young have to teach themselves and develop their own hunting techniques. The parent will shepherd them through the process, which is a kind of education in itself, but he or she never explains anything. The young receive no feedback when they fail, no tips about what they should have done. Not that this would be very easy for the poor meerkat teacher – explanations and feedback require language.

Precisely because education is important to human beings and something that language is of great help with, teaching has been put forward as a possible starting point for human language. In this scenario language would have evolved so we could explain and provide feedback when teaching.

Education need not be about hand axes either. There are a great many other matters young humans need to learn and for which

Meerkats in South Africa – an adult is keeping watch, looking out for predators, while a youngster learns what to do.

language ought to have been an educational aid. Gathering edible plants, for instance, requires extensive botanical knowledge while there are also many plants that need careful preparation and cooking to be made edible. This applies in particular to the various kinds of roots and tubers that are an important component of the diet of many hunter-gatherers. How important may recipes have been to the evolution of language?

\* \* \*

Our closest relatives are not much given to teaching, however. At most they will allow the young to look on when they are doing something, but no real teaching has ever been observed in chimps or other apes, not even at the level of the meerkats. This means that while this scenario passes the chimp test on the one hand, on the other it would have required two separate stages of evolution.

Our language-less ancestors would have had to begin to teach their children without language at first and then the needs of that education would have prompted the evolution of language in turn.

Nevertheless, the long history of hand axes shows that *Homo erectus* was the first human species we know of that could actually teach its young the kind of specific and detailed information that would have been necessary for the hand axe tradition to have remained as stable as it did for such a long time. This could scarcely have occurred without some effective means of teaching. It seems therefore natural to place this scenario among *Homo erectus* and date it to a million or so years ago.

There is a snag here, though, inasmuch as the scenario I described above of a man verbally explaining how to make hand axes does not fit with the observations made by ethnologists of the few remaining stone-age tribes that still exist on the planet. What actually happens in these tribes is that the teacher shows his pupils what to do but he does not explain while demonstrating. There is silence in class when the skill of making stone axes is being taught.

## INSTEAD OF PICKING OFF LICE

Primates devote a great deal of time to removing lice from one another. In addition to picking off vermin, grooming and generally cleaning each other's pelts make up an important social ritual among the different species, not to mention the purely practical aspect of being rid of the pests. This is how friendships are affirmed and deepened, and if you are an ape, it provides the lubricant for social relationships. But this is not the way things work among humans – I doubt whether my offering to search through a colleague's hair for lice during the coffee break would help to keep our relationship running smoothly.

Why did the grooming ritual disappear at some point in our evolutionary history? Part of the answer might of course be that we do not have fur, but that is not the reason we got rid of all those tiny pests. It would actually do us good to have our skin explored by a friend every now and then, particularly if we spend a lot of time in the woods where insects can easily be picked up. That is not something we do, however.

For primates it is just as much about keeping relationships running smoothly as it is about lice. What do human beings use to achieve the same purpose? How do humans affirm and deepen friendships and keep social relationships on an even keel? The answer is pretty obvious if you observe what goes on in an ordinary workplace canteen during the coffee break: we talk. We use language for the same purpose that apes and monkeys use grooming – apart from the lice, that is. We chat and we gossip with friends and acquaintances. Much of the chatter has little or no information content of any particular interest; this is talk for the sake of talk – the weather is a classic subject of conversation that has no real content.

Primates spend a lot of time grooming one another – the species that live in large troops may have to devote several hours a day to grooming in order to keep their friendships running smoothly. Each grooming session takes a while; you can only groom one friend at a time and you can't do anything else while you are at it. So the time this all takes increases very rapidly the more friends you acquire.

Human beings live in very large groups with many more friends and much more complex networks of social relations than any other primate has. At the time of writing I have 521 friends on Facebook. There could never be enough hours in the day to groom the fur of 521 friends even if some of them have hair that is thinning as much as mine, which would also speed up the removal of lice.

In the wild, too, in hunter-gatherer cultures, human beings have complex social networks made up of as many as 100 to 200 friends and acquaintances. That would far be too many to use mutual grooming as a means of social lubrication. That is why we needed another way of maintaining social relationships, and one that was faster than grooming.

The British researcher Robin Dunbar considers that need to be the mother of language. According to his model we evolved language as a social lubricant: so we could chat. Chatting and gossip during a break is simply more efficient that grooming. It works faster and you can chat to several people at the same time, which means you can lubricate a great many more friendships per hour with chat than you can by grooming.

Dunbar's idea is that this began with singing or moaning word-lessly to one another while grooming. The sound became part of the grooming ritual and eventually replaced it – we would just sing rather than pick off lice. The grooming song then gradually evolved to convey messages as well, and this became the origin of language.

On a number of points, Dunbar's theory has much in common with the singing theories we looked at when discussing the battle of the singers. Dunbar, however, manages to avoid the gender imbalance that is a feature of the singing battles; his theory makes no distinction between the sexes and is therefore a step in the right direction. But it falls foul of the same problem they do when having to explain the transition from lovely but meaningless song to meaningful if not particularly melodic language. Some other factor is essential for this to occur.

In terms of dating, Dunbar has calculated that the transition from grooming to small talk took place half a million years ago or so. I would actually place it somewhat earlier.

The theory passes the chimp test inasmuch as chimps have so few friends on Facebook that they have enough time to groom everyone the good old-fashioned way. The question that then arises, however, is why baboons, whose troops may contain a couple of hundred individuals, have not evolved an alternative to grooming.

## SOCIAL CONTROL

An ordinary coffee break one ordinary day in an ordinary office in an ordinary town in Sweden. Colleagues drop in to the staff room one by one and assemble around the coffee machine waiting for it to see fit to dispense its usual poison. Conversations quickly get going.

"I helped her last week when she had too much on her plate, but just yesterday when I could have done with some help myself she went and clocked off early, even though she could see me standing there surrounded by piles of letters."

"The same thing happened to me: she promised to cover for me when I had to go and pick up the kids earlier than usual, only nothing got done and she wasn't the one the boss was annoyed at."

"That's right, she makes ever so sure to keep on the boss's good side. You've got to wonder what went on between them at that after-work drink on Friday . . ."

"Something very definitely did, only trust me it wasn't just the two of them who were at it, let me tell you . . ."

The voices fade, we can no longer hear what they are saying. Gossip continues to be exchanged at each table in the staff room in any case.

\* \* \*

Badmouthing other people, absent friends in particular, is another thing language is frequently used for. A considerable portion of everything that people say consists of gossip in all its different forms. Though gossip is something many people look down on, the fact is that gossip fulfils a vital social function.

Cooperation and helpfulness were, as we have seen, crucial ingredients for making language possible. And yet cooperation is a tricky problem for Darwinian evolution – cooperating is good but parasitising on other people's collaborative efforts is even better. A human level of helpfulness and trust must therefore be based on a means of preventing freeloaders from exploiting the willingness of others to help. And that is where gossip comes in. A lot of gossip is actually about other people's failings and unwillingness to help. Gossip is a highly effective tool for spreading information about the shortcomings of other people so that the whole group gets to know who you can trust and who you can't.

Spreading information in this way is difficult without language. Apes can achieve a great deal with their limited expressive abilities but they would find it difficult to gossip about who did what to whom. Gossiping as a form of social control therefore seems entirely plausible as an explanation of language – it is of vital importance for human cooperation, and the characteristic features of language are well adapted to the kind of information involved.

But then we come up against the familiar question of the chicken and the egg. In this scenario it is language that makes human helpfulness possible – and yet we have previously observed that human helpfulness is a necessary precondition for language. So which end are we supposed to begin at? It is here that we need to imagine an interaction between language and helpfulness, in which both would have to have evolved in tandem so that the whole thing could work. In that case social control as mediated through a protolanguage would have to have started at much the same time as human helpfulness was becoming established, at some point in the time of *Homo erectus*, about a million years ago or perhaps a bit earlier.

Furthermore: even if language provides the means to get back at a certain kind of cheat, it also sets up new opportunities for cheating. Gossip is notorious for containing unfounded and occasionally malicious rumours. Given the way gossip works it is easy for the unscrupulous to spread false rumours to damage a competitor and indirectly whitewash yourself. So how do we get round that problem? Recent media attention to "fake news" and "alternative facts" suggests that the problem is not one that can easily be solved. Possible solutions may well involve what is referred to as "second order gossip", gossip, that is, about how reliable someone else's gossiping is.

## THINKING WHATEVER YOU WANT IS GREAT, BUT THINKING WHAT I WANT IS EVEN BETTER

Mum and Dad are sitting with their tiny newborn baby in their arms, the day after the birth. The whole family have turned up to the maternity ward to admire the latest addition. Grandpa (the father's father) seems thoughtful as he looks at the little tyke whose huge eyes are looking back at him. She's got blue eyes and a bit of blond fluff on her scalp, just like her mother; she doesn't appear to have inherited the darker colours of her father's skin.

Granny, Mum's mum, is as happy as can be and chattering away. "She's so sweet, and she's the spitting image of her father!" Her other daughter agrees with her, "Look, she's got her Dad's nose. Isn't she gorgeous?" and turns to the father. "You must be so proud to have such a beautiful daughter; you only have to look at her to see she's yours."

\* \* \*

We have already considered what may appear to be a paradox about our use of language – the way we compete over who is allowed to speak and who has to listen, despite the fact that listening ought to be more valuable if language transmits information from speaker to listener. As already pointed out, this suggests that the transmission of information is not the main point of language. We have already considered language as a tool for acquiring power and status as well, which is one way of getting round the paradox.

The Israeli scientist Daniel Dor has come up with a different solution. The aim of his book *The Instruction of Imagination* (2015) is to shift our perspective as to the way we use language. He poses the very pertinent question: what does a speaker want to achieve by speaking. Is the speaker's goal really to convey a particular message – or might the goal be instead to achieve a certain effect on the listener?

This touches on the difference between coded and puzzle communication that we considered previously. In coded communication the focus is on the message that is conveyed, whereas in the puzzle version it is on the reconstruction of the message by the listener. Both place the message at the centre, however, and see talking as about conveying a message. What Dor does could be described as moving one step further on from puzzle communication and shifting the focus from the message to the thoughts that the communication evokes in the listener. The goal of Dor's speaker is not to communicate a particular message, but to get the listener to think a particular thought.

Dor considers language as a social technology, a tool that we use for thought transference. We know that apes are able to think quite sophisticated thoughts; their inner conceptual world is considerably richer than they can communicate with their limited expressive abilities. An ape's thoughts therefore remain inside an ape's head and apes never enjoy the synergistic effects that humans continually benefit from as we think together and exchange ideas with one another. Dor considers this to be the key difference between ourselves and the other apes: it is possible for us to exchange ideas. In his view, language is a technology that we have created together to make possible that exchange of ideas.

An exchange of ideas presupposes rather more than my just sending you a message – it assumes that I can get you to think what I am thinking and get you to construct in your inner world a matching conceptual structure to the one I have in mine. In order to achieve this, I use language to "instruct your imagination", in

Dor's phrase, so that you will create the image I want to give you in your mind.

In its initial and most basic form, this process would have been about concrete experience. Let us return at this point to our rhinoceros scouts. When the scout was delivering her report she did her best to construct an image in her listeners' minds of the scene she had observed around the carcass of the rhino – she was using her performance to instruct them to imagine a dead rhino with three hyenas around it so that they could then plan what to do on that basis.

In practice the difference between communicating the message that there is a dead rhinoceros and instructing listeners to imagine a dead rhinoceros is an extremely fine one, but a difference in perspective is involved that becomes important when more subtle ideas than a rhino carcass are in play.

The rhinoceros scouts also fit in very well in terms of date: it should have been around a million or so years ago that Daniel Dor's social technology began to develop when *erectus* began to realise that puzzle communication could be used to construct ideas in other people's heads.

It is after all crucial to puzzle communication that you do not actually say the exact message you want the listener to receive – instead, you convey a message that you judge the recipient will interpret and reconstruct as the message you actually want to communicate. That is why you might be content to say "It's stuffy in here" when the message you actually want to communicate is "Open the window" – you are relying on the listener being able to work out that your statement has a purpose that goes beyond commenting on the quality of the air in the room.

Dor's model takes this one step further. As he sees it, the issue is not about the listener understanding your message that the window should be opened, but about getting the listener to think to themselves that it is so stuffy in here that a window needs opening. Once more the difference is wafer thin in practical terms, but it is the shift in perspective that is important. The goal of the speaker is not to convey the right message but to get the listener to think the right thought – and in this instance to perform the right action as well. It is not much of a leap from this point to use the technology of language to implant in the listener not those ideas that the speaker is actually thinking, but the ones the speaker wants the listener to think. Communication and manipulation have become two sides of the same coin.

Every good storyteller knows how to use Dor's technology and understands how a story should be told in order to construct the desired image in the mind of the listener. Imagine you are attending a job interview, or that you are on a date with an attractive potential partner. You are no doubt doing your best to make the intended employer or partner construct in their minds as favourable an image of yourself as possible. Without lying directly, you make use of all the tools language offers, all the tricks you are familiar with, to get them to imagine that you are just what they want. And they, in their turn, are doing their best to see through all your tricks while attempting at the same time to construct in your mind the best possible image of themselves.

Let's go back to that scene in the maternity ward, based on a research paper published a year or so ago. One of the researchers had been observing and recording – with the consent of all those concerned apart from the newborn babe – a conversation of this very kind in the maternity ward when the relatives get their first chance to meet the new arrival. There was an obvious and significant difference between what the relatives of the mother and the father said about the baby. The father's relatives were fairly neutral and commented on the similarities with the mother and father roughly to the same extent, whereas the vast majority of the mother's relatives stressed how like the father the little darling was. The researcher interpreted this as reflecting the fact that it is in the interest of the mother (and her family) that the father is convinced that he really is the father of the child – particularly if there is even the slightest doubt about that – whereas there is no corresponding interest on the part of the father's family to convince the mother because there cannot be any doubt as to maternity on her part. It is in the father's and grandfather's interest instead to make sure that they have not got a cuckoo in the nest.

From Dor's point of view, this can be seen as the mother's family doing their best to instruct the father to imagine he is the father beyond any doubt and to suppress any alternative notions.

## SO WHAT DID WE START TALKING ABOUT?

Each of these different ideas about the original topic of conversation may be considered more or less plausible, and each has its proponents. The subjects of conversation that have been proposed are in most instances something that human beings actually use language for today and that would also have been discussed by our ancestors in all likelihood. From a Darwinian perspective most of the ideas also describe situations in which language may have given the speaker and/or the listener a considerable evolutionary advantage in the struggle for existence.

The various scenarios above are dated to different periods of time and different stages in our evolution. Some of the scenarios can be combined, and there is nothing to say there was only a single topic of conversation that was important through all the stages of the evolution of language. If the battle of the singers were included it would have to be placed first on the timeline, probably among the habilines two million years ago, and the same would apply to Dunbar's vocal grooming, even though Dunbar himself would assign a date for it that is quite a bit later. Then there are several different scenarios that fit in well with *Homo erectus* at a point a little over one million years ago. The chronology is not particularly exact because *erectus* existed as a species for a very long time, and it is by no means evident whether the scenarios should be assigned dates at the beginning or at the end of the *erectus* period. Dessalles' idea, like many other conceivable scenarios with narrative skills at their core, ought, however, to be dated later in the evolution of language, to maybe half a million years ago. Dating scenarios of this kind to as recently as 200,000 years ago and early *Homo sapiens* would also be feasible, but that is less likely in my view.

To summarise the chronology:

- *Early* scenarios, more than two million years ago, among the habilines: Battle of the Singers, vocal grooming.
- *Middle-period* scenarios, around one million years ago, among *Homo erectus*: Carrion hunters, stone-axe classes, progression from vocal grooming to messages, simple forms of social control and mental instruction.
- *Late* scenarios, 200,000–500,000 years ago: Storytelling in various forms, both Dessalles' status building and more advanced social control and mental instruction.

These various ideas could also be categorised according to the kind of language use they prioritise.

- *Attractive*: The focus here is on the form of language; first and foremost it should sound pleasing and does not have to convey a message. Under this heading would be the battle of the singers and the most basic form of Dunbar's vocal grooming. If these are to be relevant in any way it would be to a very early stage in the evolution of language. But with a focus on form rather than content, these ideas are moving in the wrong direction, away from the construction and conveying of meaning that are so essential to language and that differentiate it from the communication systems of all other animals.

- *Instrumental*: Here the focus is on the function; language is used in practical terms to convey a message, and it is the content of the message that is important. Under this heading we find the carrion eaters, the politicians, the stone-axe teachers as well as the social controllers. Producing an evolutionary advantage from instrumental communication is not very difficult – the problem here is, rather, explaining why language failed to offer an advantage to other apes. Additionally, we need to pay attention to who benefits from the communication – the benefit needs to be reciprocal, with both speaker and listener gaining from the conveying of the message. Instrumental communication can easily become one-sided: either the speaker wants something from the listener, and in that case the benefit to the speaker is the focus, or the speaker's aim is to inform, in which case the benefit accrues mainly to the listener.

  Dor's scenario is instrumental in one sense as well, but at another level. It involves a more intimate form of thought transference than simply sending a message and, to that extent, it may be of mutual benefit – and yet it entails the manipulation of the listener by the speaker, which means that the benefit is no longer reciprocal even though the communication is still instrumental from the speaker's point of view.

- *Status building*: This is an intermediate form in which the meaning-conveying content of the language is important but in which the communication is still not primarily instrumental in practice. The evolutionary advantage is derived from the higher status a skilled narrator can acquire, and as such it calls to mind the battle of the singers – while unlike that battle, it is based on the very features that are the prime characteristics of language. Dessalles' scenario is most at home in this category.

I consider the ideas that are based on the form and beauty of language to be improbable. They postulate a stage in human evolution for which there is no evidence, and they fail to explain the most fundamental features of language. With regard to the origins of language the challenge is not to explain how we acquired beautiful voices – many animals have those – but how human language acquired its unique ability to convey complex messages. Instrumental language would therefore seem more plausible as the message-conveying aspect of language is at its core. Dessalles nevertheless has a point when he observes that instrumental communication ought to lead to competition for the listening position whereas in actual language-use, there is much more competition for the position of speaker. Status building may serve as a supplement to instrumental language, particularly because it allows the benefit of communication to be shared more symmetrically. Dor's ideas, too, may be of assistance in this area. The structure of language suggests that some form of storytelling must have played a key role, at least while grammar was developing. It is possible to accomplish the purely instrumental communication of facts more simply, without having to employ all the grammatical machinery we have today.

* * *

Gender equality poses problems for several of the theories referred to. Even though we do not know very much about gender roles in prehistory, there is nothing to suggest that other kinds of humans were noticeably more gender equal than we are. The only thing we can decipher about gender equality from fossils relates to gender differences in skeletons, in relation to childbirth and wounds and damage to the skeleton.

Chimps and bonobos have bodily differences between the sexes that are comparable to ours, while those of the gorillas and orang-utans are greater. This difference was also greater in

*Australopithecus*: the males were much bigger than the females, which suggests that relations between the sexes were more like those among gorillas than among humans or chimps. Gender differences among *Homo erectus* and more recent human species are in the same range as among modern humans and chimps, even though there is some evidence that Neandertal women played a greater part in the hunting of big game than their *sapiens*-sisters have traditionally done.

Both hunting big game and the pursuit of status are activities that are not conducted on a gender-equal basis by human beings today, and nor are they gender equal among chimps. This argues against scenarios that are structured around that type of activity, even if we ought not simply to dismiss them on that basis.

\* \* \*

Social information in various forms does not encounter the same problems of gender equality and also fits in well with the evolution of human cooperation. This can be both information for social control and information directly related to cooperation. We should not exclude some role for status-building information either – that scenario can easily be combined with the kind of information needed for cooperation and social control.

*If we put together these scenarios with the conclusions from the previous chapter on the dating of the first speaker, we arrive, irrespective of which scenario we prefer, at a functioning protolanguage that was evolved by* Homo erectus *just over a million years ago.*

Let us return to the chimp test and ask ourselves which scenarios would result in neither chimps nor any other animals having language. The scenarios that are based on social relations within groups have to explain why other social and cooperative species did not evolve language. One factor is probably the size of the group: human groups were small enough for everyone to know all the other members but too big for everyone to keep track of everyone else all the time, which creates a need for shared social control and communication about individuals who cheat. Troops of pygmy marmosets are so small that that kind of communication is unnecessary, while jackdaws live in such large flocks that it is impossible to know all the other members. The troops baboons live in are large enough but they do not possess a family structure that would provide the launch pad for cooperation to take off. There are few animal species other than humans whose social structure demonstrates just the right balance.

A language-ready brain would also be required, along with concepts, categories, mental time travel and a basic theory of mind. Our ancestors had the entire package, but it is rare among other animals, which limits further the number of potential candidates for language.

Finally, ecology may also help explain why no other species has evolved a language. Pygmy marmosets, for instance, mainly eat sap and resin from trees and would gain nothing by being able to communicate about food. Our ancestors, on the other hand, lived on food that was harder to come by and cooperation and communication offered huge gains in the business of acquiring it. The scenario of the carrion hunters accentuates that particular aspect and takes it about as far as it can go, but even though our ancestors did not live solely off rhino carcasses the principle is valid nonetheless – humans are specialists at food that is hard to get.

*The combination of trust and helpfulness, just the right family and group structure, a language-ready mind and an ecological niche in which cooperation was an advantage turn out to be unique to* Homo erectus, *and explain why no other animal possesses language.*

Homo erectus *must therefore have possessed a basic protolanguage at a minimum. And Neandertals, Denisovans and our own ancestors would therefore have possessed at least as much language when they evolved out of various* erectus-*groups just over half a million years ago.*

Even then our common ancestor may already have possessed a

fully working grammatical language with all the modern refinements; we just do not know as yet. The Neandertals cannot have
been entirely without language, as we have seen. At this point
let us take a trip into their world.

# The Cave Man

A group of people are sitting round a fire at the mouth of a cave just above a small river. Today, the river, a tributary of the Dordogne in what is now France, is called the Sourdoire. The ground is stony down by the water and dense thickets of mountain birch and willows cover what soil there is. The air is chilly even though it is only the beginning of September. The inland ice is not far away. The humans are clad in furs to protect them from the cold.

They are all light-skinned, some are blond and many of them have red hair. The four men in the group have almost identical features and appear to be closely related. Five ruddy little children are running round playing while the adults are talking. Although they all have wide noses, prominent eyebrows and almost no chin, the children could easily be European kids of today when it comes to the rest of their bodies.

The subject of conversation around the fire is the herd of mammoths a young hunter had seen from a distance earlier in the day, ten or so kilometres from the cave. A single mammoth would provide enough meat and fat for the whole group to put on a layer of flesh before the long hard winter that will soon be here, and the mammoth wool will come in very handy as protection against the biting Ice Age cold, even though the group will soon start moving south towards their winter hunting grounds near the Mediterranean. But hunting mammoth is very difficult and dangerous – more than one of their number bear old wounds, broken bones that have healed and so on, as mementos of previous mammoth hunts. What is the best way of going about it?

The oldest man gets to his feet laboriously and stands so everyone can see him. He has a wooden stick to lean on; his back is bent and he has difficulty straightening all his joints. It is obvious that it hurts when he moves. Although he will not be taking part in any more mammoth hunts, he has more experience than anyone else in the group and everyone listens when he starts speaking. He reminds them of the narrow crevice that lies a bit further along the path the mammoths usually take, and how on several previous occasions when he was younger the group had had success hunting mammoth at that spot.

A month later the group leaves the cave heading for their winter quarters. The mammoth has been completely devoured, and the group has enough mammoth fat and dried mammoth meat for their long journey on foot. But the old man will not be coming with them. He died a week earlier and was buried inside the cave. His body was interred in the floor of the cave in the foetal position, with some of the last of the autumn's dried flowers strewn over it and then covered with a small mound of stones.

\* \* \*

Sixty thousand years later, in 1908, the man's skeleton was discovered by the parish priest of the little town that had grown up in another nearby river valley, not far from the crevice where they caught the mammoth. Our view of the Neandertals would be coloured by this skeleton for a long time. The old man's appearance was reconstructed by the French scientist Marcellin Boule, who correctly concluded that he must have walked with a stoop but who, unfortunately, allowed himself to be misled into thinking that this was typical of all Neandertals. He would also reconstruct the man as much more apelike than is probable, with hairy skin and prehensile toes. This reconstruction would be extremely influential, particularly on the popular science of the time, and turned the Neandertals into the archetypal primitive cavemen who could barely walk upright and were incapable of comprehending any tool more complex than a club or saying anything more than "ugh-ugh". Even today the word "Neandertal" is used as a pejorative term for people with the kind of primitive attitudes we do not feel are appropriate for a *Homo sapiens*.

It is both bigoted and sad that another kind of human should be devalued in this way simply because they were different. Boule's reconstruction was governed as much by his own prejudices as by the actual appearance of the skeleton – but it would never have gained so much attention had it not struck a chord in a great many people's minds, the kind of chord that is very keen to distinguish between *Us* and *Them*. This is the same chord that is struck by contemporary xenophobic rhetoric – arguing that the person who is different is both inferior and dangerous can still pay off even today.

Reconstruction of a Neandertal in a modern suit, in the Neandertal Museum in Mettmann, Germany.

The Neandertals were human beings, according to every reasonable definition that can be applied to fossils. They were not exactly the same as us: a Neandertal can be recognised by certain characteristic features of the face and skull. Modern humans have faces that are rather straight and vertical from the forehead to the chin. The faces of Neandertals were convex instead: with a bulge in the middle around the nose and mouth while the brow and the chin were more receding. The shape of the skull, and thus the brain, was also different – longer and narrower than ours but just as large.

These are not dramatic differences, not even as far as the face is concerned, and below the neck our skeletons are all but identical. If a family of living Neandertals were wearing modern clothes and had paid a visit to a hairdresser, they could probably walk around our cities without attracting too much attention.

The Neandertals were Europe's original inhabitants, the only true Europeans. We and the Neandertals went our separate ways about half a million years ago. It was in Europe that they evolved from earlier forms of humans, whereas we *Homo sapiens* are relatively recent immigrants from Africa. For a very long time Neandertals were the only form of human beings present in Europe and the lands around it. They were also the original white-skinned humans, probably the first kind of humans who were not consistently dark-skinned with dark hair.

The art of making stone tools had been largely static during the time of *Homo erectus* who created millions of identical hand axes for more than a million years. But after the partition of the human family into several branches half a million years ago, technological advances progressed more rapidly. The Neandertals in particular developed new methods for effectively producing high-quality flint knives, including the "Levallois" technique, a controlled way of producing several knives or spear points of very high quality from the same chunk of flint. The Neandertals also knew how to bind the spear points onto wooden shafts to make spears, which was no easy feat. Depending on what was available they might use bitumen as glue or boil glue from birch sap. Preparing birch sap was an especially complicated process that had to be done in several stages and required particular careful control of the temperature inside the hearth.

This tells us a great deal both about the ability of Neandertals to control fire and their capacity for innovation and technological progress. Compared with the inhabitants of a modern industrial society, the Neandertals were not remarkably creative or inventive in their tool-making. But compared with their *erectus*-predecessors they made lightning advances and managed to keep up with their *Homo sapiens* contemporaries for a long time. How advanced a language would Neandertals have needed to develop and spread knowledge about new technical advances?

## FRATERNISATION

There is still some dispute about the degree to which we and the Neandertals belong to the same species. Were the Neandertals just a variant of *Homo sapiens*, or were they a separate species who would, in that case, have to be called *Homo neanderthalensis*? Does the issue of the Neandertals' language have any bearing on the species question?

This question of species turns out to be a tricky one – even when dealing with living animals, biologists find it difficult to agree on exactly how a species should be defined. Traditionally a new species has been identified as such whenever a biologist judges that the members of the species differ sufficiently from other species in terms of anatomy and appearance. But this is a rather blunt and subjective definition. The concept of species that many biologists would prefer to work with is one that considers a species as an evolutionary unit of its own, a group of animals that are evolving together along a path that is clearly distinct from other species, irrespective of the odd instance of an affair across the species boundaries. Until very recently, however, it was very difficult to examine the extent to which evolutionary lines have been kept distinct. The only effective means is to check the D.N.A. of the animals in question and see whether the D.N.A. of the two species form separate groups without too many kinship bonds existing between them after they parted company at some point in prehistory.

* * *

In 1984 a discovery was made that would revolutionise research into the recent evolution of life – D.N.A. can be preserved in fossils, and as long as the fossil is not too ancient, the D.N.A. in it can be decoded in order to compare the genes of extinct creatures with those of their modern relatives.

From modest beginnings in the 1980s, the technique for producing fossil D.N.A. has progressed rapidly. The fossil cannot, however, be any age at all, and the bones really need to have been preserved in the dry and the cold. For this reason the focus in studies of fossil D.N.A. has been on the fauna of the Ice Ages, which offers the best opportunities of making a discovery.

* * *

Neandertals are part of the Ice-Age fauna. They were contemporaries of the mammoths and the cave bears and the other well-known animals of the period. They remained in Europe and Central Asia during the bitterest periods, albeit while keeping well to the south of the ice edge. A great deal of research was therefore devoted to the pursuit of D.N.A. from Neandertal fossils, an endeavour that would soon be rewarded with success. At the end of the 1990s the first D.N.A. sequences from Neandertals were published, and by 2013 the entire D.N.A. of a Neandertal had been reconstructed from fossil fragments.

When the D.N.A. of Neandertals was compared with the D.N.A. from different groups of modern humans, it was quickly established that the two groups must have parted company about half a million years ago. A couple of years later, however, after more D.N.A. analyses, it also proved possible to demonstrate that a certain amount of fraternisation must have occurred considerably later than that. *Homo sapiens* evolved in Africa and then spread out across the world from there; those *sapiens* who remained in Africa and became the ancestors of the Africans of today never encountered any Neandertals. But the *sapiens* who left Africa would soon enter Neandertal territory in the Middle East – and apparently mutual attraction occurred often enough to have left its traces on our genes. We know that the encounters between Neandertals and *Homo sapiens* that took place between 40,000 and 100,000 years ago resulted in children. We know that Neandertals could have children with ordinary humans because Neandertal D.N.A. is still present in all human beings outside Africa.

As a group the Neandertals died out about 30,000 years ago. We are not really certain why; it may well have been because of competition from *Homo sapiens*, but it could also have been due to disease, changes in climate or something else. The Neandertals were never very prolific and that made them vulnerable to change. They disappeared at any event shortly after *Homo sapiens* arrived in Europe.

But before they disappeared they had time for a great many intimate encounters with *Homo sapiens* and a lot of children with brows that were on the low side were born as a result, children who then became relatively successful members of *sapiens* tribes and had children and grandchildren of their own with "pureblood" *sapiens*. Everyone alive today whose roots are outside Africa has a small percentage of Neandertal genes in their D.N.A. At that time, *Homo sapiens* were fully developed humans with fully developed human language. Would Neandertals have had so much success in those intimate encounters unless they had had a language as well?

Simply transferring some sperm can of course be managed without language in a wordless meeting in the forest, with or without consent. But the fact that Neandertal genes are still in circulation in modern humans is evidence that the resulting children not only survived but grew up to be fairly successful members of a group of Homo sapiens and eventually had children and grandchildren together with "pure-blood" Homo sapiens. The hybrids would inevitably have formed part of sapiens communities, and in order to survive they must have possessed some form of human language faculty. This tells us that the linguistic abilities of these children were not impaired by the fact that half the genes in their D.N.A. were Neandertal, which could hardly have been the case if the Neandertals had lacked the genes relevant for language.

Another aspect worth considering here is that in most human cultures it is not socially acceptable for a women to return home pregnant from a trip to the forest. Even in Sweden, it is not that long ago that there was a stigma attached to being born a "bastard", and these children faced an uphill struggle to achieve social and reproductive success. If the bastards in question had also had some kind of linguistic handicap, there could hardly have been any grandchildren to carry the Neandertal genes down to us.

Children of temporary liaisons tend normally to grow up in the mother's group, so any children of sapiens-fathers and Neandertal mothers would have grown up among the Neandertals, and whatever children they had in turn must have died out with the other Neandertals. In order for Neandertal genes to exist in us today the hybrid children must have been born in a sapiens-group and most probably therefore to a sapiens-mother and a Neandertal father.

Alternatively the hybrid children would have been born "in

wedlock" of a Neandertal woman who was in a stable enough relationship to a *sapiens*-man that she could move in with him as part of his *sapiens*-group. This would provide the children with a better start in life than if they were "bastards", but assumes that "importing wives" was acceptable to the group in question. That presupposes in turn that the Neandertal woman in the couple was able to communicate with the group, which she could scarcely have managed without possessing a linguistic ability of her own that was at least something like the human language faculty.

In any case, the choice of which label to apply to the Neandertals is not actually very interesting; a much more interesting question is how they thought and felt, how human they were. And they were demonstrably human enough for many a *Homo sapiens* to accept a Neandertal as a romantic partner – and vice versa. As far as I am concerned that is enough to call them human.

*And as far as I am concerned that is enough for me to conclude that they could talk like people.*

## NEANDER-TALKERS?

So what do we know about the Neandertals' language?

In Jean Auel's novel *The Clan of the Cave Bear* their language is described as follows:

> Iza used a few spoken words when she talked, but primarily for emphasis. The people of the Clan could not articulate well enough for a complete verbal language, they communicated more with gestures and motions, but their sign language was fully comprehensive and rich with nuance.[43]

43 Auel, Jean M., *The Clan of the Cave Bear* (1981).

This resembles the ideas we discussed in the section on the first signer and is entirely plausible as a description of a possible proto-language. But it does not tally well with what we know about the language faculty of the Neandertals. As we know, the Neander-tals had a vocal apparatus that was almost identical to ours, and that was adapted for speech in several ways. With those adapta-tions in place they would have had little difficulty in articulating more than the grunts they manage to produce in *The Clan of the Cave Bear*. The other side of that coin is that if all they had done was grunt, there would have been no evolutionary impetus to improve their vocal apparatus.

A protolanguage of that kind would fit rather better at an earlier stage in our history. Early *Homo erectus* may well have possessed a language like that, with signs and gestures doing the hard work. The evidence for *erectus* being able to speak is much less clear and unambiguous. And yet that ability was in place before the Nean-dertals and *Homo sapiens* went separate ways half a million years ago or so, in the common ancestor and ancestress we share with the "cave men", an ancestor and ancestress who were probably members of the species *Homo erectus*.

There is a great deal to suggest therefore that the Neandertals really were "Neander-talkers", with a spoken language that was probably as well articulated as our own and fully functional in any case. As well articulated as our own because the Neandertals also possessed evolutionary adaptations for speech in their vocal tract. Only someone who frequently produces sounds that require detailed articulation would need those adaptations. This does not necessarily mean that the language of the Neandertals was comparable to our own in every respect. It tells us nothing about their grammar for instance.

Clarity of articulation is necessary to produce and perceive dis-tinct words, and there cannot be a Darwinian pressure to evolve that kind of articulation unless the vocabulary is expanding. So the Neandertals had a substantial vocabulary and therefore probably the ability to coin new words; they could hardly have amassed a vocabulary worth the name otherwise. You can get quite far with a language like that, one with the capacity to create words for what you need even if it lacks the ability to form complex sentences with those words. If that were the case, in purely linguistic terms the language would have been on the same level as that of a one-year-old *Homo sapiens*, but with an adult brain and an adult conceptual apparatus behind it.

But would such a restricted language be enough to seduce a *sapiens* of the opposite sex? And if Neandertals lacked an ability to handle grammar, would the children of such a parent be able to manage a fully fledged *sapiens* language? The fact that their skills at seduction evidently worked suggests that the Neandertals had a more developed language faculty than that, and that they could do more than just handle a lot of words. We might also remind ourselves that they also possessed the human version of the FOXP2 gene, which clearly has some significance for the language faculty.

## IS IT POSSIBLE TO RECONSTRUCT THE NEANDERTALS' LANGUAGE?

If you ask a linguist, and preferably a historical linguist who specialises in the reconstruction of extinct languages, whether it is possible to reconstruct the language of the Neandertals, the answer would be a very definite "NO". Not so long ago, that "no" would have been completely open and shut, and anyone attempting a reconstruction of that kind would have been ridiculed by other researchers.

\* \* \*

In 2014 I was attending an international conference on the evolution of language, held that year in Vienna. Earlier in the day

I had presented a lecture of my own entitled "Did language evolve incommunicado?"[44] But now the time had come for several other researchers to make their presentations and I was eagerly looking forward to attending a lecture with the sensational title: "Detecting differences between the languages of the Neandertals and modern humans."

Could that actually be possible now? I had already met the scientists who were going to speak – there are only a few hundred of us in the entire world doing research into the evolution of language, so everyone knows everyone else – and I knew they were neither crazy nor incompetent. The speaker was a rather young man, Sean Roberts, but he was to be backed up by two very experienced colleagues who had been doing research into the relationship between language and genes for many years, and had made a number of interesting discoveries. They had also published an article on the language faculty of the Neandertals the year before, at around the same time as I had published an almost identical piece (and fortunately we had both arrived at essentially the same conclusions in our parallel contributions).[45]

Only now they were claiming to have discovered a means not just of saying something about the language faculty of Neandertals, but of gaining access to their language. It sounded almost too good to be true.

Their idea is based on the hybrid children we discussed earlier in this chapter, children with a Neandertal parent and a *sapiens* one. Many people alive today are actually the descendants of these children and carry a tiny fraction of Neandertal genes in their D.N.A.. Other humans, in contrast, never had any contact with

44 Anyone wondering what it was about can take another look at the section called "The First Thinker" in this book, which stays close to the paper I gave.

45 Dediu, Dan & Levinson, Stephen C., "On the antiquity of language: the reinterpretation of Neandertal linguistic capacities and its consequences." Frontiers in Psychology 4(397), 1–17, doi:10.3389/fpsyg.2013.00397 (2013); Johansson, Sverker "The talking Neanderthals: What do fossils, genetics, and archeology say?" Biolinguistics 7, 35–074 (2013).

Neandertals and are therefore "pure" *sapiens*. Researchers have charted in considerable detail which groups have Neandertals in their ancestry and which do not. Pure *sapiens* are everyone with recent roots in Africa south of the Sahara, while the descendants of the hybrid children are distributed throughout the rest of the world, including England and Sweden.

There are currently around a thousand languages that are spoken by human beings whose ancestors never met a Neandertal, and several thousand that are spoken by the descendants of the hybrid children. My scientist colleagues used a database containing grammatical data for roughly 2,500 languages and using sophisticated statistical techniques they tried to detect systematic differences between the grammars of the languages spoken by the descendants of the hybrids and of those spoken by "pure" *sapiens*.

If there are differences of this kind in the grammars, these could either be the result of genetic differences among the groups – perhaps the Neandertal genes have some subtle influence on the language faculty that means that particular grammatical features are more common – or of a direct influence by the Neandertal languages their distant ancestors encountered and which the hybrid children may even have acquired as their native tongue. In both cases the differences in grammar would tell us something about how the Neandertals might have spoken.

Unfortunately this *was* too good to be true. Although my colleagues did find some exciting patterns, there was nothing that was really definitive; nothing that could not be more simply explained. It was a good effort and their lecture got an honourable mention as the most ambitious contribution to the conference. But we still do not know anything about the grammar of the Neandertals.

An anticlimax, you might think. But that is how research works; a scientist cannot expect to get unambiguous results every time. On the contrary, it is perfectly normal to get ambiguous or negative results. Knowing what does *not* work also contributes to our overall knowledge. Only publishing "successful" research that comes up with the desired result would provide a distorted image of the real state of affairs. Given the way scientists' careers and research funding are orchestrated today, this is a real problem in many areas.

# Cultural "Man"

A young woman is kneeling on the ground outside a small hut. The grass that is growing everywhere else has been worn away at the entrance. The stony soil is a bit painful on her bare knees but that is something she has to ignore. In her hands is a little figurine shaped like a full-figured female body with wide hips and ample breasts that is a lot more curvaceous than her own skinny frame. The figure has been made of ivory, laboriously carved with a flint knife from a piece of mammoth tusk. In front of her in a bowl made out of a scallop shell is some pigment made from red ochre. She has already painted a ring around her belly and a pattern of stars on each breast. And now she is painting the same design on the figurine using a blade of grass for a paintbrush. She will have finished painting just as the sun sets.

This is the first time in her young life that she will spend a whole night without other people around her. She lies in the darkness of the hut and tries to sleep but she keeps hearing the sounds from the forest outside and rustling and creaking in the bushes. She is scared but the shaman has told her this is what she has to do. Once she had been with her man for two years and not become pregnant, her mother had told her to talk to the shaman and he had told her about the hut in the forest. He had explained how she had to paint both the figurine he gave her and herself, what the different patterns meant in the spirit world, and how the figure symbolised the female aspect of fertility. Then he had instructed her to spend a whole night on her own in the hut on the next night of the full moon. At that time the spirit of the forest will come to unlock her womb so she can become pregnant. But only if she does exactly what the spirit tells her and remains silent the whole time.

She has begun to doze by the wee small hours but awakens with a jolt when she sees a strange shape outlined against the entrance to the hut in the moonlit sky. It is standing erect like a human being but has huge antlers like a deer and its body is as broad and powerful as a bear's. Lying there she has to struggle to stifle her scream as she realises it is the spirit of the forest that has come at last.

The spirit lies on top of her. She can feel its thick shaggy coat against her body. Even its face is covered in hair and its eyes are just black holes against the fur. She is trembling with both fear and anticipation. The spirit pushes inside her, towards her womb. That part of the spirit feels no different at least to that of her man.

When the spirit has done what he has to, he stands up and leaves the hut as silently as he arrived. She remains lying where she is and wondering about what she has just been through, hoping that it was worth it and hoping that her womb really will open now.

The Spirit of the Forest was inspired by this image from the Trois Frères cave in France, painted approximately 13,000 years ago.

The night in the hut had the desired effect. At the next full moon she does not bleed and nine months later she and her man can celebrate a tiny new born baby who will grow up to be a strong healthy lad. No-one acknowledges the striking resemblance the boy bears to the shaman.

\* \* \*

Chimps are practical creatures with a very limited interest in the kind of things produced by humans, who produce things for aesthetic reasons. The few tools and other items that chimps make are purely functionally designed with no aesthetic ambitions. Making something because it is beautiful, or because it symbolises something, does not appear to be part of their conceptual world. Although chimps in captivity may learn to paint and at least one chimp artist has had its paintings sold at auction (anonymously) for prices that many a human artist might envy – there is still considerable doubt about how much of the works' originality is in the mind of the chimp and how much is in the eye of its beholders.

At the beginning of human prehistory, things appeared to be at much the same stage as they are among the other apes today. The oldest stone tools were also purely functional; the goal was to produce a sharp edge and what the rock looked like, beyond that, was a matter of indifference. Neither *Australopithecus* nor the habilines show any evidence at all of possessing a more sophisticated culture. Unlike us, of course – we strongly prefer to see ourselves as culturally prominent creatures.

## CULTURE AND LANGUAGE

Symbolic and aesthetic culture arose at some point during the two million years that separate the habilines from us. Language, too, arose at some point between the habilines and us. Could there be a connection? What do language and culture have in common?

Art and culture not only tell us something about the cognitive ability of the artists, but also about their ability to communicate and their desire to do so in particular. Most forms of cultural expression obviously involve communication, and yet communication is something that many animals are engaged in as well. What is new about culture is not communication as such, but rather the manner of communicating and, above all, how significant an impact the communication has on both the sender and receiver.

Culture is based on systems of symbols that create meaning. The meaning of cultural statements, or meanings, is derived from systems such as these. Certain cultural manifestations, such as figurative art, represent something in a more or less transparent way and convey their basic meaning in what they show. That basic meaning can be interpreted even by a receiver who does not share the same symbolic network. That is about as far as our understanding, as contemporary human beings, can take us in relation to cave paintings and figurines from a vanished culture. And yet even in figurative art there are normally further dimensions of meaning that cannot be deduced solely from what it represents.

It is the systems of symbols that create meaning that make culture relevant to language. Language, too, is a system of symbols that create meaning. Every word is a symbol for what that word means, and in language, too, there are various layers and dimensions of meaning. Many words are like figurative art to the extent that they refer to something concrete that exists in the surrounding world. These tend to be the first words that a child learns. But such words, with their apparently straightforward meanings, often have connotations that extend beyond their literal meaning, and they can be used metaphorically or have their meanings extended in other ways. Woman, lady, female and hag have virtually the same concrete meaning and can be used to refer to the same individuals but their connotations, symbolism and associations differ considerably.

A great number of words in any language do not have a basic meaning of this kind and cannot be explained by pointing to something. These include both a large group of abstract terms for abstract concepts and a smaller group of very frequently occurring words that have a purely grammatical intralinguistic function: all those little words, that is, that connect up our sentences to form grammatical wholes and help clarify who is doing what to whom, but do not have any actual and autonomous meaning outside grammar. These words without a concrete reference can only be explained by means of other words, and are only meaningful within a network of linguistic symbols.

The ability to handle symbols and networks of symbols is therefore a prerequisite for language, and archaeological evidence of symbol use is also evidence of a symbol-ready brain, which is already quite some way down the road to a language-ready brain. Making direct connections between a symbol and a meaning is something that apes can do as well – but constructing an entire network of symbols that create meaning is a uniquely human ability. That capacity is used in both art and language and that is why the origin of art has something to tell us about the origin of language. Art also has the advantage over language in that it may be visibly present in the archaeological evidence. That is why we will be devoting several pages to prehistoric art to see how it can shed light on prehistoric languages.

## THE CULTURAL ANIMAL

Culture is a concept that is difficult to define. Sometimes it is used as the dialectical counterpart to nature, as in the name of the eminent Swedish publishing house that originally published this book (Natur & Kultur). But there are many levels to this dialectic. Nature versus culture evokes animal versus human and, in that case, culture would be specifically human, something that differentiates us from the uncultured beasts. But it can also be associated with heredity versus environment, and then culture becomes all the various behaviours of a group that are passed down from generation to generation; passed down, however, through the social environment and not in D.N.A.. Most of what we call culture in everyday speech fits in well with that definition. Forms of cultural expression such as music, literature and art all belong to established cultural traditions that are passed on within the group by other means than genetic inheritance. The traditions of ethnic groups, which are handed down from generation to generation within the same group are also an obvious form of culture in this sense. Language, too, can become a manifestation of culture. However, applying this definition to the behaviours of other animals raises several concerns.

* * *

The female humpback is listening to the song echoing through the deeps of the ocean. A new male is singing; she does not recognise either the voice or the song itself. Both the rhythm and the theme are different from the songs of the local males.

The new male keeps to the fringes of the herd and within hearing for a while – although the hearing range for a whale can be a thousand kilometres – but well out of sight, before he swims on to new hunting grounds. The local males continue to refine their songs – they all sing virtually identical songs, variations on the same theme, but they keep refining that local theme and introducing new motifs. It is not long before the phrases they sampled from the temporary visitor have been incorporated. The songs will evolve in new directions under new forms of influence.

The adolescent calf is still swimming alongside his mother. He listens to the singing of the older males in the herd and tries to imitate them. The males respond to his attempts by singing the herd's theme back to him the way it should sound. He continues to practise and learns to sing the right way, learning to sing like a member of the herd.

* * *

Is what the whales are doing culture? Their singing is a behaviour that is passed on within the herd, but not transferred in D.N.A., and differs from one herd to another. To that extent it is clearly culture. It would be difficult to produce a definition of culture that included human singing – which we are all agreed is culture – but excluded the songs of the whales.

* * *

In this broad sense of the word, distinguishing cultural humans from animals would not be possible. Culture in the sense of behaviours that are passed down within groups without genetic inheritance, and which serve to distinguish one group from another, occurs in a variety of animal species – whales, apes, songbirds and many others. There can be little doubt that culture in this broader sense was an attribute of our ancestors as well, culture that may have ranged from various kinds of song to different ways of making a stone axe.

So culture is to be found among a range of creatures, including our relatives. And yet I wrote at the beginning of this chapter that there was *no* evidence that *Australopithecus* and their friends had any particularly refined culture at all. Culture in this narrower sense is more or less what is featured in the arts sections of newspapers – the visual arts, drama, literature, music and so on; although not just anything qualifies for inclusion here. Culture has to convey some kind of meaning. As already mentioned, it has to operate within systems of symbols that generate meaning and it must possess a clearly aesthetic element. This narrower sense of the word excludes what is purely functional, the kind of thing that is intended solely to be practical and of material benefit. Culture prefers to be seen as something beneficial in itself, but beneficial at a higher level, beneficial for the intellectual and psychological health of society and not just beneficial at a material level.

Culture of this symbolic–aesthetic kind is hard to find in other animals. As far as we can ascertain all behaviours in animals have practical motives. There are animals, however, that engage in decorating their nests and other constructions in a variety of ways, and some aspects of that process might be called art if it was done by a human being. But we have no reason to believe that animals have any symbolic or aesthetic motives that underpin their constructions.

More refined culture is limited to creatures that can handle net-works of symbols. Anyone who can do that can probably handle a language as well. Archaeological evidence of a more sophisticated culture is therefore evidence of a language-ready brain.

## CULTURAL FOSSILS

When we consider our extinct ancestors in this regard, we can, of course, only study the objects they left behind – or more particularly the tiny fraction of their property that has not been destroyed by the passage of time but preserved through the millennia and for millions of years. For very ancient times this involves only stones and bones. With a bit of luck it is also possible to find objects made of wood and horn from the last 500,000 years. But anything made of softer and more perishable material is gone. And immaterial cultural manifestations such as rituals, songs and dance cannot for obvious reasons be studied through archaeology. Furthermore, we cannot know anything directly about the way the people of that period thought and what they intended by the objects that have actually been preserved – and yet meaning and symbolism are essential elements of more refined culture. In archaeological terms culture will therefore tend to be defined simply as the non-functional, all the objects or qualities for which we can find no functional explanation but which resemble in some way what we call culture today.

Only a very small part of cultural production leaves evidence behind in materials that are sufficiently durable for archaeological study – sculptures and buildings in stone, paintings or etchings on permanent surfaces, ceramics and very little else – which means that any future archaeologists, a million years from now, will only be able to uncover a very limited view of the culture of our own time. There are ethnic groups whose entire culture will leave no archaeological traces at all because they use only perishable materials such as matting woven from leaves and wicker baskets. This should be taken into account when interpreting the cultures of the ancient past – or the lack of cultural remains from those times.

But even with that caveat in mind there is nothing to suggest that either the habilines or *Australopithecus* were any more cultural than chimps. They may have left material traces behind but these are purely functional.

Most researchers can find no clear evidence of culture in *Homo erectus* either. But the matter is much less obvious in this instance. There are disputed finds from the *erectus*-period that some researchers consider to be more than purely functional.

There are stones from the age of *erectus* that are vaguely

suggestive of human bodies and that may have been shaped by human hands. But there is no consensus as to whether they are true figurines or naturally occurring rocks. The one depicted on this page is roughly human shaped and six centimetres long. According to its discoverer, this is a stone whose natural shape was vaguely like a human and was then enhanced by someone who deepened and accentuated the grooves that make it human-like. There are also traces on the stone of what might be pigment. Other researchers, however, consider all these features to be the result of natural processes without any human intervention.

Seashells have also been found with geometric patterns scratched on their exteriors that were apparently etched by *Homo erectus* half a million years ago in what is now Indonesia. These may be uncomplicated patterns, a few zigzag lines, but they cannot

The Venus of Tan-Tan, 230,000 years old, found in present-day Morocco. Could be a hand-made figurine, or just a funny-shaped stone.

simply be explained away as the outcome of natural processes or as a functional human activity. Cutting the meat out of the shell-fish would leave a different pattern and could hardly have scratched the outside of the shell.

\* \* \*

My seven-year-old daughter Cassandra collects unusual stones, dead insects, snail shells and other odd things she comes across in nature. These might be specially shaped or coloured stones, or ones that glisten attractively or stand out from the usual pebbles in some way. Collecting things is a very common human hobby, and humans will collect absolutely anything, from pets to weapons. Collecting has no real function; it is something human beings do just for the pleasure of it. Although collecting provides no benefit, some people can become completely obsessed with it. What is it that drives contemporary human collectors and what conclusions can we draw about the way they think from their collecting?

  I used to collect stamps when I was much younger. Nowadays I do not do any collecting in that sense but devote a great deal of time to cataloguing and systematising my library and my music collection. Through a process of introspection I have been able to discern some of the factors that drive my collecting and arranging – it has a lot to do with order for me, with being systematic and exhaustive – a gap in a series causes a pang in the heart of every collector – but there is also the pleasure of owning something unusual, something not everyone else has.

\* \* \*

All that cataloguing requires an ability to be systematic, a capacity for ordering and arranging, and those qualities appear to be rare in the animal kingdom. The need to be exhaustive, the drive to fill gaps, requires an awareness of missing elements, an understanding of which additional objects the collection could contain even though they are not currently present. That kind of awareness is not something we have been able to identify in other animals either. Even when it comes to the kinds of collecting that animals should evidently have a Darwinian interest in practising – such as the collection of eggs the bird has in its nest – it has been shown that the parent birds are not good at knowing how many eggs there should be in the nest; they often fail to notice when researchers – or cuckoos – have interfered with their egg collection.

Anyone who can identify a gap in a collection demonstrates an ability to think about what is absent. And yet the ability to communicate about something absent, what is not here and now, is an essential feature of language, and one, common sense would tell us, that requires a speaker to be aware of what is missing and to be able to think about it.

But the first collections young people put together, like Cassandra's collection of natural objects just described, are not primarily characterised by their systematic quality or exhaustive nature; instead the emphasis here is on the unusual. This, too, requires a specific cognitive ability; it involves being able to distinguish between the usual and the unusual as well as an awareness of what sticks out from the herd. It requires a capacity to categorise objects based on their characteristics and an ability to notice how frequently those features recur in the surrounding world. Human language also makes use of our ability to categorise and to arrange characteristics in a sequence. And categorisation has already been proposed as an essential requirement for language by the pioneering linguist Eric Lenneberg.

To take this one stage further and not just notice things that are unusual but to pick them out and collect them requires curiosity and an interest in new things that is rare among other animals as well. For most animals the new and the unusual involve uncertainty, something to make them watch out. Collecting, therefore, is based on a combination of cognitive attributes and curiosity that seems to be uniquely human and that is of relevance to language. For this reason, prehistoric collecting may supply us with a clue to prehistoric language.

\* \* \*

It is not particularly uncommon at archaeological sites to find small stones and other minor items that have not been worked or fashioned by human hands but stand out in some way from the ordinary stones on the site, objects that have apparently been transported there from somewhere else. These are frequently stones of the type Cassandra was keen to gather, stones with bright colours or shiny patches. Do these just happen to be at the site or are they the work of prehistoric collectors?

Minor collections like these have not been found among the remains of the most ancient prehumans. They begin to appear, however, with the advent of *Homo erectus*, which could mean that *erectus* possessed both the same interest in the unusual and the same cognitive capacities as my Cassandra does.

\* \* \*

The kind of object *Homo erectus* is otherwise best known for are the hand axes we have already mentioned. These were produced in a standardised form and the vast majority are considered to be clearly functional tools, no doubt used for many different purposes just like a prehistoric Swiss army knife. Most of them are also just the right size and weight to be held in the hand while working. But that is not true of all of them. *Homo erectus* produced some gigantic "hand axes", during the latter part of their history for the most part, that had the standardised teardrop shape but were otherwise far too large and heavy to be used as tools. No-one has been able to come up with any practical function for these axes that would make sense.

It also appears as if *Homo erectus* occasionally selected unusual kinds of stone, or stones with unusual inclusions, as the raw material from which to produce their hand axes. These unusual materials were not suited at all to the tool in question. Even though *Homo erectus* mostly showed good sense with regard to the materials they used, on occasion they chose to make their axes out of rocks that were unsuitable in functional terms. The fact that these axes are made from the same kind of conspicuous stone that Cassandra collects may well be a clue.

Among millions of practical implements, why does there appear to be a tiny proportion that have been deliberately produced to be impractical? How are we to interpret this fact? It is a question that has generated a good deal of discussion among archaeologists, and the explanations that have been put forward revolve around these implements conveying some kind of meaning in addition to their function as tools. The message might be as simple as "Look how good I am at flaking stones", with the aim of increasing the status of the creator, or they may bear some deeper symbolic message or perhaps fulfil a ritual function?

All the possibly cultural objects we have discovered from the time of *Homo erectus* raise more questions, however, than they provide answers to. All these discoveries are contentious in one way or another and their interpretation is unclear. *But it is interesting that the first possible evidence of culture begins to appear among the same kind of humans that were probably the first talkers. This supports both the cultural interpretation of possible cultural artefacts and the linguistic interpretation of what may be trace evidence of language.*

\* \* \*

Eight men are slowly making their way deep inside a cave in what is now France. They all carry torches in their left hands. Even the faintest illumination fails to penetrate this far inside the cave when it is day, and night has already fallen. The torches can do no more than create tiny islands of light in the endless darkness surrounding them. Each man carries a bundle of firewood on his back, tied with a leather strap.

They emerge into a large cavern full of stalactites and stalagmites and other cave formations. The two young men who have not been here before take an inquisitive look around in the flickering flames of the torches. But as they continue on across the uneven floor of the cavern that light falls on something that will make them forget the hanging rocks.

In the middle of the vault is a circle that has been constructed from broken stalactites; the pieces have been piled on top of each other to form a wall, knee-high here and waist-high there. The men place their bundles of wood in little piles just inside the wall at regular intervals around the entire circumference. They then lean their torches cautiously against the wall. The leader of the group keeps hold of his though and moves a little deeper inside the cave to have a look round. Then he points to a stalactite that is just the right size, about as long and thick as his arm and calls over the two new men. They are told to break off the stalactite and they grab it roughly halfway up. Not too high up because then they will not have enough leverage, and not too low down because then they will just break off the tip. They need to break off a piece that is as long as possible to bring themselves and their tribe good fortune. It takes all their combined strength, but at the third attempt the stalactite cracks about four inches below the roof and they wobble at the sudden weight of a half-metre long stone column in their arms. The two young men carry their stalactite over to the circle and carefully add it to the wall where it is lowest.

The leader tells them to climb over the wall and step inside it and then kneel down with their faces to the ground. If they had had *sapiens* foreheads they could have rested on those but in their case it is their broad noses and prominent orbital ridges that make contact with the soft clay. The leader joins them inside, taking up a position opposite them. The other men, standing around the

Piece of Ochre with engraved pattern from the Blombos cave in what is now South Africa. The engraving was made between 70,000 and 100,000 years ago.

outside of the wall, pick up their torches and light the piles of firewood they brought with them. A ring of fire flares up along the inside of the wall. The two young men remain inside the circle with the leader facing them. The latter takes a piece of red ochre out of his wolf-skin cape and a sharp, newly knapped flint knife.

The initiation ritual can begin.

\* \* \*

Clearer evidence of culture that is more than simply practical handicraft begins to appear in the archaeological evidence from about 200,000 years ago, mainly among emergent *Homo sapiens* in Africa but also among Neandertals in Europe. The stalactite circle in the cave was constructed by Neandertals almost exactly 175,000 years ago. We do not know precisely what it was used for but it was found several hundred metres inside the cave, much further in than would be sensible or practical for residential purposes, and there are traces of fire on the stalactite pieces. It is

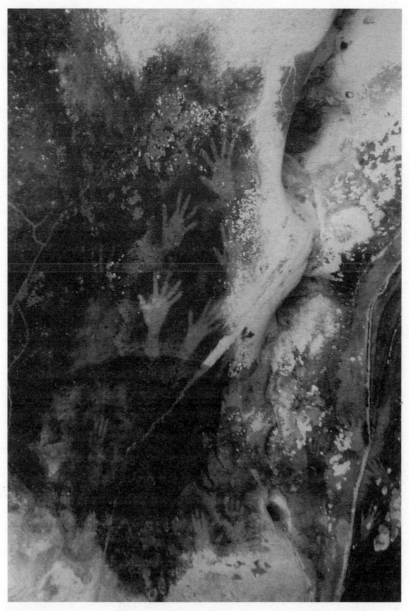

Painted handprints in the Pettakere cave on the Indonesian island of Sulawesi, one of the oldest known cave paintings, around 40,000 years old.

a reasonable supposition that a ritual of some kind took place at the site.

Interpreting the most ancient and extremely rare traces of culture remains problematic but what has gradually become increasingly clear is that the people of those times did not live by bread alone. Little by little they began to use pigment to add colour to objects and to make necklaces from seashells; they began to whittle figurines and engrave patterns on stones and fragments of bone until eventually they were able to produce the exquisite cave paintings that have been found at several sites around the world.

The view that used to prevail among archaeologists was that culture in this sense appeared rather suddenly around 40,000 years ago in Europe. But more recent finds combined with the reinterpretation of some older discoveries have proved that this is a misconception created by the predominance of Europe in the field at the time. There were quite simply so many more sites located in Europe that had already been explored and excavated that it created the impression that everything had begun in the caves on that continent. Some degree of prejudice against the rest of the world may have contributed to this, while prejudice against the Neandertals may have served to strengthen the notion that culture began among *Homo sapiens*.

In any case subsequent research, both less prejudicial and encompassing the entire planet, has demonstrated that the story is not that simple. Early forms of cultural expression are widely distributed in geographic terms, from Europe to South Africa to Indonesia. There are also no profound differences in this regard between the different varieties of humans who existed during this period, between 50,000 and 200,000 years ago.

Both Neandertals and early *Homo sapiens* used naturally occurring pigments to paint with. We have found traces of paint on seashells and other objects and we have also discovered pieces of ochre and other coloured minerals that were evidently used as chalks; they are worn at the tips the same way chalks are after use.

The Venus of Hohle Fels, a figurine discovered in Germany, carved 35,000 to 40,000 years ago.

What was coloured with these chalks is hard to say, but their wear patterns show that it was something soft, like skin or leather and not hard like rock or bone. A reasonable supposition would be that humans painted their own skin, using ochre as make-up and for body-painting. Many ethnic groups use various pigments for that purpose today. Lipstick is a Western variation on the same theme.

Ornaments and decorative objects of various kinds also have a long history. Early *Homo sapiens* liked to make necklaces of sea-shells – or we have discovered many seashells with holes in them at least – and in some of the shells the edges of the holes are worn as though a cord or a strap had run through the hole. One or two Neandertal finds of a similar kind, although not as many, have been discovered, both seashells and the teeth of predatory animals with holes in. The Neandertals would sometimes use the feathers of birds of prey as decoration instead, like the feather headdresses of the aboriginal population of North America, perhaps.

Engraved patterns of various kinds and on various surfaces also have a long history. They were etched on cave walls, on loose rocks, on bits of pigment, on seashells and no doubt on bits of wood and skins and other perishable materials. These are frequently simple patterns, of zigzag or criss-cross lines, whose meaning and func-tion are hard to interpret. But carving lines into stone is laborious and hardly something anyone would do to no purpose, without a reason important enough to justify all that labour.

Cave paintings of the classic kind, the celebrated paintings that the people of the Ice Age made in caves such as Lascaux in France and Altamira in Spain, have been found in many sites in Europe, and in recent years in the rest of the world as well. These are of a slightly more recent date than the chalks and necklaces; the oldest of them dates from around 60,000 years ago.[46] The paintings we

---

46 I should sound a note of caution here. The date of 60,000 years ago was published in a brand-new research paper shortly before the deadline for this book and has not yet been confirmed by other scientists. The oldest generally accepted date for cave paintings is about 40,000 years ago.

have discovered are often found very deep inside the caves, but is that because they were painted only there, or because what may have been painted on more exposed surfaces has not survived the elements over the millennia?

It was long believed that cave paintings were a purely European development, and this led to that continent being seen as the cradle of art. But only a few years ago, in 2014, equally ancient paintings were discovered in Indonesia, which has turned the prehistory of art on its head and demonstrated the danger of over-interpreting the absence of finds in parts of the world that have barely been explored.

Figurative art of considerable technical excellence is also a feature of some of the oldest paintings we have discovered; these

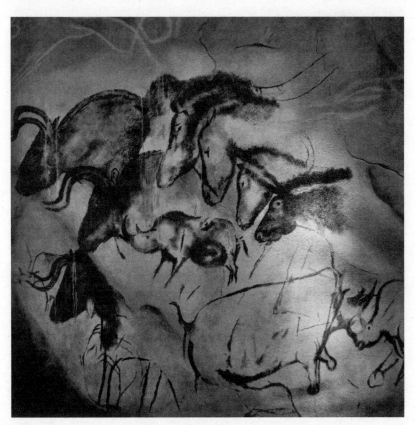

Image from the Chauvet cave in France, painted about 35,000 years ago.

are frequently of animal figures that are so well executed it is easy to identify which species they are meant to represent. Many of the oldest sculptures are so-called Venus figures, small figurines that obviously represent women but equally obviously do not represent any particular individual – no facial features are visible – and that are just the right size to fit into a pocket – if they had pockets at that time – or to be carried around in some other way. The Venus of Hohle Fels is the oldest undisputed representation of a human being.

Most cave paintings and clearly human figurines were produced by *Homo sapiens*. There are, however, some cave paintings in Spain whose date suggests that the artists were Neandertals, just as there are a small number of stones resembling humans that may have been fashioned by Neandertals.

What do these traces of prehistoric culture tell us about prehistoric language? They cannot tell us very much directly, but indirectly instead. As we noted at the beginning of this chapter, archaeological evidence of the use of symbols is also evidence of a symbol-ready brain. Archaeological evidence of art is also evidence of both the capacity and the desire to communicate – because that is what a cave painting is doing, or a face painting or a feather headdress.

*For a human who can handle symbols and wants to communicate, language cannot be far behind. And the archaeological evidence of symbolic culture ties in with the fossil evidence for language – possible traces among* erectus *and much clearer evidence among both Neandertals and early* Homo sapiens.

# The First Languages

A diverse mosaic of human languages exists at present, with thousands of languages that differ in myriad ways. That diversity is, however, not infinite, as we have seen; those languages all have a handful of features in common. Another shared facet of the languages of today is their almost infinite capacity to express human thought. All known languages possess that capacity; all languages possess enough words and grammatical refinements to express any and every thought on the part of their speakers. No-one today has a mother tongue that can reasonably be said to be more basic or more "primitive" than any other, just as no human alive today is more primitive than any other.

But things were different once upon a time. There were people then who lacked the full human capacity for language and cognition. What was their language like? This is extremely difficult to know, but we could make a start on trying to unravel its nature by looking at the problem the other way round and considering what features of today's languages really are absolutely essential for language to be language, and which features could be done without or could be different.

## WHAT ARE THE FEATURES LANGUAGE
## CAN DO WITHOUT?

A language that did not possess the features that every language has today would be a very different language from what we are used to. How different can a language be and still be called a language?

In the section on the characteristics of language we examined Hockett's list of its design features (see pp. 30–31) and concluded that it was only numbers six, ten and twelve in that list that were really essential:

- 6. Language is used intentionally.
- 10. Language can deal with matters other than the here and now.
- 12. Language is unreliable.

The list of features that all languages actually possess, and which came later in that section, looked like this:

- All languages have words in one form or another.
- All languages distinguish between nouns and verbs.
- All languages have interjections – exclamations such as Oh! Bravo! and Damn! – that exist slightly apart from the actual grammar of the language.
- All languages have a hierarchy of building blocks.
- All languages possess some kind of structure for combining the building blocks.
- All languages are open-ended systems, with the result that a speaker can coin new words.
- All languages are flexible systems, with the result that all speakers have room to manoeuvre.
- Grammatical rules apply to phrases and not to individual words.

- All languages can express an infinite number of different ideas; any human thought can be put into words in every human language.

What could we do without in this list? How much could we take away while leaving enough for what is left to justifiably be called a language?

If we take Hockett's list as our starting point, my view is that communication that is not intentional or deliberate should not be called language. This would not cause any major problems in terms of the origin of language because other apes are fully capable of communicating intentionally. What is lacking in their case is the conscious control of the speech apparatus, but language does not have to be based on the vocal tract – it could just as well be a sign language. Apes most definitely use gestures intentionally to communicate.

Hockett 10, concerning what is not here and now, is a vital feature of language. But when do children start referring to things other than the here and now? A child of just over one year of age can talk and talk a lot – but this is almost solely about what is happening in the present, or possibly about the things the child wants to exist here and now: *Mum! Biscuit!*

We call the child's communication language even though the child can only keep track of what is here and now. This is a feature, therefore, that a language need not have.

Hockett 12 is a bit trickier. If we assume, purely hypothetically, that there was a person who always told the truth we would call that person's speech language nonetheless. Lying is therefore not in principle an essential part of language. And yet what makes lying possible is that language is both flexible and cheap to use and those aspects are much harder to do without. It is hard to imagine a human language in which it was the language itself that made lying impossible.

In the second bullet list above there are several features that a basic language could in fact do without. It is possible to imagine a language that did not distinguish between nouns and verbs, or even failed to distinguish between word classes at all. It is also possible to imagine languages that are limited in some way and cannot express all the human thoughts of the day – a language, perhaps, that proved adequate for prehumans though it could only express prehuman thoughts, or one that could only be used within particular domains. All languages need not necessarily possess the range and flexibility that is the rule among the languages of today.

Interjections are another thing a language could manage without in principle. But they are an autonomous and rather primitive system that could very likely be older than existing systems of grammar. A stage in the evolution of language in which speech did not have interjections is rather unlikely.

In order to call something a language, however, I do think it must be an open-ended system. The communication systems of many animals are closed: they possess only a handful of different and innate sounds and cannot invent new ones. I would not call that a language. A communication system becomes a language only when it can be expanded with new words.

That also applies to the point that states that all languages *have* words. Without the concept of words in a language, it cannot be expanded by the addition of new ones and therefore words in one form or another would have to be part of it.

The remaining points on the list relate to hierarchy, structure and rules and they all have to do with grammar in one way or another. This brings us to the thorny problem of whether there can be a language without grammar. Views on this differ among linguists. It is primarily those researchers who are proponents of an innate grammar that consider grammar to be indissolubly linked to language. Others, including myself, do not consider grammar to be as crucial to the origins of language. In the same way that the very first linguistic utterances of babies – Mummy! – do not possess a grammatical structure, the very first precursors of language our ancestors produced may also have been unstructured.

*So if we then collect up these scattered pieces and consider what remains of language once we have taken away everything non-essential, all that is left is that language is used intentionally, that it has to be made up of words, and that the number of those words can increase. That much and no more.*

## THE SIMPLEST LANGUAGE

A language that is used intentionally, with words but no other structure and in which words increase in number: that, in my opinion, is pretty much how a one-year-old speaks. This is the simplest language that could reasonably be said to be a language, and it is also around this age that we begin to call the communication of the child a language. Could the first language of our ancestors have been something like this?

Learning to manage language at this limited level is also well within the bounds of what apes and a number of other animals can achieve. It is not something they will develop on their own, but with a bit of human help they have no difficulty understanding what the issue is and learning at least a few hundred words which they can use to communicate in a sensible way.

So the ability to manage a number of arbitrary symbols (words, signs and so on) and to associate them with as many different concepts exists in our closest relatives the primates, and probably existed in our ancestors before they had language. This may lead one to think that only fairly modest evolutionary hurdles would need to be overcome to get a language of this kind up and running.

But if it is that simple, why haven't chimps and parrots and other animals evolved language of this kind? Why did it occur only in our lineage?

In order for a language to be viable in the long term it has to be passed down from one generation to the next, with children acquiring it as they are growing up and then continuing to use it and passing it in turn on to their own children. It is not clear if this would really happen among primates. Some of the apes that have been taught a large number of signs by humans have by now had young, but even though there are anecdotal reports of the young apes in question spontaneously using one sign or another, there is no evidence that the whole system has been transmitted to any of them without human assistance. Neither the way apes communicate with their young nor the way those young apes learn from the adults favours the transmission of a sufficiently comprehensive linguistic system from one generation to the next. An infrastructure of this kind has to exist before language even in this limited form can be disseminated through the family lineage and continue to evolve.

And then we have the problem of how language could ever get started. Human children are very keen to communicate and possess sufficient linguistic drive to spontaneously invent and develop a basic language if a mother tongue is not supplied along with their breast milk – this has been observed among groups of deaf children who have had no contact with sign language. But that is not how apes operate. Even though they are entirely capable of learning words, they will not invent them out of nothing. There are, it is true, occasional reports from primate experiments of innovation in the use of signs, but these really are isolated incidents and by no means adequate to get a language started from zero.

*What is lacking among apes that is essential if the first language is to take off is not therefore something specifically linguistic. It involves creativity and social learning instead, the desire to invent something new and the capacity to transmit the new thing more widely within the group and down to future generations.*

But both inventiveness and a more reliable means of transmitting information between generations are qualities that our ancestors may have benefited from in other areas than language as well – this might have applied to the production of stone axes, or knowledge about edible roots, or anything else for that matter – and could therefore have an evolutionary explanation that need not be related to language. The first archaeological evidence we have for the stable transmission of information between generations involves hand axes as made by *Homo erectus*.

The same applies to the human cooperativeness and helpfulness we have already considered. They are essential to language and would need to have already been in place at this stage, although these traits need not have evolved for linguistic purposes.

*All the prerequisites for a protolanguage to come into being were therefore in place among* Homo erectus *– but not in any species before them.*

## WHAT FORM DID THE FIRST WORDS TAKE?

Nowadays both the words of speech and the signs of sign language are largely arbitrary as we have already observed when discussing Hockett's list of the features of language. They are therefore impossible to understand without having learned the language and without possessing it in a finished form that has been agreed upon by its speakers. There are isolated exceptions in spoken language such as the words for animal sounds (*miaow, moo*) and in sign language there are quite a few signs whose iconic origins can be guessed; the sign for "woman" in Swedish sign language, for example, is to make a rounded movement downwards across the chest with the hand, like cupping it around a female breast. Most signs in sign language cannot be understood, however, without having learned the language, and different sign languages are not mutually comprehensible.

There are a good many linguistic patterns that, while not directly imitative, are not entirely arbitrary either, and that occur in a wide variety of languages. For example while the word for "little" in most languages contains high bright vowels (such as "i") the word for "large" has dark low vowels (such as "a"). Words for round objects and qualities (round, ball, globe . . .) contain vowels that are pronounced with a rounded mouth remarkably often. And "mother" gets called something like "ma" or "na" in a huge number of tongues, even those that are not related. While all these patterns have their exceptions, like "small" and "big" in English, they are statistically significant nonetheless.

Such clues to the meaning of words are, however, a very marginal occurrence in the languages of the present day. If we want to make ourselves understood when we do not share a common language, we deploy a whole range of gestures, sounds, body language and mime instead to make our words as easy to guess as possible. We might even stage an entire little pantomime in the hope of getting our message across.

This is probably what our ancestors did too as they were getting started on communicating with something like language. Words in their modern form require us to have already reached agreement about what means what. But before that agreement could be arrived at, other ways of getting your message across had to be used and the message would have been couched in a way that made it possible to work out its meaning without any previous agreements.

The way chimps communicate demonstrates certain aspects of this process: they use various gestures in a flexible manner to make it possible for the other to work out from the context what the message is. But chimps do not seem to use the form of the gestures to assist the transmission of the message; they do not use representational (mimetic) gestures or sounds, at least not ones that we can perceive. It is as if they have failed to understand how that entire aspect of the process could help them communicate. This may have to do with the kind of creativity that chimps lack.

The very first words ought therefore to have possessed a free and creatively self-explanatory form, with the speaker using all the means at their disposal to make things easier for the listener, in what is clearly an ostensive-inferential communicative process (see pp. 41–42). But that kind of communication is slow and indirect. Modern humans in this kind of situation would quickly reach agreement on how to simplify the messages. Researchers have carried out a number of experiments in a variety of set-ups in which human beings are forced to communicate without any kind of language. A consistent result of these experiments is that while people began with the same self-explanatory messages that we discussed above, after only a few rounds of the experiment, they started making shortcuts and simplifying the forms of communication and fairly soon the participants had reached tacit agreements about what means what, and the elements of the system had become more like the arbitrary words of modern language and completely incomprehensible to anyone not party to the agreement.

Were our ancestors capable of simplifying in this way? This is hard to determine for sure, but the answer is probably yes. After all, even chimps can manage to keep track of what a basic arbitrary sign means, even though they cannot spontaneously invent signs of their own to any great extent. So there is no reason to believe that the first language remained representational and self-explanatory for any length of time; its speakers rapidly reached agreement instead about simplified and standardised forms of the most common of the first words at least.

*This protolanguage was probably neither a purely spoken nor a purely signed language. There would be no reason for speakers to limit themselves in this creative phase to one or the other.*

What may have imposed a limitation, on the other hand, is how far our capacity to imitate sounds had developed. Our ancestors would surely have possessed a range of ready-made sounds of the same kind as other apes, but using the voice in a more flexible way than that would have required an evolutionary adaptation in the control of the vocal apparatus. The demands made by that first language may have propelled the change and in that case only a limited repertoire of sounds would have been used initially before the range of options was extended. Alternatively vocal control could have evolved for other purposes – singing or call imitation or whatever it may have been – in which case both signs and speech would have been completely available from the beginning of language.

## Atomistic or Holistic?

The idea that a protolanguage existed in roughly this form, with word-like units but without an internal structure or any real grammar, is a view prevalent among researchers. Another commonly held view is that the words in this protolanguage functioned roughly like words do today, with a similar range of meaning so that every word stood for a particular concept. There may have been a word that meant "rabbit" and another word that meant "hunt" and so on. After that it was up to the speaker to use these words creatively to get his or her message across.

An alternative notion that has a good many adherents is that each word in the protolanguage stood instead for what would be a whole sentence in a modern language. In which case there would not be a word that meant "rabbit" but a word instead that meant "Let's hunt rabbits", and another word that meant "Let's hunt mammoths", and so on. These words are still supposed to have been coherent units without internal structure, just like normal words but with a more complex and composite meaning. This is referred to as a holistic protolanguage.

An atomistic language, in which each word has a basic meaning, would allow language to develop in a grammatical direction as words were combined into longer sentences. But holists propose instead that their holistic "words" were subsequently assigned an internal grammatical structure and subdivided into the standard kind of word.

When children are developing their mother tongue they do so primarily in atomistic fashion. A child's first words are atomistic words for particular concepts, not holistic ones that represent whole sentences. When children have to solve the gavagai problem we previously referred to (see p. 190), the concepts they start with are atomistic ones. The children then combine a couple of atomistic concepts at a time into their first sentences and then make progress in that way. Everything we know about the language of children argues against a holistic protolanguage.

A holistic protolanguage would also inevitably have been a restricted language that could only express a moderate range of messages. A new word would have to be invented for every new message to be expressed, unlike an atomistic language in which it is easier to repurpose words to suit new contexts.

Views are divided as to when we were supposed to have spoken holistically. According to Steven Mithen and Michael Arbib, the holistic protolanguage survived until a fairly late state in human evolution, as late as early *Homo sapiens*, while Alison Wray places the transition earlier on – among *Homo erectus* perhaps.

As envisaged, the process of moving from holistic expression to grammatical language is also problematic. The idea is that, purely by chance, expressions with partially overlapping meanings also happen to have partially overlapping forms, and it is these overlaps that would form the foundation for the division of the holistic words into part words with atomistic meanings, while at the same time the whole expression was reanalysed as a grammatical structure rather than as a single word. A considerable amount of pure luck would be required for this to work at all, and our ancestors would also have had to undergo a complete change in outlook at some point if they were to start dismantling a language that was working perfectly well.

*This is why I do not regard the idea of a holistic protolanguage as a realistic alternative but will continue to assume that the proto-language was an atomistic one. The first words ought to have had the same range of meaning as those of today.*

## THE FIRST GRAMMAR

The simplest protolanguage that I described above would not have had any real grammar. Many people imagine that every utterance in that language simply consisted of a single word, roughly the way a one-year-old talks today. Utterances made up of just one word are rarely unambiguous; they need context and puzzle communication in order to work. A one-year-old who says "milk" might mean she wants to have milk, or she has spilled the milk, or just that she can see the milk bottle – Dad has to puzzle out the exact meaning from the context, which usually works fine.

But even without grammar there would have been no real barrier to a speaker uttering several words one after the other. No grammar simply means that there are no rules for how the words may be combined; it does not mean that it is forbidden to utter more than one word at a time.

Apes that have learned sign language talk more or less like that. They can often use more than one sign in the same utterance, but their sign combinations do not follow any apparent grammatical rules. Apes seem to simply lump together a pair of signs that fit in with what they want to say and then the listener has to puzzle out how the signs are supposed to relate to each other. When chimps in the wild use their natural gestures and sounds they will also combine several gestures and/or sounds in the same utterance.

There are a handful of examples from other animals where a combination of two sounds appears to take on a meaning that is not just the sum of the separate meanings of the two sounds. The Diana monkeys of West Africa have several different warning cries, much like the vervets we have already encountered. But the

Diana monkeys have some additional sounds that are used to modify and refine those warning calls. In their "language" *krak* means acute leopard danger, and *boom* is a warning for something other than a predator, such as falling branches. But the combination *boom-boom-krak* does not mean that there are both leopards and branches in the vicinity – instead this combination means that there is a leopard in the area but the danger is not imminent. If the ending *-ooo* is added to a warning call instead, it makes it more general and less acute: *hok* on its own is a warning for eagles, but *hok-ooo* is a more general warning to keep a lookout upwards.

In all likelihood combining a couple of signs or sounds, at least in the same pragmatic fashion as the chimps, or even in the more formalised manner of the Diana monkeys, is something our ancestors could have been expected to manage without any great difficulty.

Unstructured utterances made up of several words ought therefore to have formed part of the protolanguage right from the start.

\* \* \*

What modern humans will often do when telling someone about something – and when language is not available – is to perform a mime in which gestures and sounds are used to depict the sequence of events to be described. There is a natural structure to the narrative in a mime of this kind that corresponds to the structure of the chain of events. If mime stories like this were a component of pre-grammatical language they might have provided a stepping stone to linguistic grammar as a result of that natural structure eventually becoming standardised and conventional.

But this would require that the protolanguage was used for telling stories, which cannot be taken for granted. Primates do not seem at all inclined to tell stories. Even those apes that have been given enough language training to be able, in purely linguistic terms, to provide an account of something that has occurred rarely do so. The communication systems of primates are remarkably instrumental instead: they communicate when they want something, not simply to describe something happening.

There is a clear difference in attitude between our relatives and ourselves in this regard. Human children start to tell stories as soon as they have enough language to do so, and they don't stop telling their parents about everything they are doing until they are teenagers.

Telling stories for the sake of it forms a considerable part of all human language use, whereas instrumental communication accounts for a much more modest proportion. And yet stories make very different demands on the linguistic tools at our disposal. Telling people you want something works even without any grammatical refinements, as every one-year-old knows.

*However, describing a sequence of events requires some kind of linguistic structure to relate those various events to each other, and so make clear who did what to whom and in what order. It is here somewhere that the roots of a need for grammar must lie.*

In terms of the chronology it is hard to date this development with any accuracy. It must have occurred after the first protolanguage came into being with *Homo erectus* just over one million years ago, but it is extremely difficult to say *how* long after. It is highly probable that it was before our shared common ancestor with the Neandertals roamed the earth about half a million years ago. But that still leaves 500,000 years or more in play. The issue of the dating is also dependent on how difficult it may have been for someone with an unstructured protolanguage to progress to a grammatical language, and how much biological evolution that would have required.

Grammar would probably have begun at a simple, practical level, with a few rules or formalised structures and with clauses that were constructed on a natural semantic basis. Several experiments have been conducted in which human beings have been instructed to give an account of events in mime form without using language. Irrespective of the grammatical structures of the mother tongue, one pattern has turned out to predominate in these pantomimes. The semantically pivotal noun – what the account is actually about – is presented first in that pattern, followed by any other factors, while what took place – which would correspond to the verb in a clause – is presented last. Longer stories are structured as a sequence of simple clauses of this kind, normally in chronological order.

If a protolanguage with atomistic words were available, it ought to be straightforward to replace parts of the mime with the corresponding words, particularly for concepts that are difficult to mime. Eventually, perhaps, all the mime elements would be replaced by words, and it is at this point that we can envisage a language with a minimal grammar, a language in which simple sentences containing subject, verb and object can be uttered. Clearly this would not require any advanced form of innate grammar and all that would be needed would be the kind of conceptual ability to structure a sequence of events that we spontaneously employ in a mime.

The Nicaraguan sign language we mentioned previously possessed this kind of structure in its earliest stages of development. Simple phrases could be signed, but sentences could not be put together out of clauses and the number of participants that could be described in a clause was extremely restricted. More complex sequences of events involving a greater number of participants would be described using several separate sentences. It was not possible to say, "The woman pushed the man so he fell to the ground", this had to be expressed instead as, "Woman pushes. Man falls," in two separate sentences with a tiny pause between them. The causal connection between the two sentences was something listeners had to work out for themselves in a puzzle-communicative process. A good deal can be expressed in this way with the kind of grammar a two-year-old – or maybe even a linguistically trained chimp – should be able to handle. While chimps have not shown any sign of being able to produce sentences with any real grammar, they can combine two words into meaningful utterances. What is also required, however, is the desire to tell a story and an ability to keep the thread of the story in mind that chimps evidently lack – although it is not their grammatical ability that is the primary shortcoming.

Storytelling and the ability to perform a mime were probably the parents of grammar. But how did we become storytellers? The narrative scenarios we looked at in the chapter on the first subject of conversation are looking more likely.

## THE EVOLUTION OF THE LANGUAGE INSTINCTS

So how did we make progress in our use of language? Thus far in this chapter I have not postulated any language-specific form of biological evolution; everything has been based instead on abilities that are either present in chimps or ought to have been present in our ancestors before there was language.

What happens if we assume that our ancestors had a proto-language along the lines of the one sketched out above and allow evolution to run its course from that point? Whatever the exact function of the protolanguage, let us assume that that function was sufficiently important to make being good at the protolan-guage an advantage in Darwinian terms.

Nowadays virtually every human being possesses a language faculty that is perfectly adequate, and even if there is a genetic component to the remaining amount of variation it is only of modest significance. But there is reason to believe that the differ-ences were greater when language was new because evolution usually weeds out variation for important abilities and reduces the differences within a species – not because of any inherent drive towards equality but simply because the descendants of those best adapted are soon all that remain. The modest variation that exists today is the outcome of Darwinian selection over many generations.

So what kind of characteristics would be selected for in an evolutionary process of this kind, among human beings who have recently been endowed with language? Let us recall that other primates are not good at inventing new words and that the young of other primates are not good at learning a mother tongue, even if their mother had a mother tongue they could learn. Our ancestors who first used language must have performed well enough on both counts, although there would certainly still have been both variation and room for improvement.

What is particularly striking about the language faculty of modern human beings is how quickly, easily and eagerly children learn languages. This suggests that it has long been important in evolutionary terms to acquire language quickly as children – children evidently have evolutionary adaptations for doing so.

The characteristics in children that would have been selected for by evolution are those that favour children learning languages quickly and easily: paying attention to language in the immediate environment, beginning to practise speech sounds early on, learning words easily and using the words the child knows readily and often.

These characteristics correspond closely enough to the language instincts that everyone agrees human children do in fact possess. It is likely that these language instincts evolved gradually, beginning from the protolanguage stage, so that generation after generation of children became better and better at learning their proto-mother-tongue. A good many of these instincts could be regarded as extreme versions of general cognitive faculties that were already present among primates with some degree of variation – that variation can be observed today in the apes that have been trained linguistically: some individuals are both more interested and better at learning words than others. That same variation provides useful raw material for the evolution of language instincts.

Systematic evolutionary pressure could then drive changes far and fast as long as there was sufficient variation for Darwinian forces to work with – think how humans have managed over a few thousand years to breed domestic dogs, from minor variations in wolves to extreme characteristics in all directions – and if rapid learning was important enough over a sufficiently long period, it would not be surprising for our children to have become so extraordinarily good at language acquisition.

While children were evolving to become better and better at learning languages, the evolution of language was also coming to meet them more than halfway. With each passing generation, language was becoming better and better adapted to being learned by children.

*This is a process of mutual adaptation with both children and language becoming better adapted to each other. The adaptation of language would have occurred more quickly, however, with the result that all the adaptations that could come about within language itself would probably occur there rather than through biological evolution in children.*

But there are some processes that would favour biological adaptations in children nonetheless, as they cannot be resolved by changes in language. Learning all the words of the language, for instance, must have constituted a bottleneck for children that could not be resolved linguistically unless the vocabulary of language was restricted. There must therefore have been a constant Darwinian pressure on the children to get better at learning words even at the protolanguage stage, with the result that our children can learn several new words a day without apparent effort.

## CONSTRUCTING GRAMMAR

How do we get from a protogrammar containing only simple clauses to the complex grammatical network that characterises human languages today? The possibility of stringing one clause after the other in the same utterance would be one first step that we have already considered. This is not a huge leap in itself and would not require any real grammatical advance. Both speaker and listener need to keep several elements in mind at the same time, and it is particularly important that they understand the chronological arrangement of those elements. These are not abilities that are evident in other animals but they are of key importance for both narrative and grammatical language.

Another step to be taken has to do with reference, making clear exactly what the speaker is talking about. If the speaker uses the word "woman" in an utterance, how does the listener know which woman is being referred to? The problem of reference would have been with us right from the start, even in the protolanguage where only one word is used at a time, but it becomes acute as language becomes more complex. There are several different tools in modern languages to help the listener solve these problems. Languages normally distinguish, for example, between a new addition to the conversation and what has already been mentioned; this can be done in English by using the indefinite or definite article – if you say "the woman" instead of "a woman" the listener knows that you are not referring to a new and unfamiliar woman but to someone who has been previously mentioned or who the listener can be expected to be able to identify in some way.

Languages also possess a broad range of techniques for specifying the people or things referred to in various ways – "the young woman", "the young dark-haired woman in the red dress who we saw at the party yesterday", and so on. At least some of these methods appear relatively early in a child's development of language and may also have been early components of the protolanguage as well. What children come up with first are adjectival designations – quite young children are able to say "big dog" or "red ball" – and similar variants may very well have been part of the repertoire in even the most basic sentences of the protolanguage. The example "Woman pushes. Man falls" could have started with "Woman old", "Woman pregnant", or something similar to specify which woman is being referred to.

* * *

Some of the examples of basic sentences above are a combination of what would be called a noun and a verb in modern languages. But an understanding of the parts of speech would not have been required for quite some time. Some researchers have discussed whether the first words were nouns or verbs, but this would not have been a meaningful distinction at that stage. It is possible to refer to parts of speech when grammar takes on more a robust form and various groups of words are restricted to different positions in the grammatical structure, but we are a very long way from that stage at this point in our reconstruction of the protolanguage.

A more meaningful analysis would surely involve considering the structure in the proto-sentences of the protolanguage as being of the "topic-comment" kind, where topic is what the sentence is about and comment tells us something new about the topic. Woman is the topic in both "woman old" and "woman pushes" while the comment adds the information that she is old or doing the pushing. Neither topic nor comment are fixed to particular parts of speech although the topic is often a noun.

The topic-comment structure may be linked to the linguistic patterns we described earlier that consist of correlations between word orders in different types of phrases in the same language. In a proto-sentence with a topic-comment structure, the topic can either come first or last, and it really makes no difference which as long as there is an agreement about how the arrangement is to be understood. The patterns of word order can be similarly described in relation to an underlying structure in which the most important word in the phrase comes either first or last. Perhaps this is how the topic-comment structure is reflected in modern formal grammar?

In most languages today it is possible to use small clauses of this topic-comment kind, although they are rarely described in formal grammar handbooks and are sometimes considered to be abbreviations of complete sentences. They are characterised as being restricted to two to three words, with those words not always being inflected as they normally are. Verbs are frequently lacking and the sentences will often be set phrases for use in social situations. One example of a phrase of this kind is the motto for Alfred E. Neuman, the fictitious lead character in the *Mad* comic: "What, me worry?" One pattern to emerge here is that the phrases are used either as requests or to express astonishment. While very common in speech these phrases are not often encountered in written language.

Some researchers consider these phrases to be a kind of linguistic fossil, remnants from the protolanguage phase. The Serbian-American linguist Ljiljana Progovac regards them as the key to the origins of language.[47] Other basic elements of language, such as interjections, have also been discussed as possible linguistic fossils.

\* \* \*

Yet another way of specifying the referent, and one that is far from trivial, is simply to point – if you say "woman" while pointing at

47 Progovac, L., *Evolutionary Syntax* (2015) – Progovac provides many more examples of the kind of topic-comment clause described here: "Case closed!", "Him retire?", "Everybody out!", "Me first!", "John a doctor?"

a female person in the vicinity there can be no doubt about who you mean. Pointing with the fingers continues to be used as a supplement to language: if you look carefully at people talking you will see a good many pointing gestures intended to assist with making the references specific. Pointing has also been incorporated into language itself, in the form of demonstrative expressions such as "this one" and "that one", and so on.

Methods would have been required early on, particularly in narrative contexts, for positioning an entire sentence in time and space, expressing where and when – and whether – something happened. What in both English and Swedish and many other languages is rendered by sentence adverbs such as "yesterday", "perhaps", "not", "over there" ought also to have formed an early component of the grammar.

Initially various informal methods of referring to things and people would surely have been used pragmatically and creatively; the speaker would have employed all the means to hand to give the listener enough clues as to what is being alluded to. This could still have occurred in a linguistic context of basic sentences. But if the sentences remain short, containing only two or three elements in each one, there can be so many sentences in an utterance that keeping tabs on how the sentences relate to each other soon becomes a problem. That problem can be solved either by linking the sentences to each other in an appropriate way or by combining several sentences into one.

Combining sentences can be done by permitting several components in each sentence. Instead of saying separately: "Woman old. Woman pushes," the two sentences can be joined together to make: "Woman old pushes." But as soon as we have more than two or three components in a sentence, rules of some kind are required to determine how the relationships between those components are to be interpreted. It is here we are beginning to approach true grammar even though a great deal of grammatical complexity remains to be developed.

*The logical and mathematical structure of the very first grammar was actually no more advanced than that of birdsong and would not have required any specifically biological evolution of our ancestors' grammatical abilities. In terms of date we are still in the same period as the previous section, somewhere between 500,000 and one million years ago.*

## HIERARCHICAL GRAMMAR

What has been largely absent from the protolanguage up to this point is a hierarchical structure within and between sentences. The possibility of replacing words with entire phrases has been lacking, as has the possibility of combining several clauses into a more complex sentence that contains main and subordinate clauses. Both of these make new demands on the language faculty and require above all an ability to manage larger units as just that: units, and not simply a collection of words. Speakers need to be able to juggle both phrases and clauses as entire units and to maintain a hierarchy of clauses within sentences and phrases within phrases. Now it may well be the case that not every human language has to make use of all these possibilities – the language Pirahã, which was mentioned earlier, may not do so – but every human being has the capacity to cope with hierarchies of these kinds.

Being able to handle the combination of separate elements in hierarchies is rare in the communication systems of other animals. One exception are songbirds such as the nightingale, which appears able to manipulate phrases as movable units that can be combined in its song. There are animals, however, including some primates, that can manage simple hierarchies within their conceptual framework, even though they do not employ them in communication. Baboons, for example, keep track of their social hierarchies, which among certain species are structured on two levels and function a bit like human clan societies. Each baboon is a member of a clan and has a status within the clan, but then there is also a ranking order between the clans in a troop. A conflict between two individuals from different clans becomes a conflict between those clans. This is why a baboon needs to understand status and power at both the individual and the clan level, and researchers have been able to show that they do so.

People can manage considerably more than this, both in linguistic and other contexts. We find it easy to keep track of hierarchies and handle combinations of units in many different fields. The majority of the hierarchy management that human beings do in their natural state would, however, appear to be in social situations, which makes it likely that this is an ability that evolved out of something similar to the clan awareness of the baboons. Humans can generalise and employ their cognitive abilities in new contexts, but it has proved difficult to find evidence of this among other primates. One very common trend within the cognitive evolution of humans would appear to be that we are able to extend the range of our conceptual tools for general use, the same tools that are often present in some form in other animals but which they only employ in specific contexts.

Have our cognitive skills at managing social hierarchies become generalised in similar fashion so that they can be used for other purposes, including communication?

* * *

In computing contexts it is very common to have to manage composite data structures as units while combining them into hierarchical structures. Programming languages achieve this in slightly different ways, but every modern computer language possesses the tools to do so. Behind the screen of the computer, this process is managed using pointers and dynamic memory allocation in various forms.[48]

Human memory is, however, structured very differently to that of a computer. This is not just because it is made up of neurons rather than semi-circuits – it possesses a different kind of logical structure and is addressed differently as well. It is therefore by no means self-evident how something like a pointer could be made to work in our brains. Our knowledge about how memory is managed in the brain is, moreover, far from complete. But in order for us to be able to do the kind of things we actually do with our minds, both in linguistic and other contexts, we would need something functionally equivalent to the pointer in the computer example. How these can then be implemented in the wetware of the brain is another story, which I have no intention of being drawn into.

It remains unclear to what extent other animals would need to have pointers in their head for what they do. A nightingale might need one, but then only for the sake of its singing; there is nothing to suggest that nightingales can think hierarchically about anything other than songs. The hierarchical thinking that baboons do might conceivably be more capable of being generalised:

---

48 In simplified terms, the memory of a computer can be seen as a long sequence of numbered compartments. A value can be placed in each compartment, and the number of the compartment recorded in order to retrieve the value when required. Although a pointer is an ordinary memory compartment, what turns it into a pointer is that the value stored there is the number to another compartment where the value you actually want to access is located. Dynamic memory allocation refers to a situation when a program that is running on the computer need not have specified in advance exactly how many and which particular compartments it will use; instead, while the program is operating, it can ask for a group of compartments "on the fly" when it needs them. The program can store a number of values that serve as a kind of unit in compartments of this kind. The program then keeps track of which compartments it was assigned for that group by storing a pointer in another compartment that points to the first compartment in the group concerned.

baboons appear to be better at thinking about their hierarchies than nightingales are about their songs. But there is no clear-cut evidence for the existence of more general pointer systems in the minds of other animals.

*Our ability to do with our minds what computers achieve using pointers and dynamic memory allocation may have been a vital breakthrough in the evolution of human thinking.*

The way pointers are managed opens up the possibility of both hierarchical grammar in language and different forms of abstract hierarchical thinking in other contexts, which we are significantly better at than other animals. For this reason it is unlikely that our pointer management is language-specific, even though language is a heavy user of that system.

This new system of memory allocation presumably required biological changes to occur in the brain, but we know far too little about how memory works to say anything meaningful about what such changes may have entailed or how difficult they were in evolutionary terms to initiate. It is also difficult to provide any definite answer to the question as to what would have been the evolutionary driver of such a change, even if suspicion naturally falls on the nascent hierarchical grammar.

\* \* \*

We have mentioned recursion, the concept of something referring to itself and by so doing building layer after layer of units of the same kind (see p. 169). It is primarily within the generative paradigm that the possibility of recursion within grammar is considered to be a vital and essential feature of language, maybe even its defining feature. But if we possess a general system for handling pointers and composite units then we get recursion into the bargain, or as good as. All that is really required is that the unit the pointer points to should be allowed in its turn to contain pointers that point to further units. If you can handle chains of pointers in that way, you can handle recursive tree structures. For this reason it is unlikely that recursion required any additional biological changes beyond pointer management.

*  *  *

If we now dispense with memory allocation and computer analogies and return to true grammar, there are two ways of progressing from basic sentences towards a more hierarchical grammatical structure: by linking two sentences together and by inserting a sentence within another one. Linking probably came first, as it appears to be easier.

In modern languages the relationship between sentences is normally expressed by linking words of various kinds, usually those known as conjunctions. The simplest example of a linking word of this kind is "and", which simply signals that two sentences or clauses belong together without specifying in greater detail the nature of the connection between them. Other connecting words are "but", which expresses the opposite kind of relationship between two sentences, and "then", which expresses chronological order. Most modern languages have a wide range of conjunctions of this kind that can be used to relate sentences and clauses to each other in various ways.

*  *  *

It is here that we begin to see the first function words appear: the first words that do not refer to something in the surrounding world but have a purely intralinguistic function. As previously noted, all words of this kind essentially derive from content words: they are words that originally meant something concrete, but have now been recycled to serve a grammatical function through the process known as grammaticalisation (see p. 130). Grammatical endings and other forms of morphology regularly arise in this way.

Provided our ancestors could get the process of grammaticalisation going, we no longer need to concern ourselves with the origin of function words. If the protolanguage only contained content words, the evolutionary processes of language itself would produce the functional words required soon enough.

This also turns out to be how the users of the language develop grammatical markers whenever researchers have been able to observe the birth of a language. Newborn languages, such as Nicaraguan sign language or the pidgin languages that have arisen in various parts of the world, basically start with only content words, but they rapidly convert certain content words to grammatical functions. The language Tok Pisin is currently one of the official languages of Papua New Guinea. It has developed out of the pidgin languages that came into being from the encounter between English-speaking colonisers and the aboriginal Papuans in New Guinea. It is a fully creolised language today, but many of its grammatical markers can still be recognised as English content words. For example *bilong* (from English "belong") marks the possessive and *pela* (from English "fellows") marks the plural of pronouns. In Tok Pisin a classical prayer begins *Papa bilong mipela*. *Mi* means "I" (from English "me") and that makes *mipela* the plural of "I", which is "We", and with *bilong mipela* a possessive marker is added that transforms "we" to "our" and thus we get: "Our Father".

If our ancestors were able to use their protolanguage both creatively and like a puzzle, which they would surely have had to do in order to get a working language going, I find it hard to see how anything could have stopped them from completing the same kind of manoeuvres that the Papuans performed in developing Tok Pisin.

\* \* \*

Simply connecting two sentences by lining them up side by side with a linking word between them is really not that demanding in grammatical terms. To go from "Woman pushes. Man falls" to "Woman pushes *and* man falls" hardly seems like an insurmountable challenge. Each sentence still retains the grammatical structure it had before. All that has to be added is an overarching structure that keeps the two sentences in order. If we continue with the pointer analogy, this bridging structure needs to consist of two pointers and the conjunction. This arrangement thus becomes a grammatical parallel to the overarching semantic structure that must already have existed to allow the listener to be able to keep the relationship between the sentences semantically in order. An interesting though unanswered question is to what extent the semantic structure can be used as scaffolding on which to hang the grammatical structure. The latter is after all more or less identical, at this stage at least, with the former, even though the linkage is less constrained in modern languages.

Adding new structures inside the sentence is a little more advanced. Whether we are working with a generative or a constructionist grammar, pointers will be required at the heart of the superordinate sentence, or some other comparable means will be necessary to maintain the subordinate structure as a unit.

But here, too, we can begin with baby steps. Returning to our example of the pushing woman, we can see how a coordination of "Woman old. Woman push" leads first to "Woman old and woman pushes". The speaker soon realises that it is unnecessary in puzzle-communicative terms to repeat the word "woman". It is enough to say "Woman old *and* pushes" for the listener to be able to work out that the woman is the subject in both clauses and there are two different comments about her. From there it is not too far-fetched to enclose one sentence entirely within the other so that you get: "{[Woman old] pushes}", where I have used different kinds of parentheses to show the structure of the sentence. "Woman old pushes" may initially have been uttered for purely practical reasons by lazy speakers who were relying on listeners to do the puzzling out bit, and would only be analysed as a hierarchy of clauses subsequently.

* * *

Another phenomenon that would evolve at this stage is what the linguist Tecumseh Fitch calls "dendrophilia". To those of us who know Greek this word might suggest "tree huggers", but Fitch defines it instead as a predilection for making hierarchical structures and for finding – or inventing – hierarchical structures in everything that can be seen and heard. A love of hierarchies definitely exists among humans; we are keen to discover them in all manner of things. A dendrophilia of this kind gets us past the chicken-and-egg problem that would otherwise occur in the evolution of language – when the first speaker who started to use hierarchical grammar had finished speaking, what listener would have been able to interpret what had been said hierarchically? Fitch solves that problem by having the listener be the one to begin to use a hierarchical structure by making an analysis of utterances in which the speaker has merged a couple of sentences for purely practical reasons, and without any hierarchical ulterior motives – as in the example above. In the presence of listeners who can handle that much, the speaker can go on to construct hierarchies to his heart's content.

*From this point, the continued refinement of grammar would probably have been driven largely by the cultural evolution of language rather than the biological evolution of the language users. Grammaticalisation would, no doubt, already have started but cultural evolution would also have been prompted by the creativity of the language users in finding increasingly sophisticated ways of communicating increasingly complex messages.*

As language became more complex there would also have been a continued biological evolution of our ability to learn and employ language. The language instincts we have already referred to would gradually have been sharpened and refined in an inter-action with the increasing complexity of language itself. No revolutionary biological novelties would have been required, however, once we had pointer handling at our disposal.

* * *

*What is described here was a gradual evolution rather than a sudden leap. We did not acquire grammar overnight – but it is very difficult to know whether the time it took was relatively brief or lengthy from an archaeological perspective.*

Cultural evolution can take place so quickly that it may appear sudden to an archaeologist, and fairly simple biological changes can occur in the course of a few millennia as well. But how quickly it actually happened will also depend on which evolutionary driving forces were involved. And that will depend in turn on how important it was to our ancestors, in the world they lived in, to become even better at learning and using language. This is very difficult to ascertain, and grammatical evolution of this kind leaves no archaeological evidence behind. But technological and cultural progress can provide us with clues nonetheless. To all intents and purposes, *Homo erectus* remained at the same technical and cultural level for a million years, but then progress took off about 500,000 years ago and it has been accelerating ever since. If I was forced to guess when grammar evolved, I would estimate that it followed the same chronology as technical progress: starting with a grammar-less protolanguage among *Homo erectus* and then gradually followed by more and more sophisticated grammar being used by the various humans who evolved from *erectus*. The basic grammatical machinery ought to have been in place 500,000 years ago and a fully developed human language faculty would either have appeared rapidly thereafter – in which case it would also have been shared by the Neandertals – or evolved more gradually, only to reach its fully fledged modern form in early *Homo sapiens* about 200,000 years ago. However, the dating of the most recent common ancestor to all modern humans to just over 100,000 years ago establishes a firm deadline: if the language faculty had not been fully formed by then, it would not be identical in every modern ethnic group all over the world, which it is. And the parallel technical and cultural development of both Neandertals and *sapiens* right up until almost the time that the Neandertals became extinct, together with the fraternisation that did occur, argue against there being any radical difference in linguistic ability between the two branches of our family tree.

*In any case the outcome are people like you and me who can speak a language freely and instinctively that contains thousands of words and possesses subtle rules for how those words can be combined to express each and every thought that occurs to us; a language, moreover, that we learned freely and instinctively as babies.*

## WHERE WAS THE FIRST LANGUAGE SPOKEN?

Was there one single language that was the very first language, that was spoken by a particular people at a particular place and time? If language had arisen as the result of a single supermutation, then the answer would have been a definite YES. It was really not that simple, however. Conversely, in my scenario for the origin of language, it is hard to put your finger on any particular stage in the process and say: "Here is the first language." That would be arbitrary and pointless.

The basic prerequisites for language involved trust, creativity and social learning. These traits probably arose with the arrival of *Homo erectus* as a species in Africa about 1.8 million years ago and led immediately to the *erectus* people becoming successful and "filling the earth". This package made a protolanguage possible and it may have been the case that the progression from creative puzzle communication achieved using various means, to a more or less coherent protolanguage took place so quickly that the latter could play a part right from the start. In that case the first protolanguage would have been spoken in Africa, probably somewhere on the East African savannah, by the first group of *Homo erectus*.

Not that it had to happen that way. *Erectus* may have spread across the world and populated a great many different sites, language-ready but without language, and then several groups, independently of each other, developed communication systems that tended to become increasingly language-like with the result that many protolanguages would have arisen along a broad front in the vast areas that *erectus* ranged across. In that event there would have been no clearly defined first language and no one place where language came into being.

It could also have been the case that a protolanguage first evolved among one particular group of *erectus* and then spread to all the others. Cultural transmission from group to group can occur very rapidly as measured in evolutionary terms if no biological changes are required. There would have been a first language in that event, but no conceivable way of finding out where it was spoken.

With regard to the dating of the latter two scenarios we end up somewhere around one to one and half million years ago, after *erectus* had spread across the world, that is. The place could have been anywhere from Cape Town to Jakarta.

*Erectus* would prove remarkably stable as a species for a very long period. Once they had spread across the globe they continued to live in much the same way for another million years. This argues against something as revolutionary as language having arisen during that time – it should have left archaeological traces. That is why I consider it most likely that language arose either just before or just after the stable period. The first scenario above, involving a single protolanguage occurring in Africa, therefore seems more likely than either of the others.

The subsequent biological evolution of our language instincts and the other language adaptations would then have taken place during the million years that *erectus* existed and perhaps during the final stage in particular, when the size of the brain increased rapidly in tandem with new species evolving from *erectus* some 500,000 years ago. That laid the foundation for the progression from a protolanguage to a fully fledged one. Every single mutation in that process of change would, of course, have occurred in a particular individual at a particular place even though it is not possible to determine exactly where or when or in whom, and besides, each mutation would only have been a tiny part of a larger puzzle.

# The Warp and Weft of the Protolanguage

This book has drawn on many threads and explored many different pieces of the puzzle in search of the lost protolanguage. Those various threads have gradually been woven together, but the cloth they formed has been spread across many chapters in which the same thread may be picked up, twisted round another thread and then put aside again, several times over, and in different sections. At this point therefore I would like to provide a more coherent picture of the patterns that have emerged from the fabric.

We are a long way from knowing everything about the dawn of language. But we know a great deal more today than when I first became interested in the subject in the 1990s, thanks to all the dedicated work done by many researchers in the field. Some of these scholars and scientists have been referred to by name in these pages, but they could have included many more – when I wrote a more academic book on the same subject a few years ago, it contained  well over a thousand references to the work of other researchers.[49] A great deal of knowledge that is relevant to the origin of language has come from other fields of scientific inquiry as well, produced by researchers who may not have paid any attention to language in their work.

There are still many aspects of the origin and evolution of language on which researchers hold different views. I have done my best to make it clear in the text where these areas of disagreement

49 Johansson, Sverker, *Origins of Language – Constraints on Hypotheses* (2005).

are to be found. And yet I also take a stand on most issues where I judge that there is enough evidence from which to draw conclusions.

## QUESTIONS AND ANSWERS

There are a number of recurrent issues and divergences in the literature on the origin of language that elicit a variety of responses from different commentators and researchers. My aim at this point is to summarise my own responses to those questions.

### Motivation or mutations?

One clear pattern to emerge from the development of our knowledge concerning the origins of humanity and language is that we are discovering more and more of the abilities concerned in other animals – in many respects we humans are not quite as unique as we would like to believe. Many apes in particular, as well as dolphins and some birds, possess a rich array of concepts, a conceptual world that would be perfectly adequate for a basic language and its contents – and yet they do not use those concepts in the way they communicate. While apes lack the ability to speak, they are more than capable of learning other kinds of symbols and for that matter of learning to understand spoken language to some extent. Apes can also deal with mental time travel and can conceive of other apes as thinking creatures. And even though human beings are much better at all that, the difference is a quantitative and not a qualitative one. In my scenario for the evolution of grammar there are no revolutionary biological changes in the evolution of the brain. What I consider to be most challenging from the biological perspective would be memory allocation using pointers rather than anything specifically linguistic.

The points on which we clearly differ from our closest relatives and that have prevented them from evolving language have more to do with inclination than ability. Human beings *want to* communicate; we experience a powerful need to share from a very early age and we like to communicate for the sake of communicating – something chimps never do. This is closely connected with the degree of trust and cooperation in human societies and, on this point, there truly is a qualitative difference between us and the suspicious chimpanzees. Human cooperativeness is probably one of the keys that unlocked the door to language. At the same time language helps to maintain cooperativeness and trust by facilitating coordination and the making of agreements, while also making possible a high level of social control.

*The origin of language has more to do with motivation than with mutation.*

### Early or Late?

Did humans start using the first protolanguage early on in our evolution, in some earlier form of prehuman, or was it something that appeared only recently, once we had already become *Homo sapiens?*

Proponents of the "late" scenarios often refer to an origin of language occurring less than 100,000 years ago, perhaps even as recently as 50,000 years ago, while the "early" scenarios place the protolanguage perhaps as far back in time as a million years ago or even earlier.

I consider a recent origin as completely out of the question, primarily because humanity had already begun to spread across the globe by that point and was no longer a single coherent population. The fact that we all possess the same language faculty today proves that this faculty must already have been in place before our ancestors went their separate ways.

In addition, there are more than enough signs of both culture and anatomical and genetic adaptations to language among the

Neandertals, which would suggest that some form of language must have existed among the common ancestors to both the Neandertals and ourselves maybe half a million years ago. There are signs in *Homo erectus* that indicate the species had at least a basic protolanguage; if so, this would push the chronology back another million years.

*The protolanguage arrived at an early stage in our evolution.*


## Sudden or gradual?

Was language something that gradually evolved over a long period – through several different stages of protolanguages – until our ancestors had a fully developed faculty for handling modern grammatical languages, or did we go from nothing to possessing a modern language faculty at a single stroke?

This question is related to the one about an early or more recent date for the protolanguage to the extent that it is usually the same researchers who propose either early on and gradual, or more recently and sudden, respectively. This is hardly surprising. There would scarcely be time for gradual evolution if language were only 50,000 years old, whereas many stages would seem more natural if there are a million years to play with.

This issue is also related to the way in which language is defined. Someone who considers that a particular attribute is the only one of relevance to language – what makes language *language*, that is – will find it easier to conceive of its origin as sudden than the person who considers language to be the sum of many different characteristics, all of which contribute to making a system of communication more language-like.

Consequently, the proponents of a sudden language origin are most frequently generativists who consider innate grammar to be the defining attribute of language, while functionalists prefer to see language as something that evolves gradually.

A sudden origin of language in the strict sense, with a

genetically based language faculty that appears from nowhere, pre-supposes that a single mutation would be enough to get language simply to come into being. This is, however, not a credible proposition in biological terms. While single mutations can sometimes have large effects, this would be because the mutation in question has activated already existing genetic material in a new way or at a new location. Completely new characteristics do not appear in this manner.

What is not as easy to dismiss, on the other hand, is that the origin of language can appear to be sudden in the fossil and archaeological record without being genetically sudden. If the origin of language were solely to do with its cultural evolution, without any major biological changes taking place, this might very well have occurred in such a short period that the course of events could not be followed by archaeologists. A change that took 50,000 years a million years ago would seem sudden to the researchers of today.

And yet there is no evidence of anything so sudden in the fossil and archaeological record either. What we can see is the gradual increase of both anatomical and archaeological indications of language spread out over several hundred thousand years.

*The protolanguage evolved gradually.*

### Atomistic or holistic?

In the first protolanguage, every utterance was a whole without any internal grammatical structure. But did it possess a semantic structure? Did each word in the protolanguage correspond to a semantic whole, roughly the way modern words do, or did the "words" convey a composite meaning holistically, much as a whole sentence does nowadays? And when the protolanguage then developed into a grammatical language, did this occur by putting several atomistic words together, or by the taking apart of a holistic but semantically complex phrase?

Child development in both cognitive and linguistic respects

currently begins with the combining of atomistic words and concepts to form sentences. Atomistic words that are then used employing the techniques of puzzle communication also provide a more practicable way of forming a useable protolanguage that would contain a reasonable number of words. And last but not least, combining atomistic words into sentences is a much easier process than breaking apart holistic phrases that lack any internal structure.

*The protolanguage was atomistic.*

## Communicative, musical or a purely cognitive language?

We often think of languages as something we use to communicate various messages. But it is not self-evident that this was the function of language when it first arose. Some researchers think that the first language was musical – a singing speech with much the same kind of messages as birdsong – or that the first language was a purely internal language for thinking, which did not involve communicating with the outside world.

But when we consider the characteristics of language we can find little support for these ideas. Conveying a wide variety of messages is a key attribute of language, after all, and is deeply woven into its structure, whereas birdsong points in another direction entirely. In order for language to have developed into what it is today, its meaning-conveying function must have been in existence at an early stage.

When we use language nowadays for thinking, we employ an internal version of the speech we use to communicate externally, an inner voice, with all the limitations that imposes. This is appropriate if our thinking language developed from the one we communicate with but implausible if language was originally designed to be used solely for cognition. Besides, there would be no possible way for children to learn a language that was not used for communication.

*The protolanguage was a communicative one.*

## *Spoken or signed, or a mixture, or mimed?*

Today, both spoken and signed languages exist, and both kinds are fully functional and of equal value. Spoken languages predominate, however. Groups of hearing people consistently use spoken languages, while sign languages are largely used by people who are deaf or hearing-impaired.

Other apes lack the ability to speak but their locomotor systems are perfectly capable of producing signs. Our non-speaking ancestors probably had the same level of ability as the apes of today, which makes the take-off distance for a signed language shorter than for a spoken one. That is why a signed protolanguage is a rather popular theory; the problem inherent in that theory, however, is why more or less all human populations subsequently switched to spoken languages. Moreover, anatomical adaptations to spoken language begin to appear very early in the fossil record, which argues against a recent switch from signs to speech.

Mime has also been proposed as an early form of protolanguage. Apart from when used as a party game, however, there is no reason that mime has to be silent. If our ancestors acted out mini-scenes with a communicative aim they would surely have used both gestures and sounds whenever they were suited to the story.

Nor is there any reason to suppose that the speakers of the protolanguage were purists of some kind. Particularly at the start, when the shared vocabulary was small, they would surely have used every means available to get their message across – using gestures and sounds and mime and props and anything else – much the way we do today to communicate with someone we do not share a language with.

*The protolanguage was mixed.*

## *Innate or not?*

Human beings have an innate language instinct to the extent that new-born humans differ from newborn chimps in a number of ways, which means that people and not chimps acquire language as they grow up. This is true even when both species are reared in the same environment, which proves that this difference is a matter of biological inheritance.

There is a great deal that is innate to human babies although not to young chimps, but most of this is not language specific. There are, however, some language-specific instincts:

- Babies are paying attention to language even before birth, listening to it and registering patterns of sound.
- From the age of about six months babies babble – they are practising how to produce various speech sounds, "da-da-da-goo-goo", and fine-tuning their ability to speak.
- When children hear a new word, they make specific assumptions about what the word refers to and what it means, assumptions that would appear to be innate tools for solving the gavagai problem.
- Children are remarkably good at learning many words rapidly.

Human beings also possess some social and cognitive instincts that are not language-specific but are nevertheless of great importance for language. The most important of these is shared attention. It seems natural to humans, although not to chimps, to coordinate attention so that two people interacting socially will frequently and readily direct their attention towards the same thing. Cooperation and trust are also crucial for language, but it remains unclear to what extent the trust we feel is an instinct.

All these instincts are about making it easier for children to quickly learn their mother tongue. They would not have been required for the very earliest protolanguage, but evolved subsequently, once it became important in Darwinian terms for children to acquire language rapidly.

Some researchers maintain that human beings possess a more extensive language instinct in the form of an innate grammar module. There is, however, no agreement on this matter and the issue is one that divides the different paradigms. For my part, I am not convinced by the arguments that have been put forward for an innate grammar because they take the generative paradigm far too much for granted. While there may very well be some other form of innate support for the way children learn grammar, we do not know what form that support might take,

*Although no language instinct was required for the protolanguage, it prompted the evolution of instincts for learning language. An innate grammar does not, however, form part of those instincts.*

## OUR EVOLUTION FROM JABBERING APES TO TALKING HUMANS

The baseline for the evolution of language can be established among ape-like ancestors of ours a couple of million years ago, ancestors who did not have language but possessed the same language-relevant abilities that chimps and many other primates do today. These creatures had a cognitive ability and conceptual range that would have been perfectly adequate for a basic language and they also had some ability to imagine what was not in the immediate present, to both remember the past and to plan for the future.

These forebears of ours had a basic system of communication with a few fixed sounds and a broader repertoire of gestures that were employed creatively and in a manner dependent on context to convey the message required. They had some ability to understand each other's point of view and interpret each other's messages, and they used that ability tactically in their social interactions.

They also possessed latent abilities that they evidently did not use but that would come in handy when their descendants subsequently evolved language. They were capable of learning word-like symbols and of associating them with meanings, and if someone had spoken in their vicinity, they would have been able to hear and analyse the speech sounds and discern the words. However, their own ability to produce sounds was extremely limited; they would have possessed their standard noises but could not use their voices for anything new.

The most recent of our ancestors who were entirely without language on that baseline belonged in all probability to the *Australopithecus* genus. They were, however, not entirely language-ready and a few more evolutionary steps were required before the first language could come into being.

The most important of those steps involved cooperation, helpfulness and trust. Language is based on our cooperating with and trusting each other. As it is far too easy to lie with words, language would have been stillborn as an idea had we not been able, by and large, to trust each other's words. A breakthrough in the social evolution of human beings – based perhaps on help with childbirth and childcare – that led to a new level of cooperation and trust within the group took place in all likelihood among *Homo erectus* about 1.8 million years ago. That breakthrough paved the way for language and made its emergence possible.

The ecological and social setting in which *Homo erectus* lived was such that a protolanguage would have given those who could talk an evolutionary advantage. That advantage was probably based on a combination of several of the factors we have discussed in relation to the first topic of conversation. Instrumental communication about how to subsist, social control to maintain trust and status-seeking may all have played a role.

The first step on the evolutionary ladder of the human brain, when our brains doubled in size from the ape-sized brains of our earlier ancestors, occurred with the evolution of *Homo erectus*. That increase in brain size was probably the result of an interaction between both the evolution of cooperation and of the protolanguage.

*Homo erectus* was a highly successful species that spread across large parts of the world and survived for more than a million years. Cooperation and the increased fertility that cooperation made possible were no doubt the most important reasons for their success, but a basic protolanguage would also have been a contributory factor.

The anatomy of modern humans has been adapted in subtle ways for spoken language. These adaptations were also to be found among the Neandertals and ought therefore to have evolved in the common ancestor we share with them – *Homo erectus*. This, too, suggests that *erectus* had language and that they used enough sounds in speech to prompt the adaptations of the vocal tract and so on.

Even if *Homo erectus* was effective and successful, the species was not remarkably creative or inventive. They had a stable culture with a technology that remained the same for a million years and there is no reason to believe that there were any great changes to their language during that time. But around 500,000 years ago something began to change: the fossil brains start to increase in size once more and their tools became both more varied and more sophisticated. The species *Homo erectus* separated into several different kinds of human in different parts of the world at around that time as well.

These diverse humans then evolved in parallel over a long period, and it is only fairly recently, perhaps 50,000 years ago, that any clear differences can be seen in the archaeological traces they left behind. The various kinds of human would encounter one another from time to time and the different varieties had children together, which evidently worked out well both biologically and in cultural terms. The genetic and mental differences between them – and possibly the linguistic ones as well – cannot have been insurmountable.

Traces of symbolic culture and art begin gradually to appear among the different kinds of human beings about 200,000 years ago. People who are capable of creating works of art would surely have been able to handle a more advanced language than the protolanguage spoken by *erectus*, and the Neandertals, at least, would have possessed a language with more than just a few words, but it is difficult to prove with any great accuracy when the proto-language developed into a full-blown language of the modern kind. It was, however, definitely more than 100,000 years ago because it was that long ago that the various groups of modern humans went their separate ways and spread out to different continents. The fact that people today have the same language faculty and speak comparable languages all over the world proves that language must have been fully established among the entire human race before we separated at about that time.

But all that does is establish a lower limit – language could be much older than that. We cannot exclude the possibility that both the Neandertals and the Denisovans – and perhaps even the last members of *erectus* – also spoke fully grammatical languages, even though that is not something we can currently determine. A better understanding of the genetic basis of language may produce an answer to that question at some future point because we now have access to the fossil D.N.A. of those humans.

*Homo sapiens* then spread out across the world and all the other species of human disappeared at more or less the same time. The languages spoken by the Neandertals and Denisovans vanished with them, just as the languages of indigenous peoples are currently disappearing all over the world.

So we *sapiens* began to move outward from Africa about 100,000 years ago. By then we were fully proficient speakers of completely modern languages with all the grammatical refinements and all the biological adaptations required. The first wave of this expansion reached Australia about 50,000 years ago to become the ancestors of the Aboriginals and Papuans of today. On the way there they encountered both Neandertals and Denisovans. They probably passed through the territory of the hobbits on Flores as well, even though that meeting has not left any discernible genetic traces. The next wave of emigrants expanded across Europe and Asia and supplanted or absorbed the Neandertals and Denisovans already living there. Eventually, when the inland ice receded, they also reached the Americas. All these emigrants took their respective languages with them out of Africa, but as they expanded and colonised different areas those languages would undergo changes in different ways and, through a long process of cultural evolution and repeated waves of colonisation and conquest hither and thither, ultimately become the thousands of different languages that are spoken today.

And yet during historic time that diverse range of languages has been diminishing with every passing year. Linguistic diversity may have been at its greatest just over 10,000 years ago, before agriculture was invented and large-scale civilisations became possible. Currently, languages continue to die as their speakers are culturally erased and absorbed, and unique means of expression are then lost for ever.

What does the future look like for the languages of the world? One trend that has become more pronounced is for the bigger languages to keep getting bigger while smaller ones fade away. This trend has been driven by the increasing globalisation of the way we communicate. Our conversations are no longer restricted to our own little village; instead, we both want and are able to speak to people on the other side of the world – and for that we need a shared language. If this trend continues unchecked we may be faced with a situation in which only one or a very few languages are spoken on the planet. Is that the direction we want to head in?

At the same time we are also rapidly approaching a situation when machine translation is becoming so powerful that it no longer matters whether we speak different languages – we will be able to understand one another even so. On platforms such as Facebook, I participate from time to time in conversations that are conducted in Russian or Tagalog even though I have no knowledge of these languages – the platform ensures that the communication functions well enough. Is that an alternative future, when everyone speaks the language they want to but technology helps us to build bridges and understand one another nonetheless? That may be optimistic – it would be a remarkably vulnerable world if we were entirely dependent for our everyday communication needs on an extensive information technology infrastructure. But what are the alternatives? A single world language – and in that case, whose? – or that we back away from globalisation and shut ourselves off in national and linguistic filter bubbles once again? None of these alternatives appeals to me.

The way forward in any case will have to be based on better knowledge about language and a greater understanding of the value of the linguistic diversity that we possess today. Knowledge about the origins of language will form an important part of that understanding. That is where I am doing my best to contribute.

# ILLUSTRATION SOURCES

The images in this book are taken from Wikimedia Commons. All have a Creative Commons CC-BY-SA license, unless otherwise stated. Images and diagrams not listed below are the author's own:

*Waggle dance p.66:* (https://commons.wikimedia.org/wiki/File:Bee_dance.svg) *Kanzi p.86:* Author William H. Calvin (https://commons.wikimedia.org/wiki/File:Kanzi,_conversing.jpg); *Lucy p.106:* Author Chiswick Chap (https://commons.wikimedia.org/wiki/File:Lucy_Skeleton_cropped.jpg); *Oldowan stone tool p.108:* Author Archaeomoonwalker (https://commons.wikimedia.org/wiki/File:Olduvai_Chopper.JPG); *Hand axe p.110:* Author Ángel M. Felicísimo (https://commons.wikimedia.org/wiki/File:Bifaz_achelense_(15931943729).jpg); *Homo habilis p.113:* Author Lillyundfreya & Sargoth (https://commons.wikimedia.org/wiki/File:Homo_habilis-cropped.jpg); *Map of Indonesia p.121:* Author Uwe Dedering (modified) (https://commons.wikimedia.org/wiki/File:Indonesia_location_map.svg); *Map of Russia p.125:* Author Uwe Dedering (modified) (https://commons.wikimedia.org/wiki/File:Russia_edcp_location_map.svg); *Darwin p.168:* Free image. (https://commons.wikimedia.org/wiki/File:Charles_Darwin_-_Jan_Vilímek.jpg); *The Taung child p.219:* Free image (https://commons.wikimedia.org/wiki/File:Taung%27s_child.jpg); *Brain with Broca and Wernicke areas p.224:* Author hguiney (https://commons.wikimedia.org/wiki/File:Human-brain. SVG); *Three pelvises p.252:* Author ArchaeoMouse (modified) (https://commons.wikimedia.org/wiki/File:A_Visual_Comparison_of_the_Pelvis_and_Bony_Birth_Canal_Vs._the_Size_of_Infant_Skull_in_Primate_Species.png); *The Turkana boy p.259:* Author Wolfgang Sauber (https://commons.wikimedia.org/wiki/File:MNP_-_Turkanajunge_1.jpg); *Meerkats p.306:* Author Bernard DUPONT (https://commons.wikimedia.org/wiki/

File:Meerkats_(Suricata_suricatta)_sentinels_looking_out_..._
(32413471312).jpg); *Neandertal in a suit p.325:* Author Einsamer Schütze
(https://commons.wikimedia.org/wiki/File:Neanderthal_Museum_
18.jpg); *The Spirit of the Forest p.338:* Free image (https://commons.
wikimedia.org/wiki/File:Pintura_Trois_Freres.jpg); *The Venus of
Tan-Tan p.346:* Free image (https://commons.wikimedia.org/wiki/
File:Venus_of_Tan-Tan.jpg); *Blombos ochre p.352:* (https://commons.
wikimedia.org/wiki/File:Blombos_Cave_-_3.jpg); *Pettakere cave p.353:*
Author Cahyo Ramadhani (https://commons.wikimedia.org/wiki/
File:Hands_in_Pettakere_Cave.jpg); *The Venus of Hohle Fels p.355:*
Author Ramessos (https://commons.wikimedia.org/wiki/
File:VenusHohlefels2.jpg); *The Chauvet cave p.357:* Upphovsmakare
Thomas T. (https://commons.wikimedia.org/wiki/
File:Chauvet%C2%B4s_cave_horses.jpg).

# FURTHER READING

PART ONE: ON LANGUAGE

**Human Language**

Evans, Vyvyan, *The Language Myth* (Cambridge: Cambridge University Press, 2014)

Jackendoff, Ray, *Foundations of Language* (Oxford: Oxford University Press, 2002)

**Language in Other Creatures?**

Håkansson, Gisela & Westander, Jennie, *Communication in Humans and Other Animals* (Amsterdam: John Benjamins Publishing Company, 2013)

Hauser, Marc D., *The Evolution of Communication* (Cambridge, Mass.: MIT Press, 1996)

Patterson, Francine, *The Education of Koko* (New York: Holt, Rinehart & Winston, 1981)

Pepperberg, Irene, *Alex & Me* (New York: Harper & Row, 2009)

Pepperberg, Irene, *The Alex Studies* (Harvard: Harvard University Press, 1999)

Savage-Rumbaugh, Sue & Lewin, Roger, *Kanzi P: The Ape at the Brink of the Human Mind* (Hoboken, N.J.: John Wiley & Sons, 1994)

Seyfarth, Robert M. & Cheney, Dorothy L., *Social Origins of Language* (Princeton: Princeton University Press, 2017)

Steels, Luc, *Experiments in Cultural Language Evolution* (Amsterdam: John Benjamins Publishing Company, 2012)

## PART TWO: ON ORIGINS

### The Other Apes and Us

Berg, Lasse, *Dawn Over the Kalahari* (tr. Frank Perry)
    (Kagali/Näsviken: Real Africa Books, 2011)
Dunbar, Robin, *The Human Story* (London: Faber & Faber, 2005)
Harari, Yuval Noah, *Sapiens: A Brief History of Mankind* (London:
    Harvill Secker, 2014)
Wood, Bernard, *Human Evolution: A Very Short introduction*
    (Oxford: Oxford University Press, 2019)

### Explaining the Characteristics of the Various Species and Languages

Dawkins, Richard, *The Selfish Gene* (Oxford: Oxford University
    Press, 1976)

### Heredity, Environment and Language

Berwick, Robert & Chomsky, Noam, *Why Only Us?* (Cambridge,
    Mass.: MIT Press, 2016)
Dediu, Dan, *An Introduction to Genetics for Language Scientists*
    (Cambridge: Cambridge University Press, 2015)
Kinsella, Anna, *Language Evolution and Syntactic Theory*
    (Cambridge: Cambridge University Press, 2009)
Pinker, Steven, *The Language Instinct* (New York: William Morrow
    and Company, 1994)

### The Language-Ready Brain

Ahlsén, Elisabeth, *Introduction to Neurolinguistics* (Amsterdam:
    John Benjamins Publishing Company, 2006)
Arbib, Michael, *How the Brain Got Language: The Mirror System
    Hypothesis* (Oxford: Oxford University Press, 2012)
Bouchard, Denis, *The Nature and Origin of Language* (Oxford:
    Oxford University Press, 2013)
Deacon, Terrence, *The Symbolic Species* (New York:
    W. W. Norton, 1997)

## The Cooperative Ape

Hrdy, Sarah Blaffer, *Mothers and Others* (Harvard: Harvard University Press, 2011)

Lindenfors, Patrik, *For Whose Benefit?* (Berlin: Springer Verlag, 2017)

Tomasello, Michael, *Origins of Human Communication* (Cambridge, Mass.: MIT Press, 2008)


## PART THREE: ON THE ORIGIN OF LANGUAGE

### The First Speaker

de Boer, Bart, *The Origins of Vowel Systems* (Oxford: Oxford University Press, 2001)

Corballis, Michael C., *From Hand to Mouth* (Princeton: Princeton University Press, 2003)

Fitch, W. Tecumseh, *The Evolution of Language* (Cambridge: Cambridge University Press, 2010)

### The First Topic of Conversation

Bickerton, Derek, *Adam's Tongue* (New York: Hill & Wang, 2009)

Dessalles, Jean-Louis, *Why We Talk* (Oxford: Oxford University Press, 2007)

Dor, Daniel, *The Instruction of Imagination* (Oxford: Oxford University Press, 2015)

Dunbar, Robin, *Grooming, Gossip and the Evolution of Language* (Harvard: Harvard University Press, 1998)

Mithen, Steven, *The Singing Neanderthals* (London: Weidenfeld & Nicolson, 2005)

### The Cave Man

Pääbo, Svante, *Neanderthal Man* (New York: Basic Books, 2015)

Wynn, Thomas & Coolidge, Frederick L., *How to Think Like a Neanderthal* (Oxford: Oxford University Press, 2011)

## Cultural "Man"

de Beaune, Sophie, Wynn, Thomas & Coolidge, Frederick L.,
    *Cognitive Archaeology and Human Evolution* (Cambridge:
    Cambridge University Press, 2009)

Botha, Rudolf, & Knight, Chris, *The Cradle of Language* (Oxford:
    Oxford University Press, 2009)

Dor, Daniel, Knight, Chris & Lewis, Jerome, *The Social Origins
    of Language* (Oxford: Oxford University Press, 2014)

Knight, Chris, *Blood Relations: Menstruation and the Origins of
    Culture* (New Haven: Yale University Press, 1991)

## The First Languages

Heine, Bernd & Kuteva, Tania, *The Genesis of Grammar* (Oxford:
    Oxford University Press, 2007)

Hurford, James, *The Origins of Meaning* (Oxford: Oxford
    University Press, 2007)

Hurford, James, *The Origins of Grammar* (Oxford: Oxford
    University Press, 2011)

Progovac, Ljiljana, *Evolutionary Syntax* (Oxford: Oxford
    University Press, 2015)

# INDEX

# AUTHOR'S ACKNOWLEDGEMENTS

Thank you to my Swedish publisher Anders Bergman, whose initiative this book was and who supported and encouraged me throughout the writing process.

Thank you to my late father Lars Johansson, who always en-couraged me and stimulated my curiosity. *Requiescat in pace*.

Thank you to all my children: Daniel, Cassandra, Faramir and Aina, who have contributed inspiration, anecdotes and comments on the manuscript, each according to their age and ability.

Thank you to Gisela Håkansson and Jordan Zlatev, the inspirational teachers who sparked my interest in language and its origins.

Thank you to Johan Sjons, Emelie Perland and, once again, Gisela Håkansson, for sharing their invaluable comments and views on the manuscript.

Thank you to all my other friends and colleagues doing research on the evolution of language; and to all the regulars at the Evolang conferences, thank you for many stimulating lectures, publications, discussions and conversations over a glass of wine or three whenever we have come together.

Thank you to Lorelie, for your support, patience and understanding.

Thank you to my mother, Stina Johansson, from whom I learned my mother tongue and who has always been there for me.

SVERKER JOHANSSON, Doctor of Philosophy in Physics and Master of Philosophy in Linguistics, was born 1961 in Lund in the southern part of Sweden. He is a senior advisor at Dalarna University, has conducted research at CERN in Switzerland and participated in EVOLANG, the leading international conference for research on the origins and evolution of language, since 2006.

Through a bot that he programmed, Lsjbot, Johansson is behind an estimated 8% of all articles on Swedish Wikipedia, covering everything from fungi to municipalities in the Philippines.

FRANK PERRY's translations have won the Swedish Academy Prize for the introduction of Swedish literature abroad and the prize of the Writer's Guild of Sweden for drama translation. His translation of Lina Wolff's *Bret Easton Ellis and the Other Dogs* was the 2017 winner of the Oxford-Weidenfeld Prize, and was awarded the triennial Bernard Shaw Prize for best literary translation from Swedish.